SOUTH AMERICA

A Rude Suspension Bridge in the Andes

SOUTH AMERICA

by

Nellie B. Allen

YESTERDAY'S CLASSICS

ITHACA, NEW YORK

PREFACE

South America is our nearest neighbor among the continents. It is situated largely in the Southern Hemisphere, where the seasons are the opposite of ours. Its widest mass is in the torrid zone, instead of in the temperate zone as is the case with North America. Therefore many of its products vary greatly from those of our country, while others are harvested in the nonproductive season of the north temperate zone.

Corporations from the United States are spending millions of dollars in developing the mineral wealth of South America. Some of the great packing companies in our Western cities have immense plants in this Southern continent. Reapers and harvesters made in the United States dot the widespreading plains of Argentina. Our fields are fertilized with Chilean nitrates. The material for our morning cups of coffee and cocoa comes chiefly from South American countries. The rubber for various industries, automobile tires, hospitals, and rainy-day apparel is shipped largely from South American ports.

The people of the different countries of South America need the help of the United States in developing their resources and increasing their products. They need our money, our skilled workmen, our inventions, and our manufactures. They need our help in establishing new industries, in exploiting new products, in building roads and railroads, and in financing great operations.

We need also the help of the people of South America. Their rapidly growing cities, not too far away, furnish splendid markets for our manufactures. The development of their mines and railroads and the opening up of new industries make possible the introduction of American-made machinery and tools. Their rubber, coffee, cocoa, meat, hides and skins, nitrates, dyestuffs, and other valuable products are necessary in our homes, on our farms, and in our industrial plants. Our commerce with South America will be for many years a large and ever-increasing asset.

The children in our schools, who are our business men and women of the near future, should become more intimately acquainted with the people, the countries, and the resources of South America. As a help in this direction this book has been written.

Some names of places not usually referred to in school textbooks but which are important in the industrial development of South America are mentioned in the following pages. It is not essential that children should memorize all such names. It is desirable, however, that teachers and pupils should select from the lists given at the close of each chapter the most important places—the "minimum essentials"— and should memorize thoroughly the location of these and the most important facts concerning them.

In the preparation of this book thanks are due to the following people and institutions, whose help in the shape of suggestions, criticisms, and material has been most valuable to the author: Franklin Adams, Pan-American Union; N. Albrecht, Staudt and Co., Boston; Dr. Isaac Alzamora, Ex-Vice President of Peru; Antofagasta and Bolivia R. R. Co., Antofagasta, Chile; Julian A. Arroyo, New York and Venezuela; Walter Baker Co., Boston; Adolfo Ballivian, Consul General of Bolivia; Booth S. S. Co., Liverpool, England; H. Borja, Consul of Ecuador; Boston Public Library; Bureau of Education, Washington, D. C.; Leon Campbell, Harvard College Observatory, Arequipa, Peru; Central Argentina R. R. Co., Buenos Aires, Argentine Republic; Chase and Sanborn, Boston; Chilean Nitrate Propaganda, New York; Phanor J. Eder, Author and Lecturer; Francisco Escobar, Consul General of Colombia; Fitchburg Public Library; Charles W. Furlong, Explorer and Lecturer; Domicio Da Gama, Ambassador Extraordinary and Plenipotentiary of Brazil; Mario L. Gil, Consul General of Uruguay; Colonel George W. Goethals; Goodyear Tire and Rubber Co., Akron, Ohio; *La Hacienda*, Buffalo, New York; Ernest Hallen, Balboa Heights, Canal Zone; Eduardo Higginson, Consul General of Peru; Hood Rubber Co., Watertown, Massachusetts; *India Rubber World*, New York; A. Klepstein and Co., New York; Lamport and Holt S. S. Co., New York; Liebig Beef

Extract Co., Fray Bentos, Uruguay; Lloyd Braziliero, Rio de Janeiro, Brazil; Guillermo McKissock, Vice Consul of the Argentine Republic; W. R. Martin, Hispanic Society of America, New York; M. A. Molina, Consul of the Argentine Republic; Peruvian Corporation, Lima, Peru; H. C. Martins Pinheirof, Consul General of Brazil; George E. Putnam, *Boot and Shoe Recorder*, Boston; *Revista Americana de Farmacia y Medicina*, New York; José Richling, Consul General of Uruguay; H. H. Rusby, Columbia University, New York; Ricardo C. Tort, Chancellor of the Consulate General of the Argentine Republic; United Button Co., Springfield, Massachusetts; United Fruit Co., New York; United States Rubber Co., New York; Dr. Héctor Velázquez, Envoy Extraordinary and Minister Plenipotentiary of Paraguay.

NELLIE B. ALLEN

CONTENTS

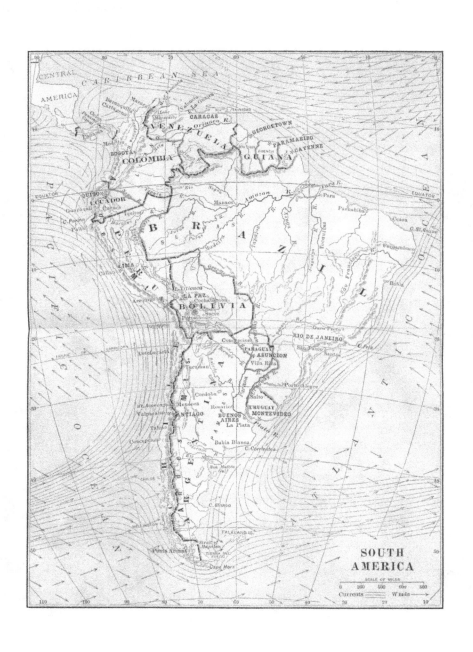

SOUTH
AMERICA

SCALE OF MILES

0   200   400   600   800

Currents ——— Winds ——→

CHAPTER I

INTRODUCTION

WE are going to visit South America, our nearest neighbor among the continents. Most people think of this grand division as being south of North America; yet this is not the case. South America is much farther east than North America—so far east that no part of the southern continent is farther west than Lake Erie. Valparaiso, the seaport of Chile, is directly south of the city of New York. The eastern point of Brazil lies more than halfway across the Atlantic Ocean, and a voyage from England to Pernambuco is about the same length as one to New York.

South America is not so large as North America but is similar in shape. Both continents are longer from north to south; both are wider in the northern part and taper to a point in the south; both have a great highland in the west, lower mountains in the east, and a great plain between. The Andes Mountains of South America are a continuation of the Rocky Mountains of North America, and the two systems extend from Alaska in the north to the Antarctic Ocean in the south. The mountains descend to low hills in the Isthmus of Panama but rise again in South America until, in Peru,

1

Bolivia, and Chile, they include some of the grandest snow-capped ranges in the world. In the great Western highland of both North and South America there are many volcanoes, and the Pacific coast of the two continents is one of the earthquake regions of the world. Many cities of South America have been destroyed by earthquake shocks, and the rumblings and shakings of the earth are very common there. The people live in low houses usually one story high. These are built in such a way that they sway and rock but seldom fall unless the shock is a severe one.

The Appalachian Highland, in the eastern part of North America, is a great storehouse of coal and iron. The Brazilian Mountains, in the eastern part of South America, are also a treasure house. They are stored with gold and diamonds, more beautiful perhaps but less valuable than the minerals found in the eastern part of North America.

Wheat and cattle are two of the most important products of both of the continents of the Western Hemisphere, and the industries of the plains of South America are carried on in much the same way that they are on the Great Western plains of the United States and Canada. So numerous are the cattle in the Argentine Republic and so great are the quantities of wheat that are shipped away from her ports that this southern republic is often called the great future rival of the United States.

The contrasts between North America and her southern neighbor are as interesting as the likenesses.

Both have a great plain in the central part, but the plain of North America is drained by the Mississippi River, a southward-flowing stream, while much of the plain of South America is drained by the mighty Amazon, which flows to the east.

The Mississippi basin lies in the temperate zone and is covered with fertile farms where wheat, corn, cotton, and sugar grow, and with immense pastures where many cattle feed. The valley of the Amazon in the torrid zone is for the most part a great tropical jungle covered with rich forests of valuable hard woods, adorned with flowering vines, and carpeted with undergrowth so dense that you would have to chop your way through with an ax. It is in these forest plains of the Amazon, known as the selvas, that millions of rubber trees grow.

The northern part of North America is the coldest part of the continent, and the widest part is in the temperate zone. In South America it is the narrow southern tip which stretches into the cold belt, while the widest part lies under the equator.

More of South America than of any other continent except Africa lies in the torrid zone, but, strange to say, the climate of a large part of this area is so cold that little or nothing will grow. This is because it is so high. Portions of Ecuador, Peru, and Bolivia consist of a plateau more than two miles high, bounded on either side by ranges of the Andes Mountains. When traveling in these bleak, cold regions it will be hard for us to realize that they are as near the equator as are the low, hot jungles of Brazil.

Figure 1—In the mountains there are a few railroads that wind in and out among the high peaks.

Nature has been kinder to North America than to its southern neighbor in thus placing the greater part of its territory in the zone best fitted for the growth of civilization and the development of commerce and industry. North America has also deeper inlets, more and better harbors, and is nearer to the great seaports of Europe and the civilization of that continent.

Another great difference between the two continents of the Western Hemisphere is in the methods of travel and of carrying freight. There are few railroads in South America, but fortunately it is well supplied with large navigable rivers. In many parts of the continent these are the only highways over the plains. The products of the inland regions are shipped down the streams by the steamers that carry provisions up to the scattered towns and cities on the banks. In the mountains there are a few railroads that wind in and out among the high peaks, up to some of the mining centers. Most of the people who live in the highlands travel on foot or on muleback and carry their provisions on mules and llamas. The llama is the most useful animal in South America. We shall see hundreds of them on the high plateaus, feeding on the scanty grass or plodding in caravans along the rough, stony trails.

In the more progressive countries of South America, such as Chile, Brazil, and the Argentine Republic, some of the larger cities are very beautiful and have all the conveniences to which we are accustomed in the United

Figure 2—A little stream flows through the narrow street and serves as a sewer and garbage pail for the houses on either side.

States. In other places we shall see strange sights. Notice in Figure 2 the little stream that flows along the middle of the narrow street and serves as a sewer and garbage pail for the houses on either side.

Most of the people who live in North America belong to the white race. In South America the majority of the people are blacks and South American Indians. South America is the nearest continent to the United States, yet few of our countrymen live there. There are many Englishmen and Germans who live in the different countries and who carry on many of the industries and much of the commerce. In recent years people both in the United States and South America have thought that there should be a closer union of the nations of the Western Hemisphere. Meetings, called Pan-American congresses, where delegates from different nations come together, have been held from year to year in various cities. Topics of common interest have been discussed, treaties made, and plans formed by which the nations of North America and South America may be more closely united.

You have all heard of the Monroe Doctrine, made years ago by President Monroe when the United States was much stronger than any of the other nations on this side of the world. The United States felt it to be its duty to defend these weaker countries from any European power which might desire some of their territory. Today some of the South American countries are rich and strong and do not like the idea of having the United States think of itself as their protector. Pan-Americanism, the union of all countries of the

Western Hemisphere for their common interest and protection, is beginning to take the place of the Monroe Doctrine. A closer relationship, increased trade, and a greater feeling of friendliness among all countries of the Western Hemisphere will doubtless be the future result of Pan-Americanism.

In the older cities of South America we shall find barred windows in the houses such as you see in Figure 3. We should not enjoy looking through these heavy bars into the streets as much as the ladies of these countries do. Neither should we like the idea of having the markets on the ground in the open squares and

Figure 3—We should not like the idea of the markets along the streets where the fruits and vegetables are so near the feet of the passers-by.

along the streets, where the fruits and vegetables are so near the feet of the passers-by.

Figure 4—The ruins in South America tell us of ancient cities, important industries, and civilized peoples who lived and worked there centuries ago.

Among the interesting sights of South America are the ancient ruins that exist there. The flights of rocky steps, the giant columns, the huge stones fitted so closely together that a knife cannot be inserted in the cracks, and the stone-terraced fields all tell us of ancient cities, important industries, and civilized peoples who lived and worked on the high, cold plateau of South America long before the earliest Spanish explorer ventured across the wide ocean to the shores of the New World.

Most of South America lies south of the equator,

and therefore the seasons are the opposite of ours. When the sun is far to the south of us, shining low at noonday and giving us but little heat during our winter season, it is high in the sky and giving summer heat to the people living south of the equator. It would seem odd, would it not, to celebrate Christmas in the summer time with firecrackers and rockets and pinwheels and to enjoy the Fourth of July in the cold weather with winter sports?

You will be interested in the animals of South America, for many of them are different from those that live in our country. The birds and butterflies are more brilliant, and the snakes and crocodiles are larger. There are bright-colored parrots and chattering monkeys. There are turtles so large and heavy that you could not lift one from the ground. You might enjoy its eggs for dinner, however, as much as the South American Indians do. There are ants of all sizes and kinds, large and small, black and brown, those that bite and sting and those that are harmless. One variety, a white ant, builds mounds fifteen or twenty feet high, the skyscrapers of the ant world. Another kind travels in armies of many thousands. They clean the leaves and fruit from every bush and tree in their route, and all the larger animals make haste to get out of their way.

There are other animals whose names perhaps you have never heard before. Among these are the tapir, which looks something like our common hog and is one of the largest animals found in South America. The jaguar is a relative of the tiger and almost as dangerous. The sloth, rightly named, is the slowest creature that

Figure 5—The tapir looks something like our common hog and is one of the largest animals found in South America.

lives; it will hang all day upside down on the limb of a big tree or, if it moves at all, it moves so slowly that it falls asleep between steps. There is also the ant bear, three or four feet long, with shaggy gray fur, which lives in the deep woods and feeds on ants. Besides these there are the cousins in the highlands: the llama, without which the South American Indians would find it hard to live; the alpaca, valuable for its fine long wool; and the vicuña, with an even silkier, softer coat.

In order to see all the interesting sights of South America we must make up our minds for a long, hard trip. We shall find the climate of the tropical plains hotter than it is in any part of the United States. When we are in the highlands we shall be too cold to be comfortable, but we shall find no stoves in the houses to warm ourselves by. Though the temperature sometimes goes below the freezing point, the South American Indians of the highlands usually go barefooted.

In order to get from the coast onto the high plateau between the mountains we shall travel higher than the top of the highest peak in the United States. In the thin air at this great height we shall probably suffer from mountain sickness. We shall be dizzy and faint and breathless, or perhaps have what seems like a severe attack of seasickness. On the long, hot river trips the flies, mosquitoes, and other insect pests will annoy us night and day, and we may have to find our way through jungles and forests and swamps where few white men have ever been before.

Not all of the trip will be full of such hardships.

Figure 6—The sloth likes to hang all day upside down on the limb of a big tree.

Figure 7—Not all of the trip will be full of hardships, for we can visit large cities with all modern conveniences.

For a part of the time we can travel in trains and steamers as well equipped and as comfortable as any in the United States; we can stop at hotels as fine as any in our great cities; we can loiter in parks more beautiful perhaps than any that our country can boast of, and shop in stores as modern as any in our large centers.

Whether a trip through South America be hard or easy, it will in any case be a profitable one. Our relations with our southern neighbor will in the future be much closer than they have been in the past. The cutting of the canal across the Isthmus of Panama has brought the countries on the west coast of South America thousands of miles nearer to our Atlantic and Gulf ports, nearer even than the seaports of Europe are. These western South American countries have great riches as yet undeveloped. In the mountains there are stores of minerals as yet untouched—tin, copper, silver, gold, and iron. There are rich pastures where today few or no cattle feed. There are millions of rubber trees as yet untapped, and vast areas where the soil and climate are well suited for the production of cocoa, coffee, sugar, and other products which we need to import in large quantities.

In the past, England and Germany have controlled most of the commerce and many of the industries of South America. These European countries are exhausted by the great war. For many years they will have little money to invest in foreign lands, and fewer men to spare from their own factories and farms to build up industries in other continents. The United States has today a great opportunity in this southern land. The people there are more ready than at any time in the past to buy what we have to sell and to send us large quantities of their productions. It is well for us to learn all that we can about this rich southern continent, which in the future may be more closely bound to us in trade and commerce than any other grand division of the world.

TOPICS FOR STUDY

Be able to spell and pronounce the following names. Locate each Place and tell what was said of it in the chapter.

Chile	Atlantic Ocean
Brazil	Antarctic Ocean
Bolivia	Lake Erie
Peru	Isthmus of Panama
Ecuador	Great Western plains
Argentine Republic	Mississippi River
England	Amazon River
Germany	Andes Mountains
United States	Brazilian Mountains
Canada	Rocky Mountains
Alaska	Appalachian Mountains
Torrid zone	Valparaiso
Temperate zone	Pernambuco
Equator	New York

CHAPTER II

COLOMBIA AND THE CITY OF BOGOTA

THE northern shores of South America washed by the Caribbean Sea used to be called the Spanish Main. From these northern ports, especially from those of Panama and Colombia, Spanish ships laden with treasures of gold, silver, and pearls sailed on long voyages to the mother country. In their home towns the sailors told wonderful stories of the new lands across the water where the temples were roofed with gold and the rulers ate from gold and silver dishes. Sometimes the ships were not so fortunate as to reach Spain with their treasure, but were pursued and captured by pirates of other nations, who sank the vessels, killed the crew, and divided the booty among themselves.

The gold and silver came chiefly from Colombia, then called New Granada, and from Peru and Bolivia, farther south. Thousands of South American Indians dug and delved in the mines to obtain the riches for their conquerors. Other Indians, footsore and weary, traveled over steep mountain trails and through hot valleys to bring the treasure to the seaports on the

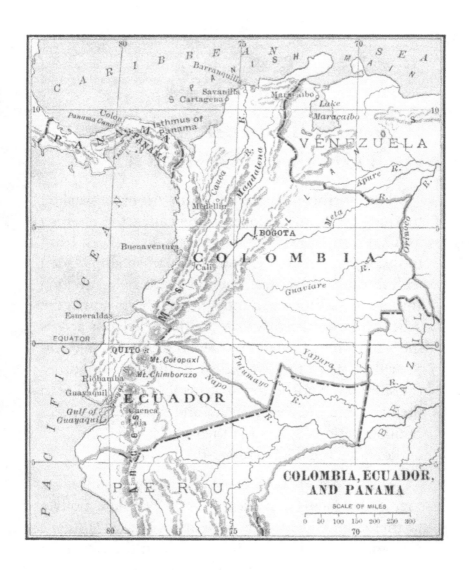

COLOMBIA, ECUADOR,
AND PANAMA

SCALE OF MILES

0   50   100   150   200   250   300

16

Spanish Main. On the coast of Colombia we shall see old forts and prisons and ruins of fortifications which, if they could speak, could tell us many a thrilling tale of these wild days of savage fighting, of horrible torture, and of long years of hopeless imprisonment.

Colombia is only about half as far from New York as London is, yet many people in the United States know very little about the country. Perhaps you do not realize how large it is. Place a map of it on one of the United States made on the same scale, with the southern point of Colombia touching the border of Mexico. The narrow northern portion of Colombia will reach to the southern boundary of Montana, and its widest part will stretch from Great Salt Lake to Omaha, Nebraska. The entire country would cover the four states of Utah, Colorado, Arizona, and New Mexico.

All of this large area lies in the torrid zone, but by looking at a map you will see that some parts of it must be much cooler than others because they are higher. The Andes Highland, which stretches along the entire western coast of South America, divides Colombia into three regions. On the low, hot coast strip we shall find tropical forests and dense jungles, cocoa plantations and fields of sugar cane. Higher on the plateau, between the mountain ranges, the climate is delightfully cool and pleasant. Here are located most of the cities and towns, and here most of the people live and work. On the eastern slopes of the Andes, well watered by many large branches of the Orinoco and Amazon rivers, are pastures of rich grass, tropical forests of valuable hard woods, and thousands of rubber trees. Like similar

*Figure 8—The homes of the natives
in this backward country are rather rustic.*

riches in eastern Ecuador, Peru, and Bolivia, these resources are as yet little known and used, and this part of the country is waiting for railroads, capitalists, and settlers.

Colombia is favored by having two front doors opening toward the ocean, one on the Caribbean Sea and one on the Pacific, and there are good harbors on both waters. The most important port on the Pacific Ocean is Buenaventura. This is the doorway through which we should enter the country if we were approaching it from the Pacific side.

One of the oldest ports on the Caribbean is Cartagena. As we enter the harbor of this ancient city we see on either side gray old forts built by the Spaniards hundreds of years ago. Down by the water are great moss-grown buildings as old as the forts. Behind these, rising from a mass of low white buildings with red-tiled roofs, are towers and steeples of ancient cathedrals standing out against a background of hills and cliffs. Around the city is a massive stone wall thirty feet high and many yards thick. Underground passages connect the town with the old forts on the hills and on the shore. It gives one a creepy feeling to walk through one of these dark, damp passages. Voices have a hollow sound, and the echoes make it seem as if the tunnel were still peopled with Spanish soldiers. We can imagine these stern warriors leading their prisoners, closely bound, through the dark passages lighted only by flaring

*Figure 9—One of the oldest ports
on the Caribbean Sea is Cartagena.*

torches and reëchoing to the tramp of heavy feet and the rattling of chains and swords. We can imagine also the despair of the prisoner, who knew that his captors were taking him to one of the dark dungeons under the old forts, where the waters of the bay rippled above his head. Here in the gloomy, filthy place he might live for years; indeed, many of the prisoners confined in these damp dungeons never again saw the light of day.

Interesting though the old city of Cartagena is, our best way of getting into Colombia is through another port a little farther to the east. This is the town of Savanilla, or little Savannah. Not so many years ago, if we had visited Colombia, we should have anchored out in the bay and have come ashore in smaller boats. Now a fine iron pier nearly a mile long stretches from the railroad station out into the water where it is deep enough for large vessels to dock.

Our first impressions of Colombia are not very pleasant, for the train which we take at the wharf runs through a low, flat, swampy jungle, and we are glad that the town of Barranquilla, the place where we shall leave the train for a river boat, is only fifteen miles away.

Perhaps you are wondering why we do not continue our trip by train. There are very few railroads in Colombia, and if we depended on them we could visit only a small part of the country. To reach many of the places which we wish to see we must travel either by river or by roads so narrow and trails so steep that we shall feel safer on a sure-footed mule than on our own feet. It is difficult and expensive to build railroads in Colombia. Much of the country is covered by ranges of mountains and by tropical forests and jungles. There are several short railroads which connect the seaports with towns a little way inland, and others which stretch from the rivers to the capital, Bogota, and some other inland cities, but as yet there is nothing like a continuous route through the country.

The little railroad from the port of Savanilla extends only to Barranquilla on the Magdalena River. This river is the chief highway of the country, and most of the commerce with the coast and with other countries is carried on its waters. A large sand bar at its mouth makes it unsafe for vessels to enter it from the Caribbean Sea. This is the reason that we took a train for Barranquilla and transferred to a river boat there. The Magdalena is a broad stream navigable for steamers for six hundred miles. At this point the course is blocked by rapids, but beyond them smaller boats can sail for two hundred miles farther.

We are glad that the steamer is waiting at the wharf of Barranquilla, for we have no desire to stop long here. We are not yet used to the tropical sun, which blazes so fiercely in the lowlands of northern and central South America. People at Barranquilla tell us that the temperature never goes below eighty degrees at any season of the year, and during some of the time it is much higher. Notwithstanding its heat, Barranquilla is an important commercial city, and two thirds of all the exports and imports of Colombia pass through it. It has electric cars and lights, a good water supply, some large business houses, and very pleasant residences built in the higher parts of the town away from the water.

*Figure 10—The tropical sun blazes fiercely down
on the wide unshaded streets of Barranquilla.*

The Magdalena is one of the important rivers of South America. Its source is about a thousand miles away to the south, nearly under the equator, and it flows entirely through Colombia. Backward and undeveloped as the interior of Colombia is, it would be much worse off if it were not for this long navigable stream. The only means of getting from the Caribbean Sea into the central part of the country is by a sail of a week or more up the wide, muddy, winding Magdalena. How hot it is! The mosquitoes are very thick, and it is fortunate that we brought plenty of netting to protect us at night from the troublesome pests. They are not only annoying, but people have learned that they carry germs of malaria and yellow fever. Drain the low, swampy region of Colombia, get rid of the mosquitoes, clean up the cities and towns and supply them with plenty of pure water, and it will be found that the white man can live here in the torrid zone and keep in good health. As we visit the different cities of South America we shall see what has been done to make them comfortable and healthfuL

The Magdalena is so wide near its mouth that it seems as if we were sailing on a large lake. On either side the broad valley stretches for miles until it is lost in the hazy distance. Parts of it are low and swampy, and parts are covered with green grass where many cattle are feeding. Farther up we come to the jungles and forests. Now we stop at a small village. Most of the blacks who live here are down at the wharf to see the boat come in or to help unload the boxes of cloth, bags of grain and other foods, and iron tools and machinery which the people of a country where little manufacturing is done need to import. A boat coming down the river will take on the bags of coffee and cocoa beans, the hides, and the sugar that are piled on the wharf.

Figure 11—A boat coming down the river will take on the bags of coffee and cocoa beans piled on the wharf.

The inhabitants of these river towns live in primitive conditions. The houses are rough wooden huts with thatched roofs and dirt floors. Some of the towns appear to be new ones. Here the houses are better, the trade greater, and a larger proportion of white men are in the crowd at the wharf.

During the rainy season much of this plain is flooded, the people go about in boats, and the cattle are driven to the higher pastures. When the water has lowered again the whole valley has received a coating of mud. Thus the soil grows richer year by year. When the flood subsides the Magdalena may perhaps plow its way through the softened earth in a new channel, and villages which a short time before stood on the banks may be some distance away. This shifting of the course of the river makes it difficult for pilots to find the channel. Sometimes it is near one bank and sometimes near the other. Navigation is often hindered, and trips upstream may take one week or two, the time depending on the condition of the river.

See those islands floating in the water. They are made of driftwood and plants worn away from the banks which have been undermined. Such islands sometimes lodge and block the current. The water swirling around them digs out the bank still further and, when the barrier is removed, the trees and plants thus torn up float down the stream, forming new islands as they drift slowly along.

Now and then we meet rude boats partly covered with oval-shaped roofs of bamboo and thatch for the

*Figure 12—We meet rude boats
with oval-shaped roofs of bamboo.*

protection of freight and passengers against sun and rain. With long poles the blacks push these boats upstream and haul them over the rapids with ropes. In the old days, before steamers sailed on the Magdalena, all the traffic was carried on in just such boats as these, but now they are not very common except on the smaller branches of the river and in its upper course, far from the Caribbean Sea.

See this little village where our steamer is stopping. The huts are made of bamboo daubed with mud and roofed over with grass. Rough boats, most of them dugouts, are drawn up on the banks. The little wharf is crowded with people who have come down to trade with the passengers. Some of the natives have delicious-looking fruit, pineapples, bananas, and oranges, besides several kinds which we never saw before. Others carry baskets, jars, hammocks, and hats which they have made and which they offer to us at prices which seem

25

very low indeed. On the wharf also there are bags of coffee and cocoa beans and bundles of hides waiting for the steamer going down to the Caribbean.

As we go farther south the river becomes narrower, and the forests, higher and deeper than those in the north, come nearer to the banks. The trees, shrubs, and vines are massed so thick as to make an impassable wall. Everywhere the twining plants and lovely flowers cover the trunks, and long vines, sometimes called monkey ladders, hang down from the branches and take root in the ground. We see large alligators sunning themselves on the banks and waiting in their lazy way for their food to find its way into their open mouths. Tropical birds of brilliant plumage flit about in the trees, and monkeys chatter in the boughs.

Ever since the time when we left the Caribbean Sea there have been palm trees in sight. Some have been short and some tall, some heavy with coconuts, and some from which the natives obtain wax to make matches. They grow in clumps and solitary in green meadows, in groves by themselves and scattered among other kinds of trees, in dry places and with their roots covered with water. There is no other tree in the world which furnishes so many millions of people with the necessities of life as the palm family. From it the people of tropical lands get wood for their houses, leaves for their thatched roofs, food to eat when hungry, and refreshing drink when thirsty.

About two hundred miles up the Magdalena we come to the mouth of its largest branch, the Cauca River.

We wish that we had time for a sail up the Cauca, for it is a beautiful stream. In the upper part of its valley, where the land is higher, the climate is delightful, never too hot or too cold. The soil is very rich, and when railroads are built and settlers take up the land, they can raise great crops of sugar, cotton, wheat, corn and other products of the subtropical and temperate zones.

One writer calls Colombia the Wonderland of Opportunity. It has all the necessary resources and advantages to become an important agricultural and commercial country and to support a dense population. All kinds of food products can be easily grown—fruits, grains, and vegetables. It contains great mineral wealth. The larger part of the world's supply of emeralds— beautiful green gems more valuable than diamonds— comes from the treasures hidden in its rocks. No other country except Russia yields such quantities of platinum.

If we wish to picture Colombia as it doubtless will be sometime in the future, we must look far ahead to the time when all the undeveloped parts of the earth will yield their treasures to feed, clothe, and house its inhabitants and furnish materials for manufacture and means of transportation. Then visitors to this Southern republic will ride in comfortable trains through what is today an untraveled, unexplored region. Great sugar-cane fields will stretch over large areas, cocoa and coffee trees will be planted by the millions, grains and vegetables will grow on fertile farms on the cool plateau, vast herds of cattle will feed in the green pastures, axes will ring and saws buzz in the tropical forests, and millions of rubber trees will yield their milky juice to the rubber gatherers. Deep shafts will be sunk in the rich iron deposits, and long trains will carry loads of coal from the mines to the steel manufactories. Mining towns will spring up near the beds of gold, silver, and copper. Stamp mills will clatter and pound as they crush the hard ore, and smelters with tall chimneys will pour out clouds of smoke into the clear air. Stores of petroleum of fine quality will furnish fuel for furnaces and engines, besides yielding quantities of gasoline, benzine, paraffin, and other by-products. Forests will furnish plenty of lumber for the cities which in future years will be found both on the low plains and on the high plateaus, where now are little villages of thatch-roofed huts.

All the necessities for such a development are close at hand. What is needed is money, laborers, good roads, railroads, tools, machinery, and a strong government to make just laws and enforce them. These things will all come in time, and the more quickly now that the Panama Canal will bring many vessels, not only from the United States but from other countries, which will use this new water route to western South America and call at Colombian ports on the way.

As we travel southward we begin to realize why very few people visit Bogota, the capital of Colombia. After spending some four or five days on the Magdalena, we leave the boat for a railroad trip around some rapids in the river. This done, we again transfer to a steamer and continue our way upstream. Again we change to a train that takes us from the low river valley up to the plateau on which Bogota is situated. It has taken us more than a week to come from the coast of the Caribbean Sea to Bogota. In the same time we could have journeyed from New York to San Francisco and back again. The interior of Colombia will not be developed to any great extent until more railroads are built and quicker means of transportation are provided.

If we contrast Bogota with our own beautiful capital, Washington, it seems but a poor place. If we think of it in contrast with the other cities and towns that we have seen in Colombia, it is very beautiful. It is astonishing to find here, in the heart of the Andes Mountains and, as one writer says, "six hundred miles from anywhere," the capital of a great republic, a city as large as Omaha, Nebraska. It is the first large city of South America that we have visited, and it is so different from the cities of the United States that we will stay here a few days and accustom ourselves to the strange sights.

There may be some things lacking in Bogota that we are accustomed to in our own home cities, but there are two things in which no city of the world rivals this South American capital. One of these is the climate. The average temperature of the year is sixty degrees, and, though it is sometimes a little chilly, in the shade and at night, for the most part it is delightfully warm and pleasant. It seems impossible to believe that we are no farther from the equator than San Francisco is from Los Angeles, but we must remember that Bogota is between eight and nine thousand feet above sea level, which accounts for the cool, pleasant climate.

The other way in which the capital of Colombia

29

excels most other cities is in its wonderful scenery. In all directions but one stretches the fertile plateau encircled in the distance by lofty mountains. Green pastures, rich farming land, and blue lakes cover the high plain, which is one of the pleasantest regions of South America.

Figure 13—The capital of Colombia excels most other cities in its wonderful scenery.

Close to Bogota on the east rise two rounded mountains, which tower two thousand feet above the city nestling at the base. On the top of each of these mountains is a large chapel which has stood for centuries gazing down on the city below. No road leads very far up the slopes, and the chapels can be reached only by some hours of hard climbing. If you are ready for a tramp, let us go a little way up one of these mountains and look down on the capital. It appears very different from a city in the United States. The streets are narrower, and some of the sidewalks are hardly wide enough for two people to walk side by side. The low buildings seem to be all joined together, and their solid walls line the streets. We see no green lawns or lovely gardens in front of them. No chimneys rise from the red roofs, and no skyscrapers tower above the lower blocks. The streets are crowded. Everybody seems to be out for a good time, but nearly all of the people are on foot, and we see few carriages or loaded wagons. Many of the

Figure 14—The streets of Bogota are narrow.

streets are covered with cobblestones, over which riding would be anything but pleasant.

Because of Spanish discoveries and explorations, all the South American countries except Brazil and Guiana were claimed by the Spanish throne and settled largely by Spaniards. Most of the cities therefore resemble those of Spain. The houses sit close to the narrow sidewalks, and a heavy door in the wall admits people to the courtyard behind. As we first walk through the streets we wonder if the people of Bogota do not like gardens and flowers and fountains and smooth green lawns. As we become better acquainted with the city we find that the gardens are behind the houses instead of in front of them, as ours usually are. Not only in

31

Bogota but in most cities of South America the houses are built around a square, called a patio. The gardens and flowers and fountains are in the patio, where the family can enjoy them in private, undisturbed by the passers-by.

The buildings are only one story or, in some cases, two stories high. Near the center of the city the lower floor is usually occupied by stores. In the outskirts, this part of the house, which is considered less desirable, is let to the poorer families, while the wealthier people live on the second floor. The rich and the poor thus mingle together in the same part of the city. The rooms on the lower floor have only one outer door, which opens on the street. A solid wall separates these rooms from the patio, which is used only by the family on the second floor. The best rooms of the house, the parlor and reception rooms, are on the street side of the patio; the kitchen is on the opposite side, in the rear; and the bedrooms are on the sides between. In the front rooms on the second floor there are balconies where the ladies sit and watch the sights. These balconies form a kind of roof which protects the people on the sidewalks from the sun and the rain. There are no stoves in the houses nor any method of heating any of the rooms except the kitchen, which is separated from the rooms where the family spend most of their time. In most of the houses of South America we find no way of heating the rooms, and in many cases they seem to us cold and uncomfortable.

Some of the buildings in Bogota are very old.

Among these are many convents and monasteries, which are now put to other uses. Some of them are used for schools, hotels, hospitals, barracks for the soldiers, the post office, and other departments of government.

In South America the public squares or parks in the cities are called plazas. Some of these plazas are very beautiful and are adorned with gardens, fountains, and statues, and surrounded by churches, stores, and government buildings. Many of the people go to the plazas in the evening to chat with friends, to enjoy the air, and to listen to the music of a military band.

In the central plaza of Bogota there is a statue of a man of whom we shall hear a great deal in our trip. This is Simon Bolivar, the hero who helped several of the South American republics to free themselves from Spain. Bolivia is named for him, streets and avenues in many countries bear his name, his image is stamped on pieces of money, and many plazas contain his statue.

There is none of the hustle and bustle in Bogota such as we are accustomed to in the business streets of our cities. No carts and drays rattle, no steam whistles shriek, no one talks in a loud, boisterous way. Everyone moves along quietly and leisurely. What is the use of hurrying? If things cannot be done today, tomorrow is coming; and if not tomorrow, the next day is sure to be here later. Not so much is accomplished perhaps by these dignified, polite people as by the quick, brusque business men and women in the United States, but they live quietly and happily and have time to enjoy their friends, their books, and their homes. Doubtless these gracious people of Bogota need to rub shoulders with the hustling business men of the United States, but it will do us good also to come in touch with these charming, cultured, soft-voiced neighbors in the South.

When railroads are built between the coast and the delightful city of Bogota many American tourists will find a trip here as pleasant and restful as to any European capital. An excursion that some of these future tourists will wish to take is to the famous emerald mines seventy or eighty miles to the north of Bogota, where most of the emeralds of the world are obtained. We should find the trip today a very hard one, for we should have to go on muleback over a rough, stony trail. One of the best-known mines is in the crater of an extinct volcano. The mining is carried on just as it has been for hundreds of years. The only machinery used to get out the gems is a pickax or crowbar in the hands of a South American Indian laborer. After the rock is broken up in this way the fragments are washed by water led down a sluiceway. The water is then drawn off and the sediment searched for the precious crystals. It was in this simple way that the largest emerald ever known was found. It was a perfect six-sided crystal, two inches long, and weighed half a pound or more.

As we leave Bogota and journey down the steep slopes to the Magdalena River we ride by acres of wheat and corn, past large ranches where cattle and sheep feed in green pastures, over meadows covered with wild flowers, through tropical forests, and past villages of mud huts green with clambering vines. Always the scene before us is very beautiful. The day is a clear one, and we can follow the windings of the river in its low valley for fifty miles or more. On the other side of the river a beautiful range of mountains rises clear and blue. Beyond them, we know, is the fertile valley of the Cauca River, the largest branch of the Magdalena, and beyond this there is another mountain range which slopes down to the Pacific.

When we were in Bogota we were between two and three hundred miles from the border of Venezuela, the country which we are to visit next. If we had attempted to reach the inhabited parts of Venezuela from the interior of Colombia our zigzag route would have measured five or six hundred miles, and the trip would have taken weeks of hard travel on muleback through deep forests and tangled jungles. Our best way is to go back to the coast of Colombia by the route which led us into the country. At Savanilla we can change to a vessel which will take us across the Caribbean Sea to the city of La Guaira, the seaport of Venezuela.

TOPICS FOR STUDY

I

1. Life on the Spanish Main.

2. Size and surface of Colombia.

3. Climate and resources of Colombia.

4. The old city of Cartagena.

5. From Savanilla to Barranquilla.

6. A trip up the Magdalena River.

7. The Magdalena and Cauca rivers.

8. Bogota, the capital.

9. Simon Bolivar.

10. The future development of Colombia.

II

1. Sketch South America. Show Colombia and the other countries spoken of in this chapter, the Andes Mountains, and the Magdalena, Orinoco, and Amazon rivers.

2. Sketch Colombia. Show mountains, two rivers, and four cities.

3. Make a sketch to show the arrangement of the rooms in a typical old Spanish house with a patio.

4. Look up the life of Simon Bolivar and tell the class something about him.

5. Make a list of the places mentioned in Topic III which you think are so important that you should always remember them.

III

Be able to spell and pronounce the following names. Locate each place and tell what was said of it in the chapter. Add other facts if possible.

Peru	Amazon River
Bolivia	Magdalena River
Ecuador	Cauca River
Venezuela	Andes Mountains
Brazil	New Orleans
Guiana	Los Angeles
Panama	New York
The Spanish Main	Omaha
Spain	San Francisco
Mexico	Washington
Montana	Grand Rapids
Utah	London
Colorado	Cartagena
Arizona	Savanilla
New Mexico	Barranquilla
Caribbean Sea	Bogota
Panama Canal	Buenaventura
Great Salt Lake	La Guaira
Orinoco River	

CHAPTER III

A TRIP THROUGH VENEZUELA

VENEZUELA is one of our nearest neighbors in South America. It is as large as all the states which lie on the western border of the Mississippi River,—Minnesota, Iowa, Missouri, Arkansas, and Louisiana,—together with Wisconsin and more than half of Illinois on the eastern side. These states are in the valley of the Mississippi, while Venezuela lies in the basin of the Orinoco—one of the three largest rivers of South America.

There is as much difference between the low tropical coast lands of Venezuela and the cool pleasant plateaus of the interior as there is between the warm, balmy climate of Louisiana and the cold, bracing air of Minnesota. The products of the different parts of Venezuela vary as much as the crops of our Gulf States do from those of the Great Lake region. Venezuela contains many mountains, some of which are so high that, in spite of the fact that the entire country lies in the torrid zone, their tops are continually covered with snow.

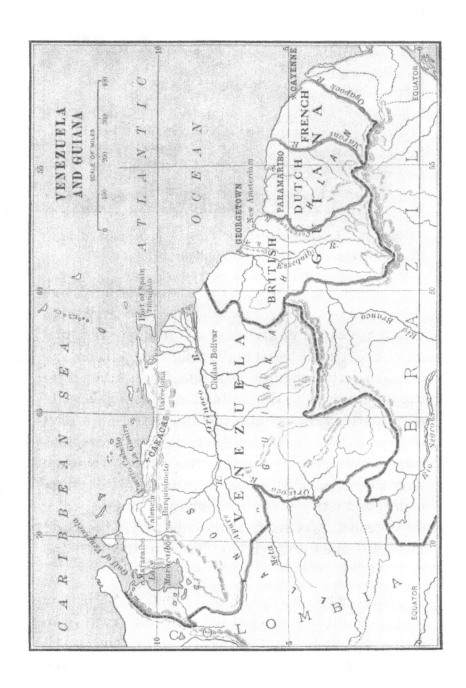

39

Figure 15—La Guaira looks as if it were being pushed into the sea by the high mountains behind it.

The states bordering on the Mississippi are all well developed, while in Venezuela there are large areas which are as yet entirely unexplored, and the total number of people living in the country is considerably less than the population of Missouri. Most of the people live on the coast and in the high mountain valleys. In some parts of the country you might travel for days without seeing a person, and you might explore regions where as yet no white man has ever set foot. There are large forests of valuable woods, many miles of grassy plains, and rich stores of mineral wealth. One writer on Venezuela says that of all the countries in the world this is the one for which God has done the most and man the least.

Venezuela has a coast line so long that if it were stretched out in a straight line it would reach from New York City to Great Salt Lake. On this long stretch of coast are more than thirty good harbors, at any one of which we might land. We will go at once, however, to La Guaira, the chief commercial port of the country. The city nestles so close to the water that it looks as if it were being pushed into the sea by the high mountains which rise directly behind it. What a pretty picture it makes! In the foreground is the deep-blue Caribbean, above which gleam bright-colored houses roofed with dull-red tiles and shaded by towering palms. Directly back of the town are steep hills, and higher still, with their heads almost piercing the sky, are green, wooded mountains.

The wharves are piled high with great bags of coffee and cocoa beans, bundles of hides and skins, and quantities of rubber. Many of these goods will come to the United States, for we buy more goods from Venezuela than any other country does—nearly

Figure 16—On the low, hot coast strip of Venezuela are large cocoa plantations, where we may see men raking up the cocoa beans in piles to dry.

as much, in fact, as all others put together. Perhaps the coffee which was on your breakfast table, the chocolate candy which you ate after dinner, the skins which were used for your shoes, or the material from which your rubbers were made came from this northern republic of South America.

If we were to journey through this low, hot coast strip of Venezuela, we should pass large plantations covered with cacao trees, which yield the beans from which cocoa and chocolate are made. These plantations thrive best along the Caribbean shore, for the cacao tree requires a warmer, more moist climate than either coffee or sugar, which are raised farther inland.

It is very hot on these cacao plantations, and perhaps even hotter in the narrow streets of La Guaira. The temperature is always high, and we wonder how the people who live here endure the heat. We are not yet used to the rays of the tropical sun, and we are glad to leave the seaport for Caracas, the capital, which is situated high in the mountains to the south.

Look carefully at a map and you will see that, besides the mountains in the southern part of Venezuela, there are in the north three ranges of the Andes system. One extends to the most northern point of South America, just west of Lake Maracaibo. Another range, east of this, stretches for some distance along the northern shore of Venezuela, while a third runs through the northern part of the country south of and parallel to the second range, leaving a long, narrow valley between the two. It is in this high valley that Caracas is situated. It is only six miles from the coast, but we shall have to ride in the train more than three times that distance and cross the second range of mountains over a pass more than half a mile above the level of the sea before we catch a glimpse of the capital in the valley between the highlands. It is a wonderful railroad that extends between La Guaira and Caracas, as difficult to build, it seems to us, as any which cross the mountains in the United States. The tracks cling to the mountain-side, and our train creeps along precipices where we can look down for hundreds of feet into deep canyons. We curve around horseshoes so sharp that we can see across narrow gorges into the cab of the engineer.

Figure 17—The tracks cling to the mountain-side.

As we climb higher we look back on the blue Caribbean and the red-roofed, cream-white villages nestling on the shore at the foot of mountains up which our track winds like a ribbon of steel. As we rise still higher we are wrapped in a thick, gray cloud which covers everything like a heavy mist and which leaves the rocks, trees, and the shining steel rails as wet as if a rain had fallen. We come out of the cloud just as we pass the crest of the mountains. The blue Caribbean has disappeared behind us, and now, below us to the south, we can see the beautiful valley in which the capital is situated.

*Figure 18—We look down into the beautiful valley
in which Caracas is situated.*

Caracas is larger than Savannah, Georgia, and is about as far from the equator as that city is from Philadelphia. The valley in which it lies is so high and the breezes that blow down from the mountains are so cool that the climate is never uncomfortable, and we shall enjoy a walk through the narrow streets more than we did through those of the hot seaport of La Guaira. The houses are similar to those of Bogota, one story high and made with very thick walls. These serve not only to keep out the heat but also as a protection from earthquake shocks, from which Caracas has suffered in times past.

Most of the buildings are painted in very bright colors,—blue, green, yellow, pink, and lavender,—and nearly all have roofs of red tiles. As in Bogota, we see no chimneys and no green lawns and beautiful gardens in front of the buildings, which in most cases come close to the edge of the pavements. This makes the streets appear even narrower than they really are and less attractive than those in our cities which are bordered with velvety grass and bright flowers. If we could enter the heavy street door of these houses and go out into the patios, we should find there pleasant open courts with gardens, fountains, and trees, which the people enjoy undisturbed by the passing in the street.

Figure 19—Some of the patios are very beautiful.

The streets in the business part of Caracas are lined with fine shops brilliantly illuminated by electric lights. Electric cars make it possible for the people living in the suburbs to enjoy all the conveniences of the city. The sidewalks are overhung with bright awnings and projecting red roofs and are filled with well-dressed, polite people, some of whom are intent on their business, while others are enjoying the open-air cafés.

Figure 20—The houses sit close to the pavements.

Caracas has more than a dozen plazas. Many of them are beautifully laid out with gardens and fountains, and nearly every one contains a fine statue in bronze or marble of some Venezuelan hero, which gives the name to the square. This evening we will go with the crowds to the Plaza Bolivar, the largest and finest in the city. It is paved with tiles, and on festive nights hundreds of electric lights hang in festoons from the many trees. In the month of May it appears like an enchanted flower garden with the orchids in full bloom. These orchids are spread all over the trunks of the trees—a single tree displaying as many as two hundred blossoms at a time. They are of the pale lavender variety sold at such high prices in the United States. On concert evenings, when the famous military band is playing, the effect of the electric lights through these flowering trees is very beautiful.

In the center of the square is a bronze statue of Simon Bolivar, the "George Washington of South

Figure 21—The statue of Bolivar in the plaza of Caracas is a very beautiful one.

America," the same hero whose statue we saw in the plaza of Bogota. Bolivar is honored as the "Father of his Country" not only in Venezuela but in Colombia, Peru, Ecuador, and Bolivia, each of which he helped to free from Spain. The statue of the hero in the plaza of Caracas is a very beautiful one, as you can see in the picture. The quiet, masterful way in which he handles his rearing horse, and the look of dignity and strength in his face, proclaim him a leader of men.

There is another plaza in Caracas, smaller than the Plaza Bolivar but which we may enjoy more. In it, shaded by lofty palms and surrounded by beautiful gardens, is a fine statue of George Washington. Simon Bolivar loved and admired our first president, and the people of Caracas were delighted to honor so distinguished a friend of their great hero. So they erected this statue and named the square the Plaza Washington. In some of the public buildings you will see the familiar pictures of "Washington Crossing the Delaware," "Washington on Horseback," and "Washington at Mt. Vernon."

On Sunday we shall enjoy going to the market, for in Caracas there is much more excitement and a greater variety of goods to be sold on that day than at any other time during the week. For miles around the city, hundreds of donkeys have been bringing to the square where the market is held all sorts of produce— loads of chickens, ducks, pigs, sheep, cheeses, vegetables, and fruit. During the night the merchants have been arranging their piles of goods, and over their little fires of charcoal the women have been making strange-looking candies, sweetmeats, and savory soups. In the

Figure 22—The people of Caracas erected this statue of George Washington in one of their plazas.

early morning the plaza and all the streets leading to it are crowded with people and donkeys. Merchants bargain over their produce, pigs and hens are killed for the Sunday dinner, and the lottery ticket venders cry to the people around to improve the last chance to purchase tickets for the great prize which is to be drawn later in the day. You can buy almost anything in the market from books and old bottles to lovely flowers and second-hand clothing. In the bird section you can have your choice of talkative parrots, lovely mocking birds, shy brown thrushes, and tiny brilliant humming birds. Women of Afrcian descent with black skins as shiny as satin haggle over the fruit, vegetable, and meat stands, driving good bargains for the families for whom they work.

Perhaps you would like to take a ride on the electric cars out into the country around Caracas. On every hand we see the level land covered with fields of sugar cane stretching away to the mountains which surround the valley. Sugar cane is raised everywhere in Venezuela except on the highlands, where it is too cold. The fields on the plantations have roadways for the wagons which carry the cane to the place where it is to be crushed. Sugar-making in Venezuela is carried on in a very different way from what it is in the United States. Let us stop at this plantation where the farmer is crushing the cane just brought in from the fields. He puts the tall stalks between rollers which are worked by oxen. As they walk slowly round and round, the juice drips out into vessels underneath the rollers. The juice is boiled down into sirup in large caldrons over a fire made of dried cane or wood. The sirup is poured into shallow wooden troughs, where it is thoroughly stirred until it is as thick as mud. Then it is turned into cone-shaped earthen molds and allowed to harden. In Venezuelan cities we shall see on the tables white sugar such as we use; but if the people in the country regions invite us to join their simple meal, we shall find only these brown cone-shaped loaves.

On the slopes of the valley in which Caracas is situated there are rows of coffee trees. Venezuela is one of the chief coffee-producing countries of South America, and on her plantations there are millions of trees. The soil is so rich and the climate so favorable that many more might be raised, but the average Venezuelan farmer is not very ambitious. He is poor and ignorant, unable to read and write, and lives with his large family in a tumble-down hut. He has no higher ideals than to exist undisturbed by revolutions, to earn enough to buy candles for his favorite saint, and perhaps now and then to indulge in a lottery ticket which he thinks may possibly bring him a fortune. His mean little home contains but few articles of furniture, he uses few and simple tools in cultivating his land, and the climate is so warm that he buys little clothing.

Figure 23—The Venezuelan peasant lives with his large family in a tumble-down hut.

Though the homes of the farmers are not attractive, the valley itself is lovely. It is green with vegetable gardens and has many large orchards of orange and lemon trees loaded with delicious fruit. Many of the orchards and gardens are irrigated, and by this means the farmers are able to raise crops in the dry season and thus make their farms productive during the entire year.

Most of the cities of Venezuela are located along the shore and in the high valley behind the coast mountains, and the most of the people live in these

Figure 24—Some of the scenes in Venezuelan cities would seem peculiar to us.

parts of the country. Let us take a trip on the railroad which runs through the valley. We ride between fields of tall, waving sugar cane, past acres of coffee plantations, near orchards of orange and lemon trees, and through dense tropical forests where in the clearing we can see little native villages. Now and then we are in the midst of pastures of rich green grass where numbers of sleek-looking cattle are feeding. We fly in and out of scores of tunnels and finally reach Valencia, one of the important cities of Venezuela. It is delightfully situated, high enough to escape the tropical heat of the lowlands and to receive the mountain breezes. From here a railroad extends to the coast between thirty and forty miles away. The coffee, sugar, and cattle are brought to Valencia for many miles around and shipped thence to Puerto Cabello, the seaport at the end of the line.

What peculiar names some of these old Spanish cities have! The Spaniard who first sailed into the harbor of Puerto Cabello found it so well protected that he gave it the name which means "The Port of a Hair," signifying that its waters were so quiet that vessels anchored by a hair would not break their moorings. The harbor is one of the finest in the world, and the city, lying at the water's edge on a long, narrow peninsula, with mountains rising behind and a stretch of shining beach in front, is very picturesque.

In coming from Colombia we might have shortened our voyage on the Caribbean Sea by entering Venezuela through the gulf of the same name and stopping at Maracaibo. This is a commercial port important not only for the products of western Venezuela but for eastern Colombia as well. The city is situated on the long, narrow neck of Lake Maracaibo and, with its low houses shaded by tall palms and surrounded by coconut groves, looks very attractive from the water.

Lake Maracaibo is nearly the size of Massachusetts. It is really an arm of the ocean, but it is so inclosed by land that it seems more like a huge lake, and is so called. It is everywhere deep enough to be navigated by ocean steamers, but its mouth is so blocked by sand bars as to prevent large vessels from entering.

The Gulf of Venezuela, into which Lake Maracaibo drains, was discovered by early Spanish explorers who arrived during the rainy season, when the country was flooded. Noticing the natives going around in boats and their huts raised on piles above the water, these European discoverers were reminded of Venice and its streets of water, and so called the land Venezuela, which means "little Venice," a name not at all appropriate for the most of the country.

Stretching from Lake Maracaibo over the mountains toward the upper Orinoco and the Meta rivers are immense tropical forests. Much of this region is unexplored, and we might travel through it for days at a time without seeing any sign of human life. Yet these forests will some day be of immense value to Venezuela. The tall, straight trunks will furnish quantities of splendid timber, some of it suitable for making the finest furniture. Some of the trees yield substances which are useful in the tanning of leather, in dyes, and in medicine. Scattered through the forests are thousands of rubber trees, which will be a great source of wealth when the region is opened up to trade.

In the country immediately surrounding Lake Maracaibo we could visit rich coffee and cocoa plantations and see acres of fertile black soil covered with the huge leaves of the tobacco plant and with tall sugar cane. In the mountains are rich stores of minerals—gold, copper, lead, and coal. If Venezuela had a strong government, so that foreigners might be sure that their property would be well protected, they would be more willing to invest money in these mines, which, with modern machinery and skilled workmen, might be made to produce many times as much as they do at present.

There is another mineral which is found around Lake Maracaibo, and in greater quantities in other parts of Venezuela. This is asphalt. It is used for paving streets, spreading on roofs, making varnishes, lining cold-storage plants, calking seams of wooden vessels, in the composition of shoeblacking, and for many other purposes.

The most noted deposit of asphalt, or mineral pitch as it is sometimes called, is the famous pitch lake on the island of Trinidad, near the mouth of the Orinoco River. This lake, composed of nearly pure asphalt, is a mile and a half across. At first sight it looks like an ordinary woodland pond surrounded by green trees, but as we approach nearer, the dark color, the thick material, and the smell all tell us that it is very different from any lake that we have ever seen before. On its borders the

*Figure 25—The most noted deposit of asphalt
is the famous pitch lake on the island of Trinidad.*

asphalt is hard enough to bear our weight, but nearer
the center it is softer, and here and there are tiny pitch
volcanoes, a foot or two high, in constant eruption.
The workmen dig out the asphalt with pickaxes and
load it onto mule carts, to be taken to the shore. In the
little shipping village on the coast of Trinidad all the
men are employed in some industry connected with
asphalt. Some are cutting it and bringing it from the
lake, some are melting it, while others are loading it
onto the vessels.

A lake of asphalt, more shallow but larger in area
than the one in Trinidad, is situated in the northern part
of Venezuela. The asphalt obtained here is of very good
quality, and has been used to protect the tunnels of the
New York subway from moisture and to make some of
the splendid avenues of our capital city, Washington.

When you ride on some smooth, hard city streets or see the workmen pouring the dark, molten mass onto some highway which is being improved, you will think of these curious deposits of asphalt in Venezuela and in the island at the mouth of its great river.

You remember that on the wharves at La Guaira we saw great piles of hides and skins and learned that these were among the principal exports of the country. Cattle are raised in great numbers on the llanos—those wide grassy plains which stretch for miles through the Orinoco valley. The mountainous regions of Venezuela are pleasanter and cooler than the lowlands, but we will leave them now and make our way back to La Guaira. There we will take a boat around to the mouth of the Orinoco and sail up the great river into its vast pasture lands. Nearly a thousand rivers rise within the borders of Venezuela, half of which are branches of the Orinoco. Seventy rivers which are wholly or partly within the country, if united and stretched out in a straight line, would furnish a navigable waterway long enough to reach from New York to San Francisco and back again. The Orinoco is the largest of them all, and is navigable for a distance equal to that from Chicago to New Orleans.

Rivers which carry large quantities of soil in their waters and which flow into parts of the ocean where the currents are not swift enough to sweep the deposits out to sea usually build deltas at their mouths. The great delta plain of the Orinoco begins a hundred and twenty miles from the ocean. Here the river, broadened out into a sluggish stream twelve miles wide, flows so slowly that it begins to drop the silt which it carries. These deposits have so filled up the channel that the river has from time to time sought a new course, and now enters the ocean in many outlets. The mouths of the two outer streams are now nearly as far apart as the city of New York is from Washington, D.C. The delta plain is cut up by the numberless channels and branches into thousands of islands which are scarcely above sea level and which, during the floods of the Orinoco in the rainy season, are entirely covered with water.

Figure 26—On the Orinoco we are shut in by the tropical forest.

Our route takes us up the most direct branch into the main river, which is bordered by the dense tropical forest. Tall trees of many kinds rear their straight gray trunks in an effort to rise higher than their fellows and so reach the sunlight. Some are covered with gorgeous flowers and look like giant bouquets. Some are festooned with a tangle of trailing vines, which hang down like so many green ropes from branches high in the air and lose themselves in the matted growth of grass and roots underfoot. In the deep shade, where scarcely a ray of sunlight flickers, there are long-legged herons, noisy parrots, and countless other birds.

The steamer that takes us up the Orinoco is clean and comfortable. There are so many passengers on board that we wonder how all of them can find staterooms and berths for the night. When bedtime comes the problem is solved. The weather is very hot, and few of the passengers, especially those who travel second class, desire staterooms. They swing the hammocks that they have brought with them to the hooks with which the deck is supplied and are soon fast asleep. Some, not so fortunate, curl up on the floor in a corner of the deck. These poor accommodations do not trouble them, for many of the people of Venezuela know no other bed than a hammock or a mat.

A two or three days' sail up the Orinoco brings us to Ciudad Bolivar, the chief city on its banks. On landing here we are as far from the coast as St. Louis is from Chicago, yet even here the great Orinoco is four miles wide. If we should sail upstream as far again, we should find that, even at that distance from the ocean, the river is only a mile narrower than at Ciudad Bolivar. If we were here in the rainy season from May to October, when the Orinoco rises so high that it spreads out for miles over the plain, we should think that we were sailing on a vast inland sea. At this time of the year the few people who live in the lowlands go about in boats,

Figure 27—At Ciudad Bolivar the river is four miles wide.

and the cattle which feed on the plain have to be taken to higher pastures.

Ciudad Bolivar is an important city, for it is the only place of any size in a district covering thousands of square miles. As we approach we see on the shore great warehouses which are filled with coffee, cocoa, rubber, hides and skins, pelts of the jaguar and other wild beasts, and beautiful feathers for millinery establishments. When our ship leaves the port for its return trip it will carry besides these products considerable quantities of gold. South of the Orinoco there are rich deposits of this mineral, and Ciudad Bolivar is the place from which miners and prospectors start for the gold fields.

Coming up the Orinoco our steamer was loaded with flour, iron manufactures, wire fencing, salt, groceries, and cotton cloth. It carried also quantities of jute bags and bagging to hold the cocoa beans and coffee berries which are exported from the country. These imports will be loaded onto smaller boats, which will sail up the Orinoco and its branches and distribute the supplies to the villages and towns scattered through the plains of Venezuela and even to parts of eastern Colombia.

The large steamers go no farther than Ciudad Bolivar, and in order to continue our trip we shall have to change to a smaller boat. While waiting here, however, we shall have opportunity to explore this Venezuelan port.

The southern bank of the Orinoco, on which Ciudad Bolivar is situated, slopes sharply up from the river so that the low, bright-colored buildings appear to rise in terraces from the water. On the crest of the slope there towers over all a great white cathedral. Near it are the public buildings of the city, inclosing a plaza. A military band plays in the evening, and hundreds of the people come here to enjoy the music, the lights, the cooler air of the night, and a social chat with friends.

How different everything seems in this Venezuelan city from a place of the same size in the United States! No chimneys rise above the red roofs, and few teams are seen in the narrow streets. All the freight is carried on the backs of donkeys or on the shoulders of blacks and South American Indians. The low houses are built around patios, and there are no front yards, green lawns, or shady piazzas. Most of the windows facing the street have heavy iron bars across them, through which we see pretty, dark-eyed young women peeping at us as we walk along.

Continuing our journey up the Orinoco, we see few people along the banks. Once in a while we pass a small village of mud huts or a group of houses raised on piles to protect them from the floods. The roofs are made of bark or are thatched with palm leaves. Some of the houses have thatched sides, while others have no sides at all—only a roof supported by four corner posts. We can see hammocks hung from the posts and occupied by one or more members of the family, who are taking their daily siesta, or after-dinner nap.

Could you build a house without using a nail? A Venezuelan native never uses one in making his hut. The long, rope-like vines which he finds in the forest serve him just as well, perhaps better, for he would scarcely know how to use a hammer.

See that woman in the small, open hut making a hammock from the leaves of the palm tree. Several of the natives have come down to the little wharf to offer similar ones for sale to the passengers on the boat. The hammocks look strong and well made and will last a long time. Another woman, squatting in front of her hut, is grinding some grain between two stones. Down in the river another is doing the family washing. The amount of laundry work to be done is probably small, for the grown people wear very little clothing and the children none at all. Groups of shy little people with their bare brown bodies and curious eyes have gathered near the wharf to see the odd-looking strangers with

Figure 28—A Solitary Hut on the Orinoco

white skins. How simple their life is! They do not have to worry about clothing, the approach of cold weather, the danger of the crop failing, or any of the many things that trouble us. On the other hand, they have no books or papers, and could not read them if they had; they have no lamps or candles or any other means of lighting their little huts, but go to bed at dark in their hammocks.

As we have come up the river the forests have been gradually growing thinner, until they form only a fringe along the banks. Back of the woods lie immense plains covered with tall grass. These are the llanos,—some of the best pasture lands in the world,— and most of the people in this part of Venezuela are engaged in cattle raising. The llanos extend from the mountain regions of the north to beyond the Orinoco and the Meta rivers, and cover a territory nearly as large as the New England and Middle Atlantic states. During a part of the year we might stand waist deep in the grass on these vast pasture lands, which stretch away on all sides to meet the sky, broken only here and there by clumps of trees or small groves. In another season on the selfsame spot we could see nothing as far as the eye could reach save a vast expanse of water out of which here and there rose the green tops of a few trees. The people go from place to place in boats, and the cattle have been driven to the higher land.

At present about two million cattle feed on the llanos, but the rich pastures would easily support many times that number. The beef which might be produced in Venezuela would make a valuable addition to the world's supply of meat, and the export of hides and skins might be greatly increased. Many of the people, however, raise just enough to support themselves. "What is the use?" they say, "We get a large herd of cattle and then there is a revolution. The soldiers come and take our animals and we never get any pay for them." We do not wonder at this feeling, for in the past fifty years Venezuela has had many revolutions, during each of which cattle and grain have been seized, property destroyed, men taken from their farms, and hundreds of lives lost. The chief need of Venezuela today is a strong, settled government in which the Venezuelans and the people of other nations may have confidence. With her fertile soil, deep forests, miles of grassy plains, rich stores of minerals, and enormous length of navigable waterways a great future lies before Venezuela, a future in which we are bound to share, for Venezuela is more conveniently situated for trade with the United States than any other South American country.

TOPICS FOR STUDY

I

1. Position and size of Venezuela.

2. Surface and climate of Venezuela.

3. The coast line of Venezuela and the seaport of La Guaira.

4. Caracas, the capital.

5. Simon Bolivar and George Washington.

6. Sugar plantations and sugar making.

7. Farmers of Venezuela.

8. Coffee and cocoa.

9. Valencia and Puerto Cabello.

10. The lake and city of Maracaibo.

11. Forests of Venezuela.

12. The pitch lakes of Trinidad and Venezuela.

13. Rivers of Venezuela.

14. The Orinoco River.

15. Ciudad Bolivar.

16. Houses and villages on the Orinoco.

17. The llanos and the cattle industry.

II

1. How large is the island of Trinidad? To whom does it belong? For what products is it valuable? What other islands of the West Indies belong to the same nation?

2. Write a list of the contrasts between the Mississippi and the Orinoco valleys.

3. Write a list of any rivers of the world which have built great deltas. Locate each river.

4. Coffee, cocoa, and other products are exported in jute bags. In what country is jute produced? Where is it manufactured? Name the waters on which it has been carried to Venezuela.

5. Why is Venezuela not an appropriate name for the country we are studying?

6. Sketch a free-hand map of Venezuela. Show the boundaries, mountains, cities, rivers, and products.

7. Why is Venezuela in such a backward condition? What does she need to help in her development?

8. Name the chief crops of Venezuela.

9. Make a list of places mentioned in Topic III which you think are so important that you should always remember them.

III

Be able to spell and pronounce the following names. Locate each place and tell what was said about it in this and in any previous chapter. Add other facts if possible.

Brazil	Llanos
Ecuador	Trinidad
Peru	Chicago
Bolivia	St. Louis
Colombia	New Orleans
Andes Mountains	San Francisco
New England States	Philadelphia
Middle Atlantic States	Washington
States west of the Mississippi River	New York
States east of the Mississippi River	Savannah
Isthmus of Panama	Bogota
Mississippi River	La Guaira
Meta River	Ciudad Bolivar
Orinoco River	Maracaibo
Caribbean Sea	Valencia
Lake Maracaibo	Puerto Cabello
Great Salt Lake	Caracas
Gulf of Venezuela	Venice

CHAPTER IV

GUIANA AND ITS SUGAR PLANTATIONS

As we journey along the coast of South America our next stop will be at Guiana, a country considerably larger than the states of Ohio, Indiana, and Illinois. Guiana is the only division of South America which is not a republic. The unequal parts into which it is divided are owned by the English, Dutch, and French. British Guiana is the largest and the most developed of the three, though much of this is uninhabited and some of it unexplored.

Our first stop is at Georgetown, the chief city of British Guiana, situated at the mouth of the Demerara River. As we land we notice on the wharves hundreds of barrels of sugar and piles of bags of cocoa beans and coffee berries.

How hot it is! We perspire at every movement, and we wonder how the laborers who are loading the vessels can continue their work. It is always hot in Georgetown, for the city is situated on the low coastal plain and is nearer the equator than Portland, Oregon, is to San Francisco. The thermometer seldom, if ever, registers

68

below eighty. The summer temperature does not run so high as that of some other tropical regions, but it never cools off.

In spite of the heat, however, Georgetown is an attractive city. The streets, laid out at right angles, are very broad and are lined with beautiful trees. Let us walk up the main street. It is more than a hundred feet wide, is lined with shops, and is lighted with electric lights. In the middle is a broad canal nearly covered with some of the biggest green leaves that we have ever seen. Some of them are three and four feet across. This plant is the *Victoria regia*, a water lily which grows in some tropical waters and which we shall see in abundance in our trip up the Amazon River and its branches.

What a variety of people there are on the streets! Chinese, Spaniards and Portuguese, Englishmen, and Dutch mingle with the native South American Indians and people of African descent. The houses look odder than the people. There are many fine, comfortable homes with wide verandas around them, as well as many poor little huts, but all of them, large and small, are raised eight or ten feet from the ground on posts or brick pillars. This is necessary on account of the dampness, the insects, and the floods. When it rains in Guiana it comes down in torrents, and although the many canals which have been built all over the city help to carry off the water, the streets are sometimes flooded.

All along the coast the land is very low, and canals must be dug and kept in repair and sea walls built in order to drain the land and to keep out the ocean. A

Figure 29—In the middle of the street is a canal covered with some of the biggest green leaves that we have ever seen.

splendid sea wall has been built in Georgetown along the shore. It is twenty-five feet wide at the top and makes a fine place on which to walk and drive. During the afternoons and evenings many of the people dress in their best and promenade on the wall or rest in the seats which are provided, while they listen to the music of the band and enjoy the sea breezes.

Behind the lowlands on the coast are swamps choked with tall sedges and reeds. Behind these are higher grassy plains where cattle are raised and where thousands and hundreds of thousands more might find pasturage. Still farther inland are dense tropical forests, largely unexplored and unoccupied, save for a few South American Indians untouched by civilization.

There are no railroads which extend any great distance into Guiana, but many rivers flow to the coast, and these are the only highways of the country. In the forests are many birds and animals, some of which are found in no other continent.

In a trip up any of the rivers of Guiana you would see but little of the larger animals, as they live farther back in the green jungle. In the early morning the deep woods are alive with their noise and chatter, but as the sun gets higher and hotter all sounds cease, and in the middle of the day the forest is very silent.

Many of the trees in Guiana, as in Venezuela, are very useful. If we were to ascend some of the streams, we should find now and then on their banks South American Indian villages. The men are employed in felling trees and floating them down to the city, in preparing charcoal, or in raising fruits and vegetables for the market at Georgetown. We may meet some of the natives in their long dugouts filled with produce or see them working on rafts of logs which are floating downstream. These rafts are very large and have come from long distances. On some of them we can see not only the men in charge of the lumber but their wives and children as well, who are enjoying the trip of a week or more on the river and the strange sights of the city, which perhaps they have never before visited.

Still farther back in the depths of the forest there are other South American Indians living in the same state as when the country was first discovered. These tribes live in huts consisting of thatched roofs supported by poles at the corners and furnished only with a rude fireplace in the center, a few earthen pots and kettles,

*Figure 30—Along the rivers of Guiana
are dense tropical forests.*

and some hammocks which serve both for chairs and
beds. The men hunt and fish, and the women prepare
the food. All meat and fish not eaten immediately must
be smoked, as in so hot a climate it would spoil in a
short time.

The men of these tribes of the interior of Guiana
often kill their prey by means of blowguns from six
to twelve feet long. These are made of reeds or young,
straight palm trunks with a hole in the center not
more than a third of an inch in diameter. The arrows,
sharpened at one end to a needle-like point, are so
small that a dozen of them tied up in a bundle would
not be much larger round than the chalk which you
use at the blackboard.

The Indian holds the gun to his mouth with both

hands, and with one powerful puff sends the arrow, straight as a dart, at the prey perhaps two hundred yards away. In some cases the tip of the arrow is dipped in poison so that its wound will cause death. In early-days the blowgun was the common weapon of all the South American Indians of Guiana, but now that some of them are able to obtain firearms it is used only by a few of the most remote tribes.

Guiana has not been thoroughly explored, but we know that in the interior of the country there are some very wonderful waterfalls, compared with which Niagara seems very small. Between fifty and a hundred miles from the coast the rivers flow from a hard granite rock onto a softer material, which they can wear down more easily. All the streams of this region, therefore, have rapids or falls, and those of the Essequibo, the largest river in Guiana, are more wonderful than any others. They are, in fact, among the grandest in the world. The river, at this place three hundred feet wide, drops over a ledge of rock more than seven hundred feet high with a roar that can be heard for several miles through the deep forest.

Gold is found in many of the rivers of Guiana and has been taken out in considerable quantities. During long ages the streams have washed out the sands of gold from the solid rock in which it was embedded. Prospectors are now seeking to find gold in the hard quartz rocks of the region, and doubtless in the future it will be a more important product of this English colony.

Instead of the fine white bread which we use in the

Figure 31—Gold Mining in British Guiana

United States, how would you like a piece of manioc bread? This is a common food of the natives of Guiana and Brazil. It is made from roots of the manioc, or cassava, plant—the same plant from which our tapioca is made. In its raw state the root is poisonous, but the natives prepare it in such a way that it becomes a nourishing food. When the plant is a year or two old the root is gathered and washed. Then it is grated and the moisture pressed out. The grated meal is then roasted, and in this state is known as manioc flour.

Manioc is raised not only in these tropical countries of South America but also in several islands of the West Indies. Not many years ago its cultivation was begun in Eastern countries. The industry there has grown rapidly, until at the present time by far the larger part of the world's supply of tapioca comes from Java and the Straits Settlements.

British Guiana is larger than Minnesota, but

it contains fewer people than live in the city of Minneapolis. Of all its area only a narrow strip along the coast is under cultivation. A little of this is devoted to the raising of coffee and cocoa, but the most of it is covered with sugar cane, and a fourth of all the people in the colony live on the sugar estates. In this coast stretch of fertile black soil there used to be many small sugar plantations. Now, however, most of these small holdings have been given up, and the land is divided into a few large estates, each containing thousands of acres.

Not more than six or seven miles from Georgetown there is a very large plantation which is carried on, as most of the plantations are, in the most up-to-date way. We shall find a visit here very interesting. The low, flat land and the many canals remind us of Holland, only, in place of green meadows dotted with black and white cows, we see instead acres of tall, waving cane.

On all the large sugar plantations in Guiana especial attention must be paid to the draining of the land. A sea wall must be built in front to keep out the ocean, and a dam must be constructed behind to keep out the floods which in the rainy season cover the higher lands of the interior and would cause much damage to the plantations. Many ditches and canals must be dug in the fields to drain off the water and keep the cane from being flooded by the heavy rains. All this work is expensive and can be done most successfully on large estates.

Approaching the plantation we go through field

Figure 32—We see acres of tall, waving cane.

after field of tall cane until we finally come in sight of the buildings, surrounded on all sides by the sea of waving green. There are so many buildings and so many people around that we should call it a village instead of a plantation. Between two and three thousand workmen are employed on this one estate. There are hundreds of laborers—men, women, and children—who work in the fields. There are the overseers to assign them their duties, the doctor to tend them when sick, the druggist to furnish them with medicines, and the teacher to look after the children. Besides these there are carpenters, blacksmiths, machinists, engineers, and other workmen to attend to the people, the animals, and the manufacturing of the sugar.

There are hundreds of families on the plantation, and, as all must have a home, of course there must be many buildings. The laborers live in those rows of cottages on either side of that long canal. The other buildings include the homes of the manager, overseers, and other skilled workmen, the schoolhouse, chapel, workshops, and factories where the sugar is made.

Figure 33—The laborers live in the rows of cottages on either side of the canal.

Let us go out into the fields and watch the cutting of the cane. Those workmen in the bright-colored robes with turbans wound around their heads do not look like blacks or South American Indians. They are Hindus from southern Asia. Large numbers of these people have come to Guiana, and they are still coming at the rate of several thousand a year. The plantation owners like to employ them, as they make dependable workmen.

Figure 34—Many of the workmen are Hindus from southern Asia.

The laborers have finished cutting the cane and have loaded it onto long boats which were waiting in the canal. Each boat is pulled to the sugar mill by two mules which walk along the path on the bank. At the mill the cane is crushed, and the juice is clarified, boiled down, and crystallized into sugar by machinery as modern as any which we might find in Louisiana or Texas.

This estate which we are visiting produces several million pounds of sugar a year, and there are so many plantations in Guiana that this colony of England is able to supply her and other countries annually with one hundred thousand tons.

We will leave Georgetown for Dutch Guiana, a little

*Figure 35—The cane is thrown onto a moving platform,
which carries it into the mill.*

farther to the east. The Dutch colony is not much more than half as large as the one which we have visited, is less developed, and is much more thinly peopled. We will stop only for a glimpse of Paramaribo, the chief city. As we walk up from the wharf it seems as if some fairy had waved her magic wand and suddenly transported us to Holland. The clean, shaded streets are lined with narrow houses with steep roofs broken by sharp little dormer windows; under shady vestibules are large green doors with enormous brass knockers; and every street has its canal flowing down the gentle slope to the river. These and many other things are very much like the home country of the Dutch settlers across the water, but we notice many contrasts also. The streets are full of dark-skinned people—blacks and natives of the island of Java—who have come to Guiana to work on the sugar plantations. Many of them are carrying heavy bundles on their heads in a way that no Dutchman could imitate. On the opposite bank of the river from the city is a dense tropical forest which would tell us, if nothing else did, that we are many hundred miles from Holland.

The third division of Guiana is smaller and of less importance than either of the other two. We shall wish to make an even shorter visit in the French colony than in the British or Dutch possessions. Several thousand of the inhabitants of French Guiana are convicts. For many years France has used this territory as a prison, where she has sent large numbers of her criminals and to which she is now sending them at the rate of several hundred a year.

Figure 36—Nearly half of the people of French Guiana live in Cayenne, the chief city.

Figure 37—The little houses in Cayenne,
clustering under tall palm trees, look very attractive.

Nearly half of the people in the colony live at Cayenne, the chief city. As we steam into the harbor through the thick muddy water we notice first the white barracks where the soldiers live, and next the tall tower of the church. The little wooden houses with their projecting roofs and broad balconies and the better plaster houses painted in light dainty colors and surrounded by palm groves look very attractive. In the early part of the day the streets are full of people— soldiers in bright uniforms, well-dressed Frenchmen, people of African descent as black as jet, Chinese in loose dark blouses, and peoples from eastern Asia in white turbans and flowing robes. From eleven o'clock until two or three the streets are deserted, the shops are closed, business is suspended, and the people spend this time in eating their breakfast, for they have had only coffee and rolls earlier in the day. After this they rest and sleep until the sun gets lower and the heat less fierce.

Much the same crops are raised in French Guiana as in the English and Dutch colonies. In the country every house has its patch of manioc. There are, besides, fields of rice and corn, sugar plantations, and orchards of cocoa and coffee trees. Gold is an important product and is being mined in increasing quantities each year.

TOPICS FOR STUDY

I

1. Size of Guiana.

2. Description of Georgetown.

3. Climate of Guiana.

4. Surface of Guiana.

5. Forests and animals.

6. Guiana Indians.

7. The cassava plant.

8. Rivers and falls.

9. Gold deposits.

10. Sugar plantations.

11. Dutch Guiana.

12. The city of Paramaribo.

13. French Guiana.

14. The city of Cayenne.

II

1. Name the chief colonies of England; of France; of Holland. Which nation possesses the most important colonies? Does the United States possess any colonies? What are they?

2. On an outline map of the world, show in color the chief English possessions; in another color the French possessions; in a third color those which belong to Holland.

3. Name the states in our country which are noted for their cane-sugar production. In what other countries of the world is cane sugar produced?

4. What other plant yields great quantities of sugar? What countries are noted for its production?

5. Name a third kind of sugar produced in the United States. What states are noted for its production?

6. Sketch Guiana; show its divisions, its boundaries, and its three cities.

7. See what you can find about the production and manufacture of tapioca.

8. Make a list of the places mentioned in Topic III which you think are so important that you should always remember them.

III

Be able to spell and pronounce the following names. Locate each place and tell what was said of it in this and in any previous chapter. Add other facts if possible.

India	Louisiana
China	Texas
Java	Niagara Falls
France	Demerara River
Holland	Amazon River
England	Essequibo River
West Indies	Georgetown
Straits Settlements	Paramaribo
Ohio	Cayenne
Indiana	San Francisco
Illinois	Portland
Minnesota	Minneapolis

CHAPTER V

A GREAT COUNTRY AND ITS GREAT CAPITAL

LEAVING Guiana, we will next visit Brazil. Few people realize what an immense country Brazil is. A trip around its entire coast would make a long voyage, for it is about as far from the boundary of Guiana to the border of Uruguay as it is from New York to Petrograd, Russia, and the distance from Bahia to Rio de Janeiro is as long as from Baltimore, Maryland, to St. Augustine, Florida.

Brazil is one of the largest countries in the world. If on a map of North America one of Brazil, made on the same scale, were laid with its most northern point on the arctic circle, its southern border would lie in the Gulf of Mexico. The distance from Pernambuco westward to the boundary of Peru is a little more than from New York to San Francisco. From this widest part the country narrows toward the southern boundary.

Brazil is larger than the United States, and there are many resemblances between the two countries. Both occupy the central part of similarly shaped continents;

85

both are drained by mighty rivers; both have in the east narrow chains of low mountains running parallel with the coast, while the main highland lies to the west.

This largest of all South American republics is made up of twenty states, one territory, and a federal district in which the capital, Rio de Janeiro, is situated, as our capital city, Washington, is in the District of Columbia. Some of the Brazilian states are very large. Amazonas, the state in which much of the basin of the Amazon River lies, includes nearly a fourth of the entire country. It is so thinly peopled, however, that it averages less than one person to a square mile. Matto Grosso, perhaps the least known of any of the Brazilian states, is twice as large as Texas. This is the state through which ex-President Roosevelt, in 1914, made his trip from the La Plata River to the Amazon. Sao Paulo, the coffee state, is the richest and the most powerful in the whole republic, while the state of Rio de Janeiro, with more than twenty people to a square mile, is the most densely populated. If Brazil were peopled as densely as France it would have fifteen times its present population.

Many people have the idea that Brazil is a low, hot country too unhealthy for white people to live in. It is true that near the Amazon River the country is both low and hot. Brazil and the Amazon are so closely connected in people's minds that, in looking at a map, they notice its low valley lying on and near the equator and think what a hot, disagreeable region this must be. They forget about the rest of the vast country, with its plateaus and mountain ranges. West of Brazil and extending in places across its borders are the Andes

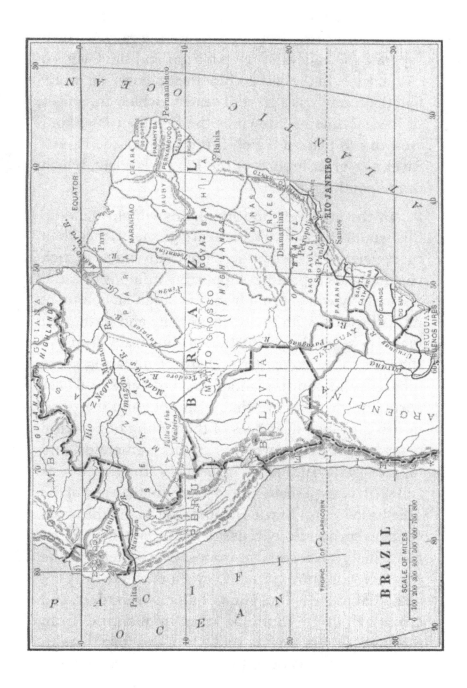

87

and their offshoots, in which the Amazon and most of its tributaries rise. In the north are the ranges which separate the valleys of the Amazon and the Orinoco rivers, while in the east and southeast, covering nearly half the country, is a great plateau on which are ranges of low mountains known as the Brazilian Highland. West of this plateau region is the valley of the Parana River, the great branch of the Rio de la Plata, which drains southern Brazil.

In the lowlands and highlands which make up this wonderful country there are greater riches than most nations possess. There are many miles of rich pasture lands capable of supporting millions of cattle. The easterly winds bring from the ocean an abundant rainfall which, with the warm climate and fertile soil, makes possible the production of almost any crop. We shall see cocoa and coffee orchards, fruit farms, sugar, tobacco, and cotton plantations, and acres of wheat, corn, and manioc. We shall visit gold and diamond mines, and shall hear tales of the finding of beautiful gems—amethysts, garnets, sapphires, emeralds, and topazes—which lie hidden in the rocks. The great forests will seem to us perhaps more wonderful than any of the other resources of Brazil. No other country in the world contains such a variety of useful and ornamental timber, medicinal plants, and dye-woods. One writer calls the great forest Nature's apothecary shop, where drugs of all kinds can be found. Gums, balsams, oils, dyes, and spices will in the future be taken in quantities from this great storehouse. As yet little of this forest wealth except rubber has been touched. Indeed, large areas have never been explored. Ex-President Roosevelt's party discovered a branch of the Madeira River longer than the Rhine, and there are many other streams in the interior of the country unexplored and unmapped. No roads or railroads run far into the interior. In many regions the waterways are the only highways, and there are few parts of Brazil not reached by some stream. No country in the world contains so many long rivers. There are some as long as the Ohio, the names of which you have never heard and which are not shown on the map. The navigable streams in the Amazon basin, if joined together, would encircle the earth twice at the equator. Besides the rivers of this one great system there are in Brazil many long branches of the Parana River and hundreds of others which flow down the slopes of the eastern highland into the Atlantic Ocean.

The banks of many of the streams are heavily wooded. In the more tropical parts of the country the woods are so dense, the jungles so matted, and the tangle of vines so thick that it would be impossible for you to make your way through them without an ax, which you would have to use at every step. The variety of animals which you would find would furnish a menagerie with interesting specimens, and the plants would be no less fascinating. Beautiful flowers, which when raised in a northern hothouse cost a small fortune, grow in abundance in the swamps and jungles of Brazil.

If you had never read or studied about Brazil, you would know by looking at a map that the interior is little known or developed, as nearly all the cities and towns are located on or near the coast. It is harder for a business man in some coast city of Brazil to communicate with the interior part of the country than for a Chicago merchant to keep in touch with Australia. Brazil is in much the same condition today that the United States was when the thirteen colonies clung to the Atlantic shore and the rest of the land was a vast wilderness.

Brazil has more to help her in her development than the United States had. When our early colonists blazed their trails through the woods and built their little log cabins in the clearings, they knew nothing of railroads, telegraphs, or the many other wonderful inventions and scientific discoveries which today unite countries and peoples, make travel a pleasure, and increase manufacturing and commerce.

Most of the large cities on the Brazilian coast are connected with the fertile plateau lying a few miles inland by short railroads, which bring the products of farm and orchard and forest to the seaports. Some of these branch railroads are connected by longer north and south lines. Today one can go by rail from Montevideo, in Uruguay, to Rio de Janeiro, and in the near future this road, connecting with the short coast lines, will be extended northward to Bahia, Pernambuco, and Para. All these railroads are near the coast. If you wish to go far into the interior of Brazil the rivers are the only highways on which you can travel.

Our first stop as we sail southward from Guiana will be at Pernambuco. This city is nearer to Europe than is any other in South America, and is usually the first port touched at by European steamers. It is the capital of the state of Pernambuco, and foreigners usually call the city by the same name. The Brazilians, however, call it Recife, which in the Portuguese language means "reef." This name was given to the city because of a low reef which runs along the shore a few hundred feet from land. This a part of the great coral reef which extends for hundreds of miles, sometimes above and sometimes below the surface of the water, along the Brazilian coast. Near Pernambuco it rises a few feet above the water and resembles a concrete wall. Against this the waves dash and the foam and spray fly in sheets, while inside the barrier the water is calm and quiet.

Pernambuco is built on long, low peninsulas nearly surrounded by small rivers and the arms of the ocean. The city is so cut up by the streams and there are so many canals and bridges that at first sight it reminds one of Venice, the Italian city of islands.

A break in the coral sea wall affords an entrance to the harbor of Pernambuco, and as we sail through the opening we catch our first glimpse of a Brazilian city—a long, low stretch of houses with red-tiled roofs nestling under tall trees. As we approach the wharves everything looks as modern as in many of the coast cities of the United States. Great improvements have recently been made in the harbor to accommodate the trade, new docks have been built, the river dredged, and large warehouses erected.

The old town of Pernambuco near the water has narrow, crooked streets lined by tall buildings. By

Figure 38—There is much sugar grown around Pernambuco.

crossing the bridge, however, to the newer part of the city, we get an entirely different idea of this South American port. Here the streets are wider, the buildings larger, and the parks finer. Electric lights and cars, paved streets, fine stone blocks, automobiles, carriages, and well-dressed people attract our attention.

A short ride on an electric railroad takes us to the suburbs, where there are beautiful residences, lovely gardens, avenues lined with tall palms, feathery bamboos, and wide-spreading Brazil-nut trees. From there we might take a trip farther out from the city, past farms where manioc, sweet potatoes, and other vegetables are growing in the rich, dark soil, to the great cotton and sugar plantations which cover much of the state of Pernambuco and the surrounding country. This is the most important sugar-producing area in Brazil. There are hundreds of sugar estates scattered through the state, some in which modern machinery is used and some in which the industry is still carried on in much the same way as it was in the early days in the United States.

Besides the sugar estates, there are other plantations in the state of Pernambuco which remind us of those in our Southern states. The pickers of African descent, with their tall baskets filled with the fluffy white balls of cotton, almost make us think that we are on a cotton plantation in Louisiana or Texas. In the city of Pernambuco we should find some cotton mills with their noisy looms and flying shuttles. At present Brazil does not rank high as a manufacturing country. Every year, however, the cities are giving more attention to manufacturing—especially to cotton manufacturing— instead of sending the raw material on long voyages to foreign countries and then buying from them the finished product.

On the higher land behind the plantations there are many acres of rich pastures, on which large herds of cattle, sheep, and goats feed. On the vessels bound from Pernambuco to foreign ports we should find great quantities of hides and skins.

After we leave Pernambuco, a pleasant sail of nearly two days takes us to Bahia. If our trip occurs during the winter months we may chance to catch sight of some whales spouting in the distance. As soon as the antarctic winter sets in, the whales migrate northward; hence whaling is an important industry in Brazilian waters.

What a magnificent harbor Bahia has! It is large

enough to hold all the navies of the world. It is guarded by strong forts, a splendid lighthouse rises near the entrance, and fine new wharves with great warehouses behind line the water front. Bahia is very different from Pernambuco. That city lay on a low, level peninsula, while Bahia is built on the cliffs which rise precipitously not far from the water's edge. The old part of the town lies on the narrow strip of shore at the base of the cliffs. Many of the houses are from three to five stories high, roofed with red tiles, and in many cases the whole front is covered in old Portuguese style with porcelain tiles— blue, brown, and green.

Figure 39—Bahia is built on the cliffs
which rise from the water's edge.

Large warehouses and wholesale establishments line the narrow, crooked streets. The air is filled with the odor of tobacco, which is piled in bags on the wharves and fills some of the largest buildings. Great quantities of cigars and cigarettes are made here and shipped to other Brazilian ports. As both men and women in Brazil smoke a great deal, it takes large amounts of tobacco to supply them.

A great deal of sugar, cocoa, and cotton is also exported from Bahia. Some of these products are brought to the city by oxcarts, some by water, and more by railroads which run back into the farming country.

Figure 40—Some of the black women carry loaded baskets on their heads.

As we walk along the narrow streets we wonder if there are no white inhabitants in the city, for we meet few people except those of African descent, and these are the largest we have ever seen. Most of the women weigh two hundred or two hundred and fifty pounds. They are of all shades, from a light cream color to jet black, and are dressed in loose, low-necked blouses, thin, full skirts, and gay-colored turbans. Many of them appear to be returning from market and are carrying large baskets of provisions on their heads. At the market we see many others squatting beside their mounds of fruits and vegetables or behind cages of chattering parrots or piles of freshly caught fish. The state of Bahia is one of the most thickly settled of Brazil and has a larger proportion of blacks than any other state in the country.

The heat and the smells in the low, sun-baked business district are not very agreeable, and we are glad to take an elevator to the upper town. At every step along the street we see something to interest us. The buildings are painted in brighter colors than are common in the United States. We mail our letters in a blue post office, shop in a pink store, and get our lunch in a lavender restaurant.

Here on the bluffs the city is delightful. Let us take a ride in the electric cars which run along the edge of the cliff. On one side we can see below us the blue harbor dotted with sails, and at our feet the business section with its rows of warehouses and narrow, winding streets, from which we have come. How different is the view on the other side! Here are broad, sunlit avenues bordered with palms and bamboos, parks ornamented with beautiful trees, plants and flowers many of which we have never seen before, and large, handsome buildings with broad verandas and cool, splashing fountains. Ladies in elegant toilets and men dressed in spotless white enjoy the piazzas or pass us in luxurious automobiles. The light-colored houses, the many churches, and the large public buildings stand out in sharp contrast to the thick masses of dark foliage by which they are surrounded.

Mother Nature has been kind to Brazil not only in

*Figure 41—One of the narrow, winding streets
leading to the upper city, Bahia.*

her wonderful forests, great rivers, and rich soil but also
in the treasures which she has stored below the surface.
For many years—until the discovery of diamonds in
South Africa—Brazil was the chief diamond-producing
country of the world. Since the beginning of the industry
it is estimated that two and a half tons of the precious
stones have been mined here. Gold is found in nearly
every state of the republic, and has been mined for two

97

Figure 42—Power house for diamond mining, Brazil. Most of the diamonds mined in Brazil are found in the loose gravel washed out by the streams.

or three hundred years in several of them. Coal and petroleum, iron, copper, and lead deposits have been discovered, and rich beds of graphite, kaolin, marble, mica, and platinum are known to exist.

Besides having these useful minerals, Brazil is a great jewel box. Not only diamonds but agates, amethysts, aquamarines, garnets, pearls, sapphires, topazes, tourmalines, and emeralds are mined in various parts of the country. A state situated near Bahia is called Minas Geraes—a name which means "all kinds of mines." This name might as well have been given to Bahia, for its deposits of minerals are nearly as rich as those of its neighbor. The city of Bahia is the diamond center of the country, and we will start from here on a trip to the mines.

Around Diamantina, just over the boundary in the state of "all kinds of mines," is one of the most important diamond fields of Brazil. The region is full of deep ravines worn by many swift-flowing streams, which are flooded during the rainy season. At this time they rush down their channels, wearing down their beds, eating into their banks, and working out deep potholes. In the loose gravel which is thus washed out by the streams the precious stones are found.

Here in the tropical heat, scantily clad blacks, with crowbars, hoes, scoops for cleaning out holes, and wooden bowls for washing the dirt, dig in the sands and gravels until the diamond-bearing clay is reached. Some of the miners dive down into the larger potholes, taking with them a canvas bag extended at the mouth by an iron ring. They fill this with gravel and rise to the surface of the water, empty the bag, and dive again, continuing this work until they have accumulated soil enough to occupy them some time in washing it. In some places around Diamantina expensive machinery is employed to wash away the surface soil and bring up the pay dirt. There are few deep mines, however, such as are common in South Africa, as the diamonds in Brazil are not found in the deep rock but in the sands and gravels of swift-flowing rivers.

Leaving the city of Bahia we sail southward along the lovely Brazilian shore. The hills near the coast grow

Figure 43—The Lovely Harbor of Rio

higher and, if possible, greener until, two days after leaving Bahia, we enter the harbor of Rio de Janeiro, the capital of Brazil. The Portuguese explorer, who in the month of January first sailed up the beautiful bay, thought that it was the mouth of a broad river and so named it Rio de Janeiro (river of January). Not many years after the discovery it was known that no large river entered the ocean at this point, but the name clung to the bay and the settlement. Today the city is popularly known in Brazil as Rio.

As we enter the harbor we notice the famous old Sugar Loaf, the mountain which guards the entrance. Rising out of the water around it are other and higher peaks, green to their very summits. Passing Sugar Loaf we find ourselves in what appears to be a calm inland sea dotted with green islands. This is the landlocked bay of Rio. At its head, nestling among the green hills, lies the city which is considered by many people to be the most beautiful capital in the world. The blue sky, rivaled by the blue water beneath it, the lovely islands around, the hills covered with terraces of light-colored houses rising out of the deep-green foliage is a picture unsurpassed in any country of the world. The city of Rio lies between the mountains and the sea. It occupies the shore, climbs the hills, and presses against the green, forested heights which lie just behind. At one end of many of the long city streets lie the blue waters of the bay, and at the other end a wall of green.

A person who visited Rio twenty-five years ago would hardly recognize the city today. It was then an unattractive, unhealthy place, and the traveler who was so unfortunate as to be obliged to stop there held to his nose a handkerchief saturated with disinfectant as he

Figure 44—Where once were swamps and lowlands is now a splendid avenue.

101

made his way through narrow, dirty, undrained streets. Today Rio is a healthful, beautiful city. Underground sewers have been built; streets have been widened and paved; low marshy areas, breeding places of disease-carrying mosquitoes, have been filled; rats have been killed off by the thousands; and many old buildings have been torn down to make room for fine modern blocks. We feel a particular interest in the improvements of Rio, for the people there learned from the United States how to make the city a pleasant, healthful place to live in.

As we near the shore we notice first of all the stone quay, more than two miles in length, extending along the water. Back of this sea wall, on land which not many years ago was washed by the tide, a splendid palm-shaded avenue three hundred feet wide has been built, on the farther side of which are fine blocks of warehouses and office buildings. There is plenty of room on this broad street for all the traffic which is carried on along the water front. It is wide enough for railroad tracks, electric-car tracks, and driveways for heavy wagons and lighter teams. On the docks and in the warehouses we see the most modern machinery for loading and unloading vessels, and we begin to realize as never before that we are in one of the great commercial cities of the world.

More wonderful than this bayside street is the Avenida Central, which runs in a straight line from sea to sea through the heart of Rio. This avenue is over a mile long and a hundred feet wide. In order to build this great artery of the city and to let in the sun and air, six hundred buildings were torn down and three thousand laborers worked day and night for nearly two years. In the center of the avenue are rows of electric-light posts of an artistic design alternating with Brazil-nut trees planted in little green plots. Splendid business blocks have been built along the street, and today the Avenida Central is the main business street of Rio.

Running between the hills and the sea is a continuation of the Avenida Central. This street is called the Beira Mar because it runs along the shore. Here, where once were swamps and lowlands in which the disease-carrying mosquito bred in enormous numbers, is now a splendid avenue. The blue waters of the bay on one side and on the other the green hills covered with lovely residences surrounded by trees and gardens make the Beira Mar one of the loveliest boulevards in any city of the world.

Figure 45—The Rua do Ouvidor is one of the oldest and most popular streets in Rio.

Let us now leave these new avenues and take a walk on the Ouvidor, one of the oldest and most popular streets of Rio. How narrow it is! Shaded by the tall buildings on either side, it is somewhat cooler than the wider, newer streets in which the hot sun beats down. During most of the day it is crowded with people. There are fine shops on this street,—jewelers, tailors, milliners, and others,—and many of the wealthy people prefer to trade here rather than in the larger department stores on the new avenues. So many others come to chat with friends, to promenade, and to see the crowd that during business hours no teams are allowed to pass through.

There are other things in the city in which we shall be interested. One of these is the Bangu cotton mills, employing three thousand hands. We have never thought of Brazil as doing much manufacturing, and we are surprised to learn that there are nearly two hundred cotton mills in the country and that this number is increasing year by year. Around Rio and Sao Paulo especially, factories of various kinds are growing in numbers. When we think of the great fields of cotton, sugar, and tobacco in Brazil and the wheat farms and cattle ranches in the countries to the south, we can readily see that manufacturing will be an important industry in the future.

The opera house in Rio is a wonderfully fine building, more beautiful than any structure of the kind in the United States. The railroad station is a palace which nearly four hundred trains enter and leave each day. Of special interest to anyone from the United States is the famous Monroe Palace, built for the Brazilian exhibit at the World's Fair at St. Louis, taken apart and carried back to Brazil, and again erected in the capital city of that country.

Before leaving Rio we must be sure to see the view from the Corcovado, the hunchback-shaped mountain that towers above the city. This peak, twenty-five hundred feet high, is the loftiest in the vicinity. When seen from the bay it appears to rise out of the very houses which nestle in the woods at its base. On all sides save one it is very steep, much too steep to climb. Zigzagging up the more slanting face is a cogwheel railway which takes us almost to the top.

The view of Rio from the water was lovely, but the outlook from the top of the Corcovado is even more beautiful. The blue waters of the bay dotted with green islands sparkle in the bright sunlight. The many boats with gleaming white sails look like huge tropical birds skimming over the water. The grim war vessels riding at anchor remind us that Brazil is an important nation with a large navy to help her maintain her position in the world. Beyond the narrow channel through which we entered the harbor stretches the wide expanse of ocean, until in the far distance the sky drops down to meet the water. Nearer the shore old Sugar Loaf rises a thousand feet in the air, its gray-green cone standing out in sharp relief against the blue, while at our feet lies the city in its bed of green.

If our trip to Rio is in the summer season we shall find the city very hot, and we shall prefer to stay in some one of the pleasant resorts in the mountains or on the bay. One of the coolest and most interesting of

*Figure 46—The view from the top
of the Corcovado is beautiful.*

these suburbs is Petropolis, where during the hot season
many of the government officials, foreign ministers,
and wealthy people live. Petropolis is situated high
on the slopes of the mountains a few miles from Rio.
Perhaps we shall like this charming resort even better
than the capital itself. We can drive on broad, shady
avenues through the middle of which, in stone-curbed
channels, flow streams of clear mountain water. We
can wander for hours in winding paths through the
deep woods, and ride to the tops of some of the peaks

where we can enjoy the cool breezes and lovely views. The beautiful residences are surrounded by gardens filled with flowers larger and more brilliant than those which bloom in our gardens at home. There are hedges of dainty heliotrope, beds of tall waving lilies, orange trees filled with luscious fruit, and tall geranium bushes with their gay blossoms peeping in at the windows.

A trip which no visitor to Rio ever misses is to the Botanical Gardens. The electric car takes us out through narrow, crowded streets into wider avenues, where beautiful houses are surrounded by shade trees and lovely flowers. Reaching the gardens we alight before a massive stone entrance. Inside this gateway we pause in wonder at the beauty before us. Every park which we have seen in the tropical countries of South America has seemed extremely beautiful to us. In all of them there have been trees, shrubs, and flowers which we have never seen before, and many others which we recognized as our choicest hothouse products. The sight which greets our eyes in the Botanical Gardens of Rio, however, is far more wonderful than anything we have yet seen. Leading into the gardens for half a mile or more from the entrance is an avenue of royal palms one hundred feet high. As we follow it we feel as if we were walking down the aisle of some magnificent cathedral. On either side of us rise tall, straight columns of silvery gray, each topped with a huge green tuft of long, waving leaves, which cast flickering shadows on the graveled walk beneath.

In another part of the gardens is a single huge palm tree taller than any in the avenue and more than a century old, called the "mother of palms." All the trees in the magnificent avenue near the entrance came from its seeds.

Figure 47—An Avenue of Royal Palms

There are other paths in these wonderful gardens through which we shall wish to stroll. Many people think that the avenues where the feathery fronds of giant bamboos meet in a graceful arch overhead are as beautiful as the palm walk.

These famous Botanical Gardens of Rio occupy more than two thousand acres, and had we time to spend we could count more than fifty thousand kinds of plants and flowers here. Many of these grow in Brazil, and others have been brought from countries in different parts of the world. We can see a variety of spice-bearing trees—cinnamon, nutmeg, and clove.

Another interesting specimen is the cow tree, which on being tapped yields a fluid which looks and tastes like milk. Lovely orchids, which are raised at great expense in the hothouses of the North, are blooming here in profusion. Tall poinsettias with their huge, scarlet blossoms make us think of our Christmas decorations. We see huge tree ferns taller than a two-story house and trees two hundred feet high covered with brilliant blossoms. Long vines like green clotheslines hang from some of the forest giants or wind themselves closely around their trunks.

Scattered through the gardens are many different specimens of rubber trees. Rubber is such an important product that we will take a trip into the tropical forests to see how it is obtained, and watch the natives prepare it for market.

TOPICS FOR STUDY

I

1. Size and position of Brazil.

2. The states of Brazil.

3. Climate and surface.

4. Resources and products.

5. Rivers and forests.

6. Plants and animals.

7. Development of Brazil.

8. Railroads and transportation.

9. The city and state of Pernambuco.

10. The city and state of Bahia.

11. Mineral resources and diamond mines.

12. The capital, Rio de Janeiro.

II

1. What countries of South America does Brazil touch?

2. What countries of the world are larger than Brazil?

3. Find and compare the number of people to a square mile in Brazil, the United States, England, and Belgium. How does the density of population affect the industries of a country?

4. On an outline map of South America color the country of Brazil. Write the names of the countries and waters bounding it. Show the highlands, the rivers, and the cities mentioned. Draw the equator and the tropic of Capricorn.

5. Draw a circle and show the zones and their boundaries. Sketch in the circle a map of South America in its proper position. Shade the part occupied by Brazil.

6. Make a list of the minerals found in Brazil.

7. Make a list of the chief countries of the world which produce cotton, sugar, coffee, rubber. How does Brazil rank in each of these products?

8. What is a coral reef? See if you can find where the largest one in the world is located.

9. What countries have the largest forest areas in the world?

10. See what you can find about the manufacture of tapioca.

11. Describe diamond mining in South Africa. How do the methods differ from those in Brazil?

12. Fill the blanks in the following sentences:

a. The United States stretches east and west from the _____ to the _____; Brazil stretches from the _____ to the _____.

b. The United States lies in the _____ zone; Brazil lies in the _____.

c. The United States touches _____ countries; Brazil touches _____ countries.

d. The most important river in the United States flows _____; the most important river in Brazil flows _____.

e. In North America there are _____ republics; in South America there are _____.

f. List three languages spoken in North America: _____, _____, and _____. List three languages spoken in South America: _____, _____, and _____.

13. Make a list of the places mentioned in Topic III which you think are so important that you should always remember them.

III

Be able to spell and pronounce the following names. Locate each place and tell what was said of it in this and in any previous chapter. Add other facts if possible.

Guiana	Brazilian Highland
Uruguay	Arctic circle
Peru	Diamantina
Australia	Bahia
Louisiana	Rio de Janeiro
District of Columbia	Pernambuco
Texas	Petropolis
Florida	Para
New England	Montevideo
South Africa	Chicago
Parana River	Washington
Madeira River	San Francisco
Rhine River	New Orleans
Ohio River	New York
Amazon River	St. Augustine
La Plata River	Baltimore
Orinoco River	Petrograd
Andes Highland	Venice
Guiana Highland	London

CHAPTER VI

THE AMAZON VALLEY AND ITS RUBBER TREES

LET us take a trip up the Amazon, the most wonderful river and one of the longest in the world. It is wider, deeper, carries more water to the ocean, has more large tributaries, and by means of them drains more land than any river in any other country. One writer calls the Amazon the "king of rivers" and the area which it drains the "queen of basins." In places the river is between fifty and sixty miles wide and looks much more like a sea than a river. For this reason the Brazilians often call it the "Rio Mar" (the river-sea). During the wet season, from November to February, there is a daily downpour of rain in its valley, and the main stream and its tributaries rise from twenty to fifty feet above their usual level. The country for hundreds of miles is covered with water. The people living in the flooded areas go to the higher lands, and all communication is by boat. Can you imagine sailing on such an inland sea, which is everywhere shaded by tall trees growing in the water? It is very different from the sunny, open stretches of lake or sea or ocean in other parts of the world, and it gives one a queer sensation to glide along under the thick, green foliage.

The mouth of the Amazon from shore to shore is as wide as the Hudson is long, and the muddy waters of the mighty river discolor the ocean for more than a hundred miles from the coast. Lying in its wide mouth, as the prey might lie in the open jaws of a great serpent, is the island of Marajo, more than twice the size of Massachusetts. It is covered with lakes, swamps, fertile pastures large enough to support thousands of cattle, and hundreds of acres of dense tropical forests. Not all the rivers of the Amazon basin are shown on the maps in your textbooks. Hundreds of streams whose waters pour into the Amazon itself or into its branches flow through regions that are as yet little known or in some cases entirely unexplored. The Indian names of some of these streams are interesting, for they tell us something of the rivers themselves or describe the region in which they lie. The name of one river means "the place of mosquitoes"; another, "the river of alligators"; a third, "the river of the ax"; and still another, "the shrieking monkey."

The Amazon enters the ocean through many channels. Some of these are unnavigable because of the swift current, sand bars, and floating islands. The Para River, one of the southern outlets, has a deep, navigable channel. We will choose this route into the great river, stopping for a while on our way to visit the city of Para. The banks of this delta stream are densely wooded. When we think that one can travel for days on the Amazon itself and journey for weeks up dozens

Figure 48—The Armadillo in its Horny Covering—
One of the Unusual Animals of Brazil

of its branches and be all the time in the midst of these dense tropical forests, we begin to realize something of the vast extent of the selvas, as the wooded plains of Brazil are called.

A forest of the United States is made up of one or two kinds of trees, or possibly of half a dozen varieties. We speak of our hemlock woods, our maple groves, or our pine forests. But here on the banks of the Amazon there are twenty, thirty, or even forty and fifty varieties, each trying, it would seem, to make a forest of its own.

Then, too, no forest in the United States is so dark and has such deep shadows as this hot, damp Brazilian jungle. The trees are so thick, the vines so many, and the leaves so large that no sunshine can penetrate to lighten the gloom or to dry the ground. In the middle of the day the bright tropical sun blazes overhead, but in the depth of the forest there is only a dim, shadowy twilight.

The tall trunks of these jungle giants rise straight and clean for fifty or even a hundred feet without a branch. Some are covered with smooth, silvery-gray bark, and some are entirely hidden by big-leaved vines with stems as large as a man's arm. The clinging vine, climbing upward toward the sun and air above, slowly but surely chokes the strong tree which supports it. Not all the trees and vines blossom or lose their leaves at the same time, and this wonderful forest is always green and always brilliant with flowers. Can you imagine a tree as large as a good-sized maple covered with big red blossoms, or a vine which has climbed as high as the chimney of your house gay with bright yellow flowers? You will have to try to picture these and many other strange sights if you are to have a true idea of this wonderful Amazon jungle.

It is hard to estimate the value of these Brazilian

*Figure 49—The peccary is somewhat the size
and shape of a small hog.*

forests. The bark, sap, seeds, and fruit of many of the trees and plants in this great storehouse of Nature yield useful oils, dyes, and gums, and the lumber that might be obtained in the Amazon valley is sufficient to supply the world for years. We have all seen furniture and other articles made from the hard wood of the mahogany, rosewood, and ebony trees. In the Brazilian forests there are many other kinds of fine hard woods as durable as these and as capable of taking a fine polish. Most of the cloth manufactured in the world today is made from the fiber of the cotton and flax plants, from that spun by the silkworm, or furnished by the warm coats of animals. In the Amazon forests there are plants and trees that yield fibers as fine as silk and as strong as linen. The natives use these for clothing, hammocks, and baskets, but sometime in the future, people of other countries may dress in cloth woven from the fibers of some of these South American trees.

The famous scientist Agassiz, who traveled in South America many years ago and explored parts of this Great Brazilian forest, in his account of the region wrote as follows: "The woods of the basin of the Amazon have an almost priceless value. Nowhere in the world is there finer timber either for solid construction or for ornament, and yet it is used but little even for local buildings and makes no part of the exports. The rivers which flow through these magnificent forests seem meant to serve, first as a water power for the sawmills which ought to be established along their borders, and second as a means of transportation for the timber. Setting aside the woods as timber, what shall I say of the mass of fruits, resins, oils, coloring matter, and textile fabrics which they yield?" These words were written many years ago when the world knew but little of Brazil and the great river which it contains, but they are as true today as when they were penned by the great explorer.

Most of you have eaten the delicious meat of the hard, three-sided Brazil nuts. We shall see the tree which bears them not only in the Brazilian forest but along the streets of the cities, in plazas and gardens, and around some of the houses. It is a splendid shade tree,

Figure 50—The brazil nut tree is one of the tallest of the tropical giants.

for it is one of the tallest of the tropical giants and has wide branches covered with large, dark-green leaves. It is scattered through the forest in great numbers, and the gathering of the nuts is an industry of considerable importance. Fifteen or twenty of these nuts grow in a round, hard shell larger than an apple. They are packed in so closely that if you once took them out you could never replace them. The South American Indians who live in the scattered huts and villages near the rivers gather great quantities of these nuts, which they store away until a steamer stops at the little wharves to get the harvest and carry it down to Para. The Indians on the many smaller streams which the steamers do not enter load the nuts into their dugouts and make several trips downstream to the nearest port.

Many large ocean steamers from European countries and the United States sail for a thousand miles or more up the Amazon, and if we wished, we could make our trip up the great river without changing boats. Before going farther, however, we will stop for a few days at the city of Para. It lies only a few feet above sea level and almost under the equator, so we must make up our minds that it will be very hot. If we go slowly and rest indoors in the middle of the day, as the Brazilians do, we shall probably get along very comfortably.

Para is probably, next to Rio de Janeiro, the most attractive city in Brazil. The trees and shrubs and plants are much larger and have bigger, brighter blossoms than those in our gardens at home, and they make the whole city look as if it were decorated for some festival. Many of the streets are lined with magnolia trees, which

Figure 51—Fifteen or twenty brazil nuts grow packed closely together in a round, hard shell.

are covered in the early spring with large, dainty pink blossoms, and the houses are surrounded by spreading shade trees. Nothing looks dry or dusty, for there is plenty of rain—too much, it seems to us, for a heavy shower interferes with our sightseeing every afternoon during our stay in the city. After the rain, however, a sea breeze usually springs up which lasts well into the night. This makes the evenings delightful, and crowds of people throng the brilliantly lighted plazas and chat and walk and listen to the music.

Para is already a city the size of Portland, Oregon, and in spite of its heat will in the future be known as one of the world's great ports. It is situated at the mouth of the Amazon, where the trade of the rich valley must pass its doors. One writer says of the city, "Three thousand miles from New York, three thousand miles from Buenos Aires, and three thousand miles from

London sits Para, at the only navigable mouth of the great river, without a possible rival on a coast of nearly a thousand miles."

The harbor of Para is crowded with craft. Large ocean steamers fly the flags of many different countries; smaller vessels have come from hundreds of miles up the Amazon; and scores of small native boats, many of them with colored sails—blue, green, or yellow, softened into duller hues by the sun and rain,—have come from villages and towns on the banks of the great river. Many of the boats carry cocoa beans, Brazil nuts, gums, and oils, but the most of their cargoes is made up largely of black biscuits of rubber. It is rubber that has made Para such an important port. Thousands of tons are shipped from its wharves every year. We can

Figure 52—Busy workers are everywhere handling the big black biscuits of rubber.

smell rubber and see rubber everywhere. All along the water front are great warehouses, some of them several hundred feet long, filled with this one product. Huge electric cranes rattle back and forth loading and unloading the vessels lying alongside the wharves, and busy workers are everywhere handling rubber—cutting up the big black biscuits, packing them in large bags, carrying them to the warehouses, and taking them from the storehouses to the ships.

The industry is such an important one that we are not satisfied to see simply the shipping of the rubber biscuits at Para. We will sail up the Amazon River, see the trees growing in the forest, and watch the natives gather the milky fluid and prepare it for market.

As we leave the Para River and enter the Amazon we understand better why the South American Indians call it the "Rio Mar." In places here it is ten miles wide. Sometimes the distant shore is but a hazy line of green, and sometimes we lose sight of it altogether. There are numerous islands in the river, which we often mistake for the farther shore. The water is so full of mud that it is a dirty yellow color. What a long journey some of the soil must have taken since it was washed by the rain and the streams from the mountains of Peru, Ecuador, Bolivia, Colombia, Venezuela, and Guiana.

We have heard of people who did not know that islands were the tops of hills and mountains rising out of the water, but who thought that they were floating bodies and wondered how sailors could find their way to them so easily. Here in the great river-sea are islands that really float. When the Amazon is flooded it often washes away pieces of its bank, uproots trees, and carries along trunks and branches. More and more material becomes entangled in the mass, which grows larger and larger as it reaches the lower course of the river.

We pass but few towns on the way, and these not attractive ones. We enjoy seeing these places, but we have no desire to make our home in any of them. Here is one near a branch river on the southern bank of the Amazon, where our steamer ties up for a little while to leave supplies of food and clothing. Down near the shore are some wooden cabins and mud huts where the blacks live. Leading up to the town from the wharf is a broad street of reddish-colored soil which the sunlight, flickering through the tall trees, carpets in strange, wavering patterns. The houses where the white people live are low white buildings with the whole front open to the air. In the clearing behind these are the huts of the South American Indians, shaded by palm trees, and a little farther away are fields of manioc, maize, and vegetables. Still farther inland are plantations of bananas, pineapples, cocoa trees, and sugar cane, while inclosing everything—houses, gardens, and cultivated fields—rises the green, impenetrable forest wall.

From time to time on the edge of the river, separated from one another by miles of water, we see the huts of the solitary rubber gatherers. Now and then we pass a rough shack close to a huge pile of logs. Here the small boats which go up the side streams to collect rubber stop to get fuel. One thing which we are sure to find at every hut is a boat. No route is possible through the forest,

*Figure 53—Now and then we pass the huts
of solitary rubber gatherers.*

and the river is the only means of communication. If roads were made in the dense jungles they would have to be constantly cared for, as in six months they would be entirely hidden by the new growth of trees, shrubs, and vines.

During the wet season in the Amazon basin it rains every day. The morning dawns fair and pleasant, but soon the clouds begin to form and the rain comes pouring down. The trees drip, and steam rises from the hot, moist land. Every day the showers grow longer, the river rises higher, the shores disappear, and the trees seem to be growing out of the water. Everything made of metal takes on a coating of rust, and every morning we should find our shoes covered with mildew. After several weeks the sun shines again for a part of the day, the showers gradually become shorter, until they cease altogether, the water grows lower, and later the soaked land appears.

In our sail up the Amazon we shall learn a good deal about its tributaries. We had scarcely entered the main river when we passed the mouth of the Xingu, a large branch on the south. On your map the Xingu may be shown without a single tributary; in reality it has thirty or forty, any one of which is a good-sized stream, larger than some of the important rivers of Europe. Some hundred miles farther on is the Tapajos, a branch over eight hundred miles long and in places from eight to ten miles wide. Still farther up the Amazon we come to the mouth of its most important tributary, the Madeira River, one of the longest waterways of South America. The name means "river of wood," and was given to the stream because of the large number of uprooted trees which are thrown up on the banks or float on the water. The Madeira is navigable for seven hundred miles. Its course is then interrupted by rapids, but above these it is navigable for large boats for several hundred miles farther.

On the map on page 87 you will find a region marked Acre. This territory was formerly claimed by both Bolivia and Brazil. Neither nation was willing to give it up to the other on account of its great forests and its millions of rubber trees. It was finally given to Brazil on the condition that she should pay Bolivia a large sum of money and should build a railroad around the rapids of the Madeira River. There are few railroads in the world that have been built in an unpeopled tropical jungle like this part of the Amazon basin. A company from the United States had charge of the very difficult work of building the road and are now operating it. The line will be of great use not only to Brazil but to Peru and Bolivia as well, for you will notice in looking at a map that large areas in both of these countries lie east of the Andes Mountains. In these regions there are miles of grassy pastures, great forests some of which contain millions of rubber trees, and rich deposits of minerals. The soil and the climate are well adapted to the production of cocoa. As yet there are no roads or railroads in eastern Peru and Bolivia which lead over the mountains to the Pacific ports, and until the building of the railroad around the rapids in the Madeira River there was no connection with the seaports of the Atlantic. These rich lands were therefore of little value to either country. With the opening up of the Amazon and its branches and the building of railroads over the Andes, the eastern slopes of the mountains and the fertile plains at their feet will form some of the most desirable portions of South America.

As you see on the map, the northern branches of the Amazon are shorter than those flowing from the south. This is because the Guiana Highland lies nearer to the main river than do the Brazilian Mountains, where the southern tributaries rise. The largest branch on the north is the Rio Negro, named from the dark color of its water. This great river, probably as long as the Columbia, enters the Amazon by several mouths, one of which is more than a mile wide. So near together are the headwaters of the Orinoco River and the Rio Negro that in the rainy season it is possible to go by boat from the mouth of the Orinoco through the Venezuelan wilderness into the Rio Negro and thence to the mouth of the Amazon. We could go even farther than this by water through the interior of South America before sailing out into the ocean. Instead of following the Amazon out to the Atlantic we could go on down the Tapajos River and its branches. Then by carrying our boat a short distance we could enter a branch of the Paraguay River, sail across the country of Paraguay into the Parana River, and finally arrive at the mouth of the La Plata, thousands of miles farther south on the Atlantic coast from the mouth of the Orinoco, where we started on our long river trip.

As we proceed on our trip up the Amazon, we know when some miles away that we are approaching the Rio Negro, as its inky waters discolor the Amazon for a long distance. Eight or ten days after leaving Para we turn northward into this dark stream. Proceeding a few miles up the river, we rub our eyes and stare in astonishment. Here, a thousand miles up the Amazon, in the midst of a tropical jungle surrounded by a wall of green forest, with no neighbors for hundreds of miles, is a large city with fine buildings, electric lights, waterworks, ice plant, sewer system, paved streets, schools, and newspapers. Manaos, for this is the name of the city, has one of the finest theaters in either North America or South America. Its palace of justice is built of fine white marble, and its museum is filled with Amazonian curiosities. We can ride on electric cars, as comfortable as those in our own cities and towns, out into the suburbs and visit the truck farms which supply the city markets with fresh fruits and vegetables. In the river are vessels from England, Germany, France, and the United States taking on cargoes of rubber from the great warehouses which line the water front. The secret of the growth of this mushroom city from a little Indian village of mud huts to an important commercial center is rubber. Formerly the rubber was collected in the region and sent down the river to Para to be shipped abroad. Now ocean steamers come up the Amazon River and the Rio Negro directly to Manaos, and many rubber firms of Para have made their headquarters here.

Let us visit a rubber gatherer's hut and go with him into the forest. We must start before the sun is up, for he has many trees to visit and much to do in preparing the rubber after he returns. It would make the work easier and the price of rubber cheaper if the trees grew in forests by themselves instead of being scattered through the tropical jungle. The worker must first chop his way through the forest from tree to tree, making his route a circular one so that when he finishes his rounds he will be near home. As he walks ahead of us in the narrow path we notice his tools. He has a small, odd-shaped ax, some little cups, and a lump of clay. Arriving at the first tree he makes a gash in its bark, being careful not to cut into the wood. Beneath the gash he puts a lump of clay, and to this he sticks the handle of a cup so that the liquid will run into it. He repeats the process in several places on one tree and then goes on to the next, and so on until, after visiting the last tree on his route, he returns to his cabin. Before starting out in the early morning he took only some black coffee. Now he eats his breakfast, and then, taking a pail on his arm, he makes his second round. He goes from tree to tree, emptying into his pail the milky fluid which he finds in the cups. Returning a second time to his hut, he makes a fire between two forked stakes which he has fastened into

the ground. For fuel he likes best the nuts of a palm tree which grows in the forest. These burn with little flame and a dense smoke. When the fire is well started he puts over it a funnel-shaped cover with an opening in the top, through which the smoke rises. Then he lays a long pole across the forks in his stakes. He dips some of the milky juice from his pail and pours it slowly over the part of the pole which is directly above the

Figure 54—He empties into his pail the milky fluid which he finds in the cups.

smoke hole, turning the stick round and round as he does so. The heat hardens the juice, and the smoke darkens it. He keeps up the pouring and the slow turning of the pole until the hardened layers have formed a big, black ball, which he either cuts off or shakes off the pole. He then begins on another, and continues his work until all the material which he has collected that day is used. In order to make the best rubber it is necessary to make the balls on the same day that the liquid is taken from the trees. Sometimes, instead of making large balls on a pole suspended by forked stakes, the Indian uses a smaller stick one end of which is shaped something like a paddle. He dips this into his pail

Figure 55—A Rubber Gatherer at Work in His Hut

and twists it back and forth over the smoke. When the rubber has hardened he dips it into his pail again and so continues until he has a ball which will weigh five or six pounds.

The rubber season lasts only half the year. During the other half the workmen harvest Brazil nuts or gather vanilla beans, sarsaparilla roots, or some other useful plants. Instead of remaining in the woods, some of the laborers go down the river and spend the rest of the year in the large cities, spending their hard-earned money. The next summer they go again into the forests and begin their solitary work. Most of the rubber stations are near the banks of the Amazon and its branches, and the gatherers go only a few miles into the woods. In the unexplored parts of the forests of Brazil, Peru, Ecuador, and Bolivia there are probably millions of rubber trees undiscovered and untapped. At present the expense of getting the rubber to the streams is so great that the business is not profitable. As the region is developed, roads opened, and railroads built, much greater quantities of rubber than are obtained at present will be taken out of the forests. These improvements will come slowly, and many years must pass before all the riches of the deep forests will be used.

India rubber, or caoutchouc, has been known for years, but since the uses of electricity have increased so greatly and the number of automobiles has multiplied, the demand for rubber has grown to enormous proportions. In parts of Mexico, Africa, India, Ceylon, the Malay Peninsula, and the East Indies, where the soil and climate are favorable to their growth, millions of rubber trees have been planted, and the production from these plantations has increased by leaps and bounds, so that today other parts of the world are as famous for their rubber exports as are the regions around Manaos and Para.

There are many other trees and shrubs that yield a liquid which may be made into an elastic substance similar to rubber. The trees which we have described in the Amazon forest produce the best rubber, and these are the kind which are being planted in different parts of the world, though experiments are being tried with other varieties.

Figure 56—The rubber gatherers bring the big black biscuits down the smaller streams to some collecting point.

The first account that we have of rubber is one written by a companion of Christopher Columbus, in which he tells of seeing the natives of South America playing on the seashore with a ball which when thrown to the ground bounded to a great height. Another early explorer speaks of a substance with which the Indians smeared their garments to make them waterproof. These were the only uses to which rubber was put for many years. Today we should hardly know how to get along without our balls, raincoats, overshoes, rubber bands, erasers, and tires for carriages and automobiles. The uses of rubber are as many and as varied as those of iron and copper. What would our fire companies do without rubber hose, our manufactories without tubing and belting, our hospitals without rubber bandages, sheeting, and hot-water bottles, our telegraph and telephone companies without rubber insulators, and our motor cars and bicycles without rubber tires? It would be impossible to mention all the uses of rubber, which, with new inventions and new appliances, are increasing every year.

We should find it interesting to follow the big black biscuits on their long voyage from Manaos to some great factory in the United States where rubbers are made. There are many processes through which the hardened juice must be put before it is useful for manufacture. No articles are made of pure rubber. It would melt with the heat, harden with the cold, and be so sticky and inconvenient that it would be of little use. On arriving at some Northern factory after their long voyage from the tropical plains of South America the biscuits of rubber are first cut up, washed, and then thoroughly dried. After this the rubber is mixed with sulphur and other substances and then rolled out into thin sheets and put through machines called calenders. Here it is again rolled into special shapes of varying thickness and finish, some to be used for the soles of your rubbers, some for the uppers, and some for linings. The different parts of a rubber, some fifteen in all, are then cut out by machinery and fitted smoothly together on the last. The seams are all covered and rolled firmly down. Then the rubbers are sent on the lasts to another department where they are varnished and then given their final vulcanizing or baking. The packing department of a great rubber factory is a busy place. Here the rubbers are removed from the lasts, inspected to see that they are perfect in all respects, sorted, tied in pairs, and packed. In the shipping room other workmen nail up the boxes, label them, and start them on their way to the firms which have ordered them from the factory.

The next time that you buy a pair of rubbers perhaps you will think of the many processes which have been necessary to change the milky juice of a South American tree to the trim, glossy foot-covering which you buy in the store. You will think, too, of the number of people— the South American Indians tapping the trees in the Amazon forests, the sailors manning the ships that sail up the great river and that bring the cargoes of rubber across the ocean to our ports, and the workmen in the large factories—who have spent their time in order that you may be protected from the wet.

TOPICS FOR STUDY

I

1. The size of the Amazon River.

2. Branches of the Amazon.

3. Forest plains, or selvas.

4. Brazil nuts.

5. Para, the rubber city.

6. A trip up the Amazon.

7. The Rio Negro and Manaos.

8. With the rubber gatherers.

9. Rubber-producing countries of the world.

10. In a rubber factory.

II

1. Name and locate the five largest rivers of the world. Name a large city on each one.

2. Write a list of the ways in which the Amazon and the Mississippi differ; of the ways in which they are alike.

3. Draw a map of South America. Show the Amazon River and some of its large tributaries; the La Plata and its branches; the Orinoco and the island of Trinidad near its mouth.

4. Why is the rainfall heavy in the Amazon basin?

5. Ship a cargo of rubber from Manaos to Hamburg, Germany. On what waters would the vessel sail?

6. Write a list of articles made of rubber. Learn to spell the words in the list which you have written.

7. Write a list of the places mentioned in Topic III which you think are so important that you should always remember them.

III

Be able to spell and pronounce the following names. Locate each place and tell what was said of it in this and in any previous chapter. Add other facts if possible

Brazil	Amazon River
Venezuela	Hudson River
Guiana	Para River
Peru	Xingu River
Ecuador	Tapajos River
Bolivia	Madeira River
Colombia	Orinoco River
Mexico	Paraguay River
United States	Parana River
Africa	La Plata River
India	Columbia River
Ceylon	Rio Negro
Malay Peninsula	Para
East Indies	Rio de Janeiro
Acre	Manaos
Marajo	Buenos Aires
Selvas	Portland, Oregon
Andes Mountains	London
Brazilian Highland	New York
Guiana Highland	

CHAPTER VII

A VISIT TO
A COFFEE PLANTATION

As the land of great rivers, deep forests, diamonds and other valuable minerals, and millions of rubber trees, we have thought Brazil a wonderful country. We shall think it even more wonderful when we visit its coffee plantations and see the millions of bags of coffee berries piled high on the wharves, packed in large warehouses, and stored in the deep holds of vessels. There are between one and a half and two billion people living in the world today. In Brazil and other South American countries, in Central America and Mexico, in the East and West Indies, in the Hawaiian and the Philippine Islands, and in parts of Asia and Africa, enough coffee is produced annually to give every man, woman, and child in the world a cup of coffee every morning for nearly three months of the year. Of this immense quantity Brazil supplies about three fourths.

In our visit to Rio de Janeiro we saw many things that told us we were in a coffee-producing country. A great deal is raised in the region around the capital, and large quantities are shipped from its wharves. The most important coffee region of Brazil lies a little southwest of Rio, in Sao Paulo, a state about the size of Arizona. This one state fills half the coffee cups of the world. In Sao Paulo there are more than fifteen thousand coffee plantations, two thirds of which average more than fifty thousand trees each. Nearly six hundred plantations contain more than five hundred thousand trees each, and one estate, the largest of them all, has so many trees that it would take you more than three months, counting steadily day and night, one every second, to count them all.

Instead of taking a water trip we will go by train on a three-hundred-mile ride from Rio to the city of Sao Paulo, the capital of the state of the same name. A few miles back from the coast of Brazil a high plateau slopes sharply down to the Atlantic, and to get to any inland city we have to climb up onto this plateau. The train shoots in and out of tunnels, and we catch glimpses of green mountains, dashing streams, and deep valleys. As we proceed we notice the peculiar reddish color of the soil. Everything inside the car and out is covered with a red-brown dust which sticks to our faces and our clothes. The cars are hot, but we should be more thickly dusted than we are if we opened a window.

After a long day's ride we arrive hot and dusty at Sao Paulo. The city is situated on the tropic of Capricorn, but, as it is about two thousand feet high, the climate is delightful. The summer days are hot, but the nights are nearly always cool, and one can enjoy a refreshing sleep. In the winter, in July and August, frosts are not uncommon. We are surprised at the size and beauty

Figure 57—Sao Paulo is the second largest city in Brazil.

of Sao Paulo. It is larger than San Francisco, and has magnificent buildings, splendid parks and avenues, and fine schools. Several lines of steam and electric cars run in various directions out into the country around. It is said that Sao Paulo is built of coffee, for it is the income from this one product that has made this beautiful city possible.

We are more interested in the plantations around than in the city itself, so we will go at once to see them. How lovely everything is! The hillsides are so green with coffee trees and the roads winding in and out among them are so red that the whole country looks like a picture. Can you imagine a plantation larger than a whole city, larger in fact than several cities? The estate which we will visit employs eight thousand workmen, contains eight million trees, has eighty miles of telephone wire, from forty to fifty miles of railroad track, thirty railroad stations, and, more wonderful than all this, it produces twenty million pounds of coffee in a year.

We can ride for hours on the red roads that wind through the plantation and see on either side nothing but coffee trees—some full grown and pruned back to about ten or twelve feet high, some slenderer and smaller (only half grown), and still others (just transplanted) only a foot or two high. A well-kept farm in any country is always a fine sight, but a coffee plantation is exceptionally beautiful. The leaves of the coffee tree are such a glossy green that they look as if they had been varnished. In September the trees are covered with small white flowers, and the air around is filled with their fragrance. Soon the blossoms fade and drop, and the berries begin to form. You know how green and glossy are the holly

Figure 58—We can ride for hours on the red roads and see nothing but coffee trees on either side.

leaves with which we decorate at Christmas time. Can you picture to yourself a tree like the holly with shiny green leaves hung thick with clusters of dark short-stemmed cherries or bright red cranberries? Then imagine, if you can, sloping hillsides, broad valleys, and level fields of brick-red soil covered as far as you can see with thousands of such trees, and you can realize something of the beauty of a coffee plantation when the berries are ripe and ready to pick.

Figure 59—The glossy green leaves of the coffee tree are hung thick with red berries.

There are many buildings on a large coffee plantation. High on the slopes of a beautiful valley, with a magnificent view spread out before it, is the long, low white house of the owner. It does not look especially attractive from the outside, but within we should find it beautifully furnished. Some of the coffee kings are very wealthy; their children are educated abroad, their homes are palaces, and their lives are filled with every luxury. The owners of the smaller estates live comfortably, but a poor year makes many debts which must be paid off when better crops are gathered. Some little distance from the owner's residence are many other buildings. There are barns for the horses, mules, and oxen, hundreds of which are needed on the estate. There are blacksmith shops, machine shops, sheds in which the farm machinery is stored, a bakery, a drug store, a sawmill, and many other buildings, to say nothing of the mills and factories in which the coffee is prepared for market, and the houses for the workmen and their families. We walk past long rows of the little whitewashed brick or mud cottages of the laborers; but at the harvest time especially we see few people in them, for not only the men, but the women and children as well, are hard at work out in the fields gathering the berries from the low bushy trees.

Many of the laborers on the coffee plantations in

Figure 60—Picking the Coffee Berries

Sao Paulo are Italians. Thousands of them come to Brazil every year to find work on the great estates. Each family is given a certain number of trees to care for. A large family is expected to tend eight or ten thousand trees, and their work is looked after by an overseer. A good deal of hoeing and weeding is necessary, as the warm climate and abundant rainfall cause weeds and grass to grow rapidly. During almost any month of the year we could see dozens of workmen, their faces and clothes stained with the red soil, loosening the earth around the trees, pulling the weeds, or leaning on their hoes to rest for a minute.

A workman is paid a certain amount of money a year, perhaps from twenty to thirty dollars for each thousand trees that he cares for, and extra wages during the harvest season; he has his house to live in, though it may be a poor one, and a little piece of land which he can cultivate for his crops of corn, beans, and manioc.

Let us get onto this little car which will take us around the plantation. We enjoy the ride over the red earth and in and out among the trees. As far as we can see stretch the reddish soil and the rows of glossy green trees covered with the red, cherrylike fruit. We are glad that our visit comes in the harvest time—the busiest time of the year on a coffee plantation. During this season thousands of laborers come to the state of Sao Paulo, just as the workmen pour into the central part of the United States during the wheat harvest. Some come on the railroad, some in slow ox-teams, and others on foot, but no matter how many there are, there is always a demand for more.

Figure 61—Brushing up the Coffee Beans

The coffee trees blossomed in September, and now in May they are covered with their dark-red fruit. The planters in this region have an advantage over those of Mexico and Central America because the berries here in Brazil all ripen at once and the trees can be stripped at one picking. In more northerly countries a single tree has to be gone over several times and the picker must be careful each time to select only the ripe fruit.

The workmen are paid according to the quantity of berries which they gather in a day, and this causes a good deal of rivalry, as it is an honor to be considered the fastest picker on an estate. Good workers sometimes pick as much as fifty pounds in one day. The pickers let the berries fall onto the ground, and other laborers rake them into piles from which they fill the tall baskets that they carry to the waiting carts.

Perhaps you are thinking how different these dark-red berries are from the brown coffee beans which we buy at the store, and you are wondering what is done to them before we can use them for our morning cup of coffee. In the center of each berry are two beans lying with their flat sides close together, somewhat like the two halves of a peanut. Several processes are necessary to remove the pulp and prepare the beans for market. The fruit as it comes from the tree is first passed over large cylinders fitted with teeth which mash the pulp without crushing the seed. From the pulping machine the seeds are carried over other cylinders, filled with holes through which they drop into water beneath. In the water they are carried next to great tanks where they are thoroughly washed and scoured to remove the last bits of the sticky pulp.

Figure 62—The coffee berries are spread to dry in the sun.

When we arrived at the plantation we noticed some large cemented yards near the mills. On these paved floors the berries are spread to dry, for no artificial heat equals the rays of the tropical sun. Here the beans remain for days or even weeks. Workmen with long wooden rakes turn the berries over and over until every bit of moisture is gone and every trace of the pulp is removed. During this time the berries are very carefully watched, and if a shower comes up they are hastily covered. At night they are raked up in heaps and covered, to protect them from the dew or rain.

Figure 63—At night the berries are raked up in piles.

Take one of the berries in your hand and examine it closely. Under the thick outside skin you will find another, thinner covering. Both of these are removed by passing the berries between heavy grooved rollers which break the dried skins. Large ventilators then blow the waste into another room, while the beans, now a light-green color, drop into great bins. You will notice that the coffee beans which you buy are all about the same size. These which we are watching go next to the separator—a kind of sieve with different-sized holes through which the beans drop.

Let us follow the beans into another room, where at long tables we see rows of dark-eyed Italian girls and wrinkled-faced Italian women with bare feet and bright-colored handkerchiefs on their heads. An endless stream of berries flows down a chute in front of each worker, whose fingers fly as she picks out the imperfect ones and allows the good ones to drop through a hole in the table into the bag which is tied underneath. When full, the bags are taken to still other workers, who sew them up, after which they are ready to be sent away. Even now the coffee is not ready to use, and you would not recognize in these greenish-gray berries the brown coffee beans with which you are familiar. It is the roasting which turns the bean dark and gives it much of its flavor. The roasting is not done on the plantations, as the beans keep much better and make a better-flavored drink if they are not roasted too long before using. It is said that Brazilians make the best coffee of any people in the world. They usually roast and grind the berries just before they use them and so are able to obtain their full flavor.

Let us follow the bags of coffee from this estate to Sao Paulo, one of the largest cities of South America. Perhaps one of the reasons for its rapid growth and the

*Figure 64—Let us follow the bags of coffee
from the estate to the city of Sao Paulo.*

business enterprise and energy of its people is due to
its situation on the plateau instead of on the low coastal
plain where most of the Brazilian cities are located.

We enjoy Sao Paulo more than any Brazilian city
that we have yet visited. Except in the older parts of
the city the streets are wide and paved, the blocks are
large and well built, and the schoolhouses are finer
than we should find in some cities of the United
States. The railroad station where we take the train
for the coast is the finest in Brazil, while the cars, the

engines, the stations on the route, and everything else connected with the railroad are the best of their kind. Not only does the city itself owe its growth and wealth to coffee, but it is coffee also which has built and which supports the railroad that leads down to the seaport. It is probably the richest railroad in the world. It pays large dividends to its stockholders, and it is said that at times the income from it has been so great that it has been hard to know how to spend it. Everything has been done to improve the line except, as one writer humorously says, to gild the telegraph poles. The railway is a remarkable one in many ways. To get from the low coastal plain to the high plateau behind, it was necessary to climb some twenty-five hundred feet in a distance of six miles. This required skillful planning and the building of several tunnels and bridges. The scenery as we descend the steep slope from Sao Paulo toward the shore is wonderfully beautiful. Leaving the plateau with its clear bracing air we run swiftly down, now peering into deep wooded glens, now skimming on slender bridges over narrow gorges, now winding along cliffs down which leap sparkling cascades, until, after a two hours' ride, we arrive at Santos, the greatest coffee port in the world.

Not many years ago Santos was one of the most dreaded seaports in South America. Travelers avoided it, sea captains made their stay there as short as possible, and hundreds of sailors entered it never to return to their ships. Stories are told of vessels lying in the harbor because nearly all of their crew were dying of yellow fever. Learning of the wonderful work which the United

States had done in Cuba in driving out sickness and disease, the people of Santos decided to do the same. Today the city is a thriving, healthful place with clean streets, modern buildings, great warehouses, and fine docks. The coffee industry is the one great business of the city. If we should take the bags of coffee that are shipped from Santos each year and place them end to end, they would stretch around the entire boundary of Brazil, a distance of six thousand miles.

Figure 65—If the bags of coffee that are shipped from Santos each year were placed end to end they would stretch six thousand miles.

All along the water front are the large warehouses, where we see dark-skinned Portuguese laborers emptying coffee beans from the bags into great piles on the floors. Other workmen are busy cleaning, sorting, grading, and packing the berries into other bags.

*Figure 66—All along the water front of Santos
are large warehouses filled with coffee.*

These are either stored in the warehouses or loaded onto vessels waiting at the wharves. The narrow streets are filled with wagons and men, and everyone whom we see is employed at some work connected with the coffee industry. Coffee agents from foreign countries are bustling about or are hard at work in their offices; laborers trot along with bags on their heads or on each shoulder; heavy wagons filled with coffee block the way; black women with sieves and brushes in hand dodge in and out among the teams, brushing up the beans which fall in the streets. They shake out the dirt through the sieves, wash the beans, and make their living by selling them.

The harbor of Santos is full of vessels, and several are tied up at the wharves to receive their loads of

*Figure 67—Vessels are tied up at the wharves
of Santos to receive their loads of coffee.*

coffee. We see the Stars and Stripes and the flags of
many foreign nations flying from the masts, and we
know that these ships will carry Brazilian coffee all
over the world.

The people of the United States use more coffee
than those of any other nation. We drink about half of
the world's crop. We buy nearly enough coffee annually
to supply every man, woman, and child in our country
with two cups for every day in the year. Nearly all of
this immense amount comes from Brazil, the greater
part of it from the port of Santos.

The next time that your mother makes coffee you will picture to yourself the great plantation with its red roads and its rows of glossy green trees loaded with bright-colored fruit. You will think of all the work necessary before the berries are ready to leave the estate, of the millions of bags in the warehouses and on the ships in the harbor of Santos, and of the long voyage from this Southern city to the ports of the United States. You will realize, more than ever before, the time, the labor, the cost, and the number of workmen that are necessary in order that we may enjoy our morning cup of coffee.

TOPICS FOR STUDY

I

1. World production of coffee.

2. The state and city of Sao Paulo.

3. The railroad trip from Rio to Sao Paulo.

4. A coffee plantation.

5. Processes in curing coffee.

6. The port of Santos and the railroad to Sao Paulo.

II

1. Sketch a map of Brazil. Draw the equator and the tropic of Capricorn. Show the states and cities mentioned in the chapter; the railroad from Rio to Sao Paulo; from Sao Paulo to Santos.

2. For each of the Brazilian cities mentioned find a city in the United States which is about the same size.

3. In each case find a city as far north of the equator as the Brazilian city is south of it.

4. Ship cargoes of coffee from Sao Paulo to France, Germany, England, Italy, and the United States. Tell in each case the waters sailed on and the receiving port.

5. Write a list of the coffee-producing countries of the world. Beside each name write the name of a city from which the coffee might be shipped. Be able to trace the route from each port to New York.

6. Make a list of places mentioned in Topic III which you think are so important that you should always remember them.

III

Be able to spell and pronounce the following names. Locate each place and tell what was said of it in this and in any previous chapter. Add other facts if possible.

Brazil	United States
Central America	Africa
Mexico	Texas
East Indies	Tropic of Capricorn
West Indies	Rio de Janeiro
Hawaiian Islands	Sao Paulo
Philippine Islands	Santos
Asia	

CHAPTER VIII

THE PLEASANT LAND OF URUGUAY

WE will leave Santos and the coffee country and continue our journey southward. Large, comfortable steamers run from Brazilian ports to Montevideo and Buenos Aires, and the ocean trip of several days will be very enjoyable. While waiting for our vessel to sail we interest ourselves by watching the scenes on the wharves. Lying near our steamer are several others, which are being loaded with coffee. Long lines of black men, each one carrying two large bags of coffee on his shoulders, are passing between the warehouses and the ships. The lines seem endless. All day long in the hot sun the workmen plod up and down the wharves, and all day long the bags of coffee disappear one after another in the deep holds of the vessels.

Santos is situated near the mouth of a small river, and we follow its winding course between green banks covered as far as the eye can see with coffee plantations. Gradually the river grows wider and the banks less distinct until, after a sail of two or three hours, we find ourselves on the broad Atlantic. We have left behind us the torrid zone with its heat, its jungles, its coffee plantations, and its rubber trees. To the south of us we shall find lands more like our own, with wheat, corn, and flax fields, and vegetables and fruit of the temperate zone.

In our visit to Venezuela we spent some time in the valley of the Orinoco River; in Brazil we took a trip on the Amazon; now we are going to visit the countries that lie in the basin of the La Plata, the third great river of South America. The early explorer who first sailed up this river named it the Rio de la Plata (the river of silver), not on account of the color of its muddy waters or because he had found any silver in or near it, but because the South American Indians whom he met seemed to be well supplied with the precious metal and he supposed that deposits of it would be found farther upstream.

The Rio de la Plata is the broad mouth of two other rivers, the Parana and the Uruguay, which join about as far from the ocean as Boston is from New York. The Parana River (in the Indian language "mother of the sea") is two thirds as long as the Mississippi. In its middle course it flows westward and forms the boundary between Paraguay and the Argentine Republic. Just as it bends sharply to the south it receives the waters of the Paraguay River, a waterway as long as the Columbia in the western part of the United States. These two rivers, the Parana and the Paraguay, open the way into the very heart of South America.

The Uruguay River is shorter than either the Parana or the Paraguay, being about the length of the Ohio. For a considerable distance it forms the boundary between the Argentine Republic and Uruguay and receives the trade of both of these countries. Farther up in its course it flows between the Argentine Republic and Brazil.

These three rivers of the La Plata system drain more than a fourth of South America. Uruguay, Paraguay, and northern Argentina lie in their valleys, and much of the traffic of these countries is carried on their waters. Large areas in each of these three countries would even yet be unsettled if it were not for these fine navigable highways which drain this part of South America. Towns and villages lie along their banks, and beyond these are rich pasture lands dotted with cattle, and level fields covered with grain lying yellow in the sunshine. The only connection that many of these settlements have with the outside world is by means of the rivers and their branches, and many of the products of the plains are shipped by water down to Buenos Aires and Montevideo, the two great ports at the mouth of the La Plata.

Our first stop in the La Plata basin is at Montevideo, the capital of Uruguay. Every time you pronounce the name of this city you say the same thing that Magellan did when he sailed along the low, flat shore on his way around the world. The words *monte video* mean "I see a mountain." You can see in Figure 68 the famous mountain which gave the city its name. It is really only a low, cone-shaped hill three or four hundred feet high, and it would receive little attention if it were not for the fact that it is the only hill in sight along the level shore. Approaching by day one notices the fort that crowns its summit and by night the lighthouse on the top, which throws its beams out over the water.

Montevideo is a very pleasant city, the one perhaps in all South America that we should best like to live in. It is not as hot as Santos, as picturesque as Rio, or as beautiful as Sao Paulo, but it is modern and handsome and seems to have a more wide-awake, bustling appearance than the cities in the torrid zone which we have visited. Its people claim that it is the healthiest city in the world. It is situated on a slope that rises gently from the river, and every heavy rain gives its streets a thorough washing and the water drains quickly off into the sea. The ocean breezes that blow through it temper the heat of summer and moderate the cold of winter, and the climate is so delightful that the city and the suburbs which lie along the coast have become popular resorts for the people from both Brazil and the Argentine Republic.

Figure 68—You can see the famous mountain which gave Montevideo its name.

159

Figure 69—Drying Hides in Uruguay

Montevideo is a comfortable city. Our vessel stops at large docks, we walk along broad paved streets, we enjoy modern hotels, we start on trips into the interior from one of the finest railroad stations in South America, and we ride on electric cars to beautiful suburbs and shore resorts nestling on white sandy beaches. We walk down the Boulevard 18 de Julio, the main street of the city, and admire the display in the shop windows and the fine stone buildings made from material quarried in the hills of Uruguay. We loiter in the Prado, a lovely park with ponds of clear water, avenues of giant eucalyptus trees, gardens of beautiful flowers, and smooth, velvety stretches of grass.

We like the people of Montevideo. They seem cordial and hospitable, they are well dressed and businesslike, and they look as if they enjoyed life. They are interested also in people from the United States, for some of the important industries of the city are in their hands. Some of the great meat-packing houses which ship large quantities of beef to northern countries are owned by companies from the United States. People from our country have helped to develop the schools of Montevideo, and one of the first playgrounds ever started in a South American country is located here and is directed by a man from the United States.

Uruguay, the smallest of the South American republics, is larger than New England. It is a lovely, rolling country, never very hot except in the north, nor yet cold enough to make stoves for heating necessary. It has broad valleys, low hills, fertile plains, pleasant groves, and clear-flowing streams. It has no mountains, no deserts, no barren land, but is one great pasture covered with rich green grass. One writer calls it a

Figure 70—A Pleasant Street in Montevideo

garden wedged in between the plantations of Brazil and Argentina. Refreshing sea breezes blow over it, navigable rivers flow through and around it, and railroads cross it.

Stock-raising is the chief industry in Uruguay. The grass is green the year round, and the cattle can always, except in times of severe drought, find food for themselves. No barns are necessary or crops of alfalfa for winter feeding. If the animals in the country were divided equally among the inhabitants, there would be enough to give each one six cows and twenty sheep, and a horse to every two people. As the country becomes more thickly populated, agriculture will become more important, and wheat, corn, flax, and other products will be raised in increasing quantities. At present, however, most of the wealth is invested in cattle. Cattle products of all kinds—live animals, horns, meat, beef extract, hides and skins, grease and tallow, fertilizers, and wool—are exported in large quantities.

In the town of Fray Bentos on the Uruguay River, two hundred miles from Montevideo, is one of the largest establishments in the world for the preparation of beef extract. Let us take a short trip there and see what we can learn of the country and the industry.

As we leave Montevideo the river is so wide that we catch no glimpse of the Argentine shore. On the Uruguay side we see broad pastures, low hills, and here and there groves of trees surrounding the buildings of some large plantation. Not far from the capital we pass a large establishment for preparing frozen meat—a

Figure 71—Stock-raising is the chief industry in Uruguay.

frigorífico, a Uruguayan would call it. Several hundred cattle and two thousand sheep are killed here every day, and the meat is chilled in a modern way by the most recent inventions. Refrigerator ships take the beef and mutton on the long voyage across the equator to European countries, where it is received in as good condition as that sent by rail from Chicago to New York.

Continuing our voyage, we see at intervals low buildings, which mark the location of slaughterhouses and meatpacking establishments. In the green pastures around, hundreds of cattle feed peacefully in the tall grass happily ignorant of the fact that in a short time their bodies will be hanging in the cold-storage rooms or will furnish the cargo of some vessel bound across the Atlantic.

We meet many vessels on the river, some loaded with lumber or fruit, some with dried beef, and some piled high with horns of thousands of cattle. There are large ocean-going craft and small river boats, but it is a safe guess that each one carries, as a whole or a part of its cargo, some animal product; it may be the animals themselves, or it may be hides for your shoes, meat for your dinner, wool for your clothes, horns for your knife

Figure 72—A Solitary Life on the Uruguayan Plains

handle, fertilizer for your garden, canned meat for your picnic, or beef extract for your sick friend. You would be surprised at the variety of fruit carried by some of the steamers. In a trip through Uruguay we should find orchards of apple, pear, peach, plum, lemon, and orange trees. In parts of the country quince trees are so thick as to form forests rather than orchards, and great quantities of quince preserves are made throughout the country. We should see fine beds of strawberries, large cocoa plantations, and heavily loaded banana trees.

Rounding a sharp bend in the river we see a collection of tall chimneys glistening in the sun. A decided odor of soup in the air tells us that we have reached Fray Bentos and that the buildings and chimneys that we see are a part of the establishment of the famous beef-extract company. The buildings are situated on the shore a little way to the south of the town and form a little village by themselves. At the wharves there are vessels which have brought coal, salt, lumber, machinery of different kinds, and tin plate to be made into cans and boxes. The ships will carry away horns, hides, tallow, bones, fertilizers, bone meal and dried blood for chicken food, and thousands of jars of beef extract and canned goods, soups, tongues, boiled beef, and corned beef,—all the products of this one establishment.

Figure 73—The Water Front at Fray Bentos and the Buildings of the Beef-Extract Company

Going up from the wharves we get a better view of the place. There are cottages for the several thousand employees, and larger houses for the managers and foremen. There are the slaughterhouses which the cattle from the pastures around and from other ranches in Uruguay and the Argentine Republic enter one by one through a narrow fenced lane. There are sheds for salting and storing the hides, factories for making tallow, buildings filled with machinery for cutting and cooking beef, for making tin cans, and for canning the products. There are shops for carpenters,

Figure 74—The cattle enter the slaughterhouses one by one.

tinsmiths, and machinists. There is the plant where the electricity is made which lights the houses, runs the cars, and moves the machinery. The company has also its own gasworks and waterworks. It supplies a church, a hospital, and a good school for the children of its operatives. Its employees receive good pay, are well cared for, are pensioned in their old age, and their children are trained in many ways so that they will make good workmen in the future.

In the busy season more than a thousand cattle are killed daily in the great slaughterhouses of this one establishment. So organized is the work, so powerful is the machinery, and so skillful are the workmen that it takes only eight minutes to kill an animal, skin it, and cut it into large sections to be hung in the refrigerating room.

Most of the cattle products of Uruguay are sent to Europe, but some are imported by the United States. As our country becomes more thickly settled and the cattle ranches give place to farms which must supply grains and vegetables for the people, we shall import more and more of these South American products.

TOPICS FOR STUDY

I

1. The La Plata River and its branches.

2. Montevideo, the capital of Uruguay.

3. Size and surface of Uruguay.

4. The cattle industry in Uruguay.

5. Fray Bentos and its great industry.

II

1. Bound Uruguay.

2. Name the chief cattle-producing countries of the world. What is the capital and most important seaport of each?

3. Write a list of the parts of animals that are used in manufacturing. Write a list of the articles which are made from these parts.

4. Sketch a map of the La Plata river system. Write the names of the rivers that belong to this system. Write the names of the countries which lie in its basin.

5. Write the letters of the word Uruguay in a vertical column.

Beside each letter write a word or phrase beginning with that letter descriptive of the country; for example,

U—undulating, or, used for pastures

R—rivers navigable, or, rich pasture land

U

G

U

A

Y

6. Do the same as in Topic 5 with the name La Plata.

III

Be able to spell and pronounce the following words. Locate each place and tell what was said about it in this and in any previous chapter.

Venezuela	Mississippi River
Brazil	Columbia River
Argentine Republic	Ohio River
Paraguay	Santos
New England States	Sao Paulo
New York	Montevideo
Orinoco River	Rio de Janeiro
Amazon River	Buenos Aires
La Plata River	Boston
Parana River	New York
Uruguay River	Chicago
Paraguay River	Fray Bentos

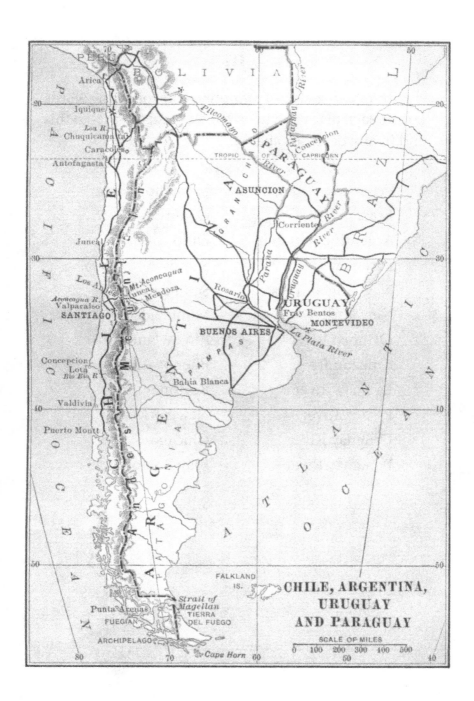

CHILE, ARGENTINA,
URUGUAY
AND PARAGUAY

SCALE OF MILES
0   100   200   300   400   500
          50

170

CHAPTER IX

THE ARGENTINE REPUBLIC AND ITS "CITY OF GOOD AIRS"

THE Argentine Republic is a large country between a third and a half the size of the United States. A line drawn through its widest part between Brazil and Chile, passing through the city of Corrientes, would reach from New York to Minneapolis, while the distance from its northern boundary to the southern tip of the continent is nearly as long as from New York to the Panama Canal. There are many things which will seem odd to us in a visit to Argentina, as the Argentine Republic is sometimes called. In the United States people go south in December and January to avoid the cold winter months of the North. In Argentina people go north in July to avoid the winter season of the southern part of the country. If you lived in this part of South America you would grow your plants in a sunny north room instead of in a south window, and your garden would flourish best on the north side of your house. At noontime in the United States your shadow always points to the north, because the sun is south of you; while at twelve o'clock in Argentina your shadow will lie to the south of you, because the sun is in the north.

In this great country, the second largest in South America, we shall find a variety of climate and surface. We can go from the tropical jungles of the North to the bitter cold of the antarctic regions; we can ride for days over its vast plains or climb some of the grandest mountains on the continent; we can endure the discomforts of the dry, dusty pampas or enjoy the delicious fruit of orchards and vineyards watered by clear, trickling canals at our feet; we can mingle with the gay crowds on the splendid boulevards of the capital city or live for weeks on the remote plains with no buildings in sight save those of the ranch where we are staying, no people save those employed on it, and no animals except the flocks and herds of the owner. We can shiver with the Scotch shepherd on the wind-swept hills of Patagonia in the Far South or wander in palm groves and enjoy the tropical fruits of the warm lands in the North. Truly the Argentine Republic is a wonderful country. It is developing more and more every year, and its industries and products are constantly increasing. Of all these, two are more important than any others. These are the cattle which feed in the rich pastures and the wheat which covers millions of acres.

One fifth of all the people of the republic live in Buenos Aires, the capital. Before going out into the plains to see the wheat fields and visit the cattle ranches we will stop for a while at Buenos Aires, the largest city in South America. From Montevideo a night's sail

Figure 75—An Isolated Ranch in Argentina

westward in a large, comfortable steamer across the La Plata River brings us to the city. The name *Buenos Aires* means "good airs," and so far as the healthfulness of the situation is concerned nature has done well by the city. It has not been so generous, however, in its gifts of beauty. From the muddy, brown waters of the river the low, flat shore stretches back as far as the eye can see, with not a hill in sight. As if to make up for the lack of natural gifts, its people have given the city everything possible in the way of beauty and of conveniences for carrying on the great trade which comes to its doors. For miles along the water front are splendid docks crowded with steamers, while among the forest of masts and funnels other vessels anchored in the river are awaiting their turn to unload. Giant cranes rattle to and fro over our heads, bringing up from the dark holds of the ships clothing and other manufactures of cotton and wool from France and

Germany; wine and silk from France; iron and steel manufactures from England; plows, forks, shovels and other farming tools, and harvesting machinery from the United States; and railroad cars from the United States and England. There are many kinds of food products also: fish from Norway; sardines and olives from Spain; sugar from Germany; and cocoa, bananas, and coffee from Brazil. Into other vessels are being lowered endless bags of wheat, bales of wool, bundles of hides, and great quarters of chilled beef. Trucks crowd the wharves; heavily loaded wagons rumble toward the warehouses; drays are loading and unloading; cars piled high with grain or animal products are pulled by puffing engines into crowded freight houses.

As we look at the miles of docks, the numbers of vessels lying alongside, the cranes, warehouses, freight depots, and all the other modern equipment of a great seaport, it seems hardly possible that, had we visited this Southern capital fifteen or twenty years before the

Figure 76—Giant cranes rattle to and fro over our heads.

Figure 77—Back of the wharves are lines of tall elevators.

beginning of the present century, our vessel would have anchored some distance out in the La Plata, which here is thirty miles wide from bank to bank, while we should have been lowered into small boats and slowly rowed toward shore. On reaching more shallow water we should have been obliged to climb from the boats into high carts with very large wheels, that had been driven into the water to take the passengers and the freight to land. Today Buenos Aires is one of the great shipping ports of the world. Many vessels, coasting and river craft and large ships from other continents, enter and leave the harbor every week, yet its commerce is so great that seventy million dollars was recently appropriated to extend and enlarge the docks.

Back of the wharves are lines of tall elevators which shut out a farther view of the flat city beyond. Even if we knew nothing of the country of Argentina, the great numbers and the large size of these grain elevators would tell us of the immense plains covered with millions of acres of wheat and corn which stretch away for mile after mile toward the lofty Andes Mountains.

Along the water front there are also warehouses filled with great piles of wool, the warm coats of thousands of sheep. Other storehouses filled with hides and skins, cold-storage plants bursting with tons of beef and mutton, and buildings crowded with horns, tallow, fertilizer, bone meal, and many other cattle products, all tell us of the rich pasture lands to the west, of which this great city of Buenos Aires is the chief outlet.

Behind the elevators and warehouses, where in former years were mud flats washed by the dirty brown

Figure 78—Buenos Aires is one
of the great seaports of the world.

*Figure 79—Elevators and warehouses
line the water front of Bahia Blanca.*

waters of the river, there are now beautiful gardens with shaded avenues, fine statues, and lovely flowers.

The Argentine Republic has more miles of railroad than any other country of South America. From the splendid station in Buenos Aires we shall find trains as comfortable and as well equipped as those in the United States, which will take us to other parts of the republic and to other countries. Later we will take a train and go across the plains and over the mountains to Chile. We might travel by rail toward the less developed regions in the North or go along the coast to Rio de Janeiro. Some shorter trips would also prove interesting. We should like to go south past cattle ranches and wheat farms to the seaport of Bahia Blanca. Since the wheat and wool industries have spread farther and farther south, Bahia Blanca has become the port for many of the products which formerly were shipped to Buenos Aires and from there sent on their long voyages to European countries.

Railroads radiate from Bahia Blanca north, west, and south, and are adding to their own wealth and to that of the city also by pushing their lines farther and farther out into the plains. They bring into the seaport immense quantities of grain and many tons of wool. As in Buenos Aires, elevators and warehouses line the water front, and vessels are loaded by means of the most modern machinery. Bahia Blanca has a splendid harbor, the best in the republic, and the government has made the city the naval port of the country. Great gray battleships lie at anchor in the harbor, and the arsenals and government docks make the place an important one.

Interesting as the trips from Buenos Aires would be, we are not yet ready to leave the capital, as there are many parts of the city that we have not visited. So we pass the railroad station and wander on to explore some of the streets. Buenos Aires has fewer skyscrapers than our cities contain. They are coming slowly, though at present most of the tall buildings are only seven or eight stories high, not tall enough perhaps to be called skyscrapers, yet they are giants compared with the low one-story houses with which many of the older streets are lined. As the city grows and land becomes more valuable the needed space may be found, as it has been in our large cities, by building higher structures.

Some of the streets of Buenos Aires are very narrow. When the city was small these narrow streets, shaded by the buildings on either side, were more comfortable in the hot summer than wider ones would have been, and were sufficient to accommodate the traffic which passed through them. Now that street cars, automobiles, heavy wagons, trucks, and carriages have become a necessary part of the city life, these older streets are very crowded. In many of them, as in certain streets in some of our large cities, the teams are allowed to move in only one direction, and in this way accidents are avoided and blockades prevented. All the newer streets are wider, and a law now in effect forbids the opening of any less than sixty feet wide.

Let us walk down the Avenida de Mayo, the finest and widest of the new streets and the main thoroughfare of the city. It is lined with trees and has very wide sidewalks. In front of the restaurants are open-air cafés much like those in Paris. These are flanked by spacious

Figure 80—The newer streets of Buenos Aires are wide and lined with trees.

Figure 81—The Plaza de Mayo

stores, fine hotels, and business blocks. As you can easily guess, *Avenida* is the Spanish word for *avenue*, and Mayo for the month of May, so the name means "the Avenue of May." It was so named because it was in that month that the Argentine war for independence began. Several South American cities have also an Avenida de Julio, as it was in July that their independence was declared.

The Avenida de Mayo extends for a mile from the Plaza de Mayo, the great square in the heart of the city, to the new Chambers of Congress, or the new Palace of Congress, as we might very well call it. This magnificent building, with its great dome similar to that which crowns our capitol at Washington, cost so much money that it is sometimes called the "Palace of Gold."

To make some of our purchases we will go to the Calle Florida, the fashionable shopping street of the city.

In the late afternoon it is so crowded with people that all vehicles are kept out. It is a narrow street, as many of the streets of Buenos Aires are, but some of the finest stores in the city are situated on it.

There are many beautiful parks in and around Buenos Aires, and we will ride out through a fine, broad avenue, past splendid mansions with gardens and fountains and groves of shade trees, to the loveliest one of all, Palermo Park. If we come late in the afternoon, especially on Sunday or a holiday, we shall find the avenues crowded with some of the finest turnouts that we have ever seen. Costly motor cars and luxurious carriages drawn by splendid horses are filled with ladies dressed in the height of fashion. Gardens and lawns, trees, lakes, fountains, and flowers make Palermo Park one of the most beautiful in South America, although

*Figure 82—Palermo Park is one of the loveliest
in South America.*

it is only a few years ago that it was a part of the bare level pampas which covers much of Argentina.

The part of Buenos Aires where the poor people live is very different from this beautiful modern section. The tenement houses, or conventillos, as you would call them if you lived in the Argentine capital, are large, low, buildings surrounding small courts. In each building there are many small rooms, each one the home of a family. In many cases the only light and ventilation comes through the door which opens on the court. The rooms are so small that the washing, the cooking, and much of the family life is carried on in the courtyard, which is usually swarming with children. In sections of the city where wide streets have been made and avenues built many of these conventillos have been torn down, but there are many left, crowded with people whose life is a sharp contrast to the gayety and luxury of the wealthy a stone's throw away.

The source of most of the wealth represented in Buenos Aires lies in the campo, as the Argentines call the level, fertile plains which stretch for hundreds of miles to the north, west, and south of the city. A few years of poor crops, of droughts, or of visitations of locusts, and prices in the city would be lower, luxuries would be fewer, and business in the great city would be lessened. There are very few capitals of the world where so many of the people are so directly dependent upon the occupations of the country around. Let us, therefore, take a trip out across the level plains to the cattle ranches and wheat fields and see what the life on the campo is like.

TOPICS FOR STUDY

I

1. Size of the Argentine Republic.

2. Contrasts of climate and surface.

3. Railroads of the Argentine Republic.

4. The port of Bahia Blanca.

5. The capital city, Buenos Aires.

II

1. Sketch a map of the Argentine Republic and show the land and water boundaries.

2. Show in the map the rivers that drain the pampas. Indicate the important cities situated on these rivers.

3. Write a list of some contrasts between New York and Buenos Aires.

4. Ship a cargo of goods from Buenos Aires to France; to Germany; to England. At what ports would the vessels discharge their freight? What waters would be sailed on in each voyage? What cargoes would be carried?

5. Name several reasons why Buenos Aires has grown to be the largest city in South America.

6. What connection do you see between the railroads of the Argentine Republic and the growth of the country?

7. Make a list of places mentioned in Topic III which you think are so important that you should always remember them.

III

Be able to spell and pronounce the following names. Locate each place and tell what was said of it in this and in any previous chapter. Add other facts if possible.

Chile	The campo
Brazil	Panama Canal
Bolivia	La Plata River
Patagonia	Corrientes
Norway	Buenos Aires
Spain	Montevideo
France	Bahia Blanca
Germany	Rio de Janeiro
England	New York
United States	Minneapolis
Andes Mountains	Washington

CHAPTER X

CATTLE RANCHES AND WHEAT FIELDS

WE will take a train at Buenos Aires for our visit to the ranches and farms of the Argentine Republic. Since the country has grown so rapidly land near the capital has risen in value, and the great cattle ranches are for the most part more than two hundred miles away.

Perhaps you are thinking that an automobile ride would be far pleasanter than one by train. The pleasure of riding in motor cars depends on good roads, and Argentina has but few such outside of her cities. In her great plains the villages and towns are widely separated by miles of open country, and the immense size of the ranches and farms, some of which contain many square miles, puts great distances between the dwellings. During part of the year, when there is little rainfall, the dust on the wide plains flies in clouds, and at other times of the year the track is deep in mud. So for a long trip we shall find the train much more comfortable than an automobile would be.

For some distance out from the city we glide by fine

large farms which supply the capital with vegetables, milk, and fruit. The country is as flat as a floor, and the soil is rich and well cultivated. As we go still farther west we find ourselves surrounded by a sea of wheat. On either side, stretching away to where the blue sky dips down to meet the flat plain, the yellow grain stands tossing and bending, rising and falling, and looking, as the wind blows over it, like the waves of a great yellow ocean. If we had taken a train at Buenos Aires which went north toward Bolivia we should have ridden through miles of similar wheat fields. If we had journeyed southward into the narrower part of the continent we should have found the same level land, the same rich soil, and the same great stretches of waving grain.

Argentina is one of the most important wheat-producing countries of the world. In any direction in which we might travel from Buenos Aires we should meet long trains of cars piled high with bags of grain. At nearly any station where we might stop we should see mountains of wheat, and on the remote plains we should meet processions of high oxcarts filled with grain creeping slowly over the dusty land. Yet these millions of bushels of wheat that are produced in South America today are only a fraction of the amount that will be grown in the future when the countries are more developed, when railroads reach out to every section, and when settlers from European countries take up the millions of acres on the plains which now lie bare and brown. For many years immigrants from Italy, Spain, Germany, and Russia have come by thousands into Argentina, but she needs many more

Figure 83—A Stagecoach on the Pampas

settlers, and she offers every inducement to persuade them to come. Steamship companies bring immigrants at low rates. Railroads charge very small fares, and in some cases none at all, to carry them to the part of the country where their labor is most needed. The immense immigrant hotel in Buenos Aires is the finest building of the kind in the world, and is so large that several thousand people can be accommodated at one time. Deserving immigrants are given their room and board free of charge until they can get work.

As in Kansas, Dakota, Texas, or any other of our great grain states, the harvest time in the Argentine Republic is the rush season of the year. At this time laborers from Italy flock into the country by hundreds and thousands, for there is plenty of work and good wages for all. Some of the largest landowners own their harvesting machines. Those on the smaller estates hire the machines that go through the country from farm

Figure 84—We shall see mountains of wheat.

to farm. These reapers and harvesters and threshers are just as large and just as modern as those that are used in our country. We never tire of watching these wonderful machines at work. They cut the grain, thresh and bag the seed, and stack the straw in a way that seems almost miraculous.

Now we have left the wheat ranches and are running through large flax fields. What a pretty sight they are! Hundreds of acres on either side of the track are covered with delicate blue blossoms. We find ourselves repeating the line, "Blue were her eyes as the fairy flax," and we do not wonder that Longfellow thought that the blue flowers of the flax plant were the best comparison that he could make with the eyes of the little daughter of the captain of the Hesperus.

Argentina is a great flax-producing country. Perhaps you wonder why you have never heard of Argentine linen as you have of Irish and French linen. The people of Argentina do not raise the flax plant so much for the fiber as for the seed. The oil pressed out from the seeds is used in making paints and varnishes, printer's ink, linoleum, and medicines. When flax is raised for the fiber it is harvested before the seeds are ripe. When it is raised for the seed it is allowed to stand in the field until the fiber is of little value for spinning and weaving. Therefore the countries which are noted for the production of the fiber and for the manufacture of linen do not as a rule produce much valuable seed. The amount of flaxseed, or linseed, as it is usually called, which is exported from the Argentine Republic is so great that if it were sent away in cars rather than in ships it would require a train so long that it would extend more than a hundred miles.

Still the level land stretches on and on. Now it is covered with acres of tall Indian corn, or maize. As far as we can see on either side are the slender waving blades and nodding tassels. The United States raises more corn than any other country in the world, but we use large quantities to feed cattle and hogs, so that no great amount is exported. Argentina does not raise nearly as much corn as the United States does, but the greater part of the crop is sent out of the country, so that she ranks today as the greatest corn-exporting nation of the world.

The fields through which we are riding look green and flourishing. They would appear very different if our trip occurred after a swarm of locusts had passed that way. When these pests make their appearance, the flax has usually been harvested and the beads of wheat are too ripe and hard for them to eat. But the juicy kernels and the fresh green leaves of the corn are a tempting meal to the hungry creatures. They swarm over the fields until every plant is thickly covered. After they leave, not a kernel or a green blade can be found; nothing but dry yellow stalks are left.

The locusts come from the north and fly over the land in clouds sometimes thick enough to darken the sun. They destroy every green thing in their path, eating the fruit, and sometimes even the bark, from the trees. Once in a while they stop trains from running. They cover the tracks in such numbers that when they are crushed by the wheels, they make the rails so greasy that the wheels slip round and round without making any progress.

As we get farther west we leave the grain fields behind and ride for mile after mile over the level land covered with nothing but brown grass. In the distance we catch glimpses of large herds of cattle and flocks of sheep such as we might see on our Western ranches. There are large numbers of horses also. The colts caper about their mothers or kick up their heels and gallop away as the train goes by. As in our Western states, the old days of the open ranch in Argentina are passed; the fields are now separated by miles of wire fencing and the same material borders the roads and the railroad tracks. Here and there we see fields of alfalfa, its deep purplish tint making a striking contrast with the brown grass.

*Figure 85—On every side of the buildings
stretch the vast pasture lands.*

At long intervals we notice in the distance clumps of trees standing out against the sky. These locate for us a pampas home, for there are no trees on the plains except those that have been planted by the people who live in these solitary places. If we were nearer to them we could see rows of poplar, eucalyptus, and willow trees shading the low, white buildings of an estancia, as the people of Argentina and Uruguay call their large farms and ranches. On every side of the buildings stretch the vast pasture lands on which thousands of cattle and sheep find food the year round. Here and there, like black dots scattered over the plain, are the little mud huts of Italian laborers. On many of the ranches we see the tall, waving arms of American-made windmills, and great stacks of wheat straw rise like giant mushrooms from the floor of the plain. But what seems odd in a land of cattle and grain, we see few, if any, barns. There are great sheds where wheat, corn, and linseed are stored until they can be shipped away, but the animals live out of doors the entire year.

Let us leave the train and visit one of the estancias. The owner is very wealthy, and the house is large and fitted with every modern convenience. The grounds are beautifully laid out with gardens, groves, and tennis courts, and there is so much land belonging to the estate that it is reckoned in miles rather than in acres. The family usually spend only a few weeks or months on the ranch, living the rest of the time in Buenos Aires or traveling in Europe. The children are educated in European universities, speak several languages, and live and dress as do the children of the millionaires in our country. It is said that there are more millionaires in Buenos Aires than in any other city of its size in the world, and nearly all of these owe their wealth to the

Figure 86—A Home of Immigrants on the Campo

great plains over which we have been riding.

Great changes in the methods of ranching have come with the passing years. Formerly the cattle on the estancias roamed at will over the unfenced land, cared for by the gauchos (the Argentine cowboys) in much the same way as was done on our great Western plains. The care of the cattle, the round-up, the separating of the animals to be shipped away, the branding, the long days of hard riding in all kinds of weather, made up some of the hard work of both the gaucho and the cowboy.

Except in the very southern part of the country, the winters in Argentina are not so severe as in some parts of the United States, but they are often cold enough and stormy enough to cause great loss among the cattle. Today all the large ranches are inclosed with miles of wire fencing, and many of the cattle owners raise several acres of alfalfa for winter feeding.

As more and more of the land in central Argentina is being taken each year for grainfields and vegetable farms, the cattle ranches have moved farther west and the sheep ranches farther south. In old geographies you will find the southern part of South America set off as a separate country called Patagonia. This southern region is now divided by the crest of the Andes Mountains between Chile and Argentina. On the Atlantic side the level pampas continue southward, rising higher toward the west and becoming interspersed with rivers, lakes, and swamps until in the western part of Argentine Patagonia the blue, cold Andes stand out against a

Figure 87—Great Cattle Pens in Argentina

bluer sky. In the high valleys of the mountains there are giant glaciers and ice-cold lakes, and on the lower slopes there are thousands of miles of forests as yet almost entirely unexplored. Much of Patagonia has a smaller rainfall than the countries farther north, but there is sufficient to support the coarse bunch grass on which increasing numbers of sheep feed every year. These sheep ranches cover immense areas, one of them being larger than the entire state of Rhode Island. Life on them is lonely, for the nearest neighbor is usually miles away. Many of these shepherds are Scotchmen, some are Germans, and others are natives and mestizos.

Even though the land is cold the sheep live in the open all the year round. In the summer they feed on the bleakest portions of the ranches, the part most exposed to the piercing winds. In winter they roam over the more protected areas where the snow is not deep enough to prevent them from getting at the grass. Even with this and other precautions hundreds of sheep on every ranch die during the winter, and at the beginning of spring the shepherds go out over the plains to get the wool from the dead animals.

We should not enjoy a trip through Patagonia, for it would be a hard, lonely journey. For hundreds of miles in the interior we should meet only an occasional tribe of wandering South American Indians and now and then a herder in his little shack with no company save his sheep and his dog. In this far southern land there are miles of forests, open plain, desert stretches, cold lakes, and rushing streams which as yet no white man has ever seen. As South America develops, as the countries become more thickly settled, as many agricultural nations in other continents turn their attention more and more to manufacturing, and as the world calls for larger and still larger supplies of bread and meat, we shall find ever-increasing areas in Patagonia devoted to cattle and sheep raising and much greater stretches than at present covered with the grain which furnishes the bread of civilized nations.

In the early days of ranching in the Argentine Republic the flesh of the animals raised there was considered of very little value, and the wealth of the owners came entirely from the wool and the hides and skins. Today every part of the animal, except the bleat and the bellow, is made use of as carefully in the Argentine slaughterhouses and meat-packing

*Figure 88—There are great warehouses
filled with piles of wool.*

establishments as in our Chicago stockyards. The animals are killed—in one establishment at the rate of between two and three thousand a day—and the meat is hung in cold-storage rooms where the temperature is below freezing even on the hottest summer day. We could make a long list of animal products which are shipped away from Buenos Aires, from Bahia Blanca farther south, from Rosario in the north, and from other cities on the seacoast and the rivers.

At these ports we should find vessels loading with dried beef for Brazil, horses for Uruguay, frozen beef and mutton, smoked tongues, tallow, and grease for England, hair and bristles for Belgium, and goat skins, sheep skins, and cattle hides for the United States. Besides these products vessels bound for many different countries carry soups, canned meats, glue, bones, fertilizers, bone meal, glycerin, oils of various kinds, and many other products made from the bodies of the animals which feed on the pampas.

When you sleep on a hair mattress, lace up your shoes, put on your woolen sweater, eat some canned beef, feed some bone meal to your chickens, or dress your garden with fertilizer, you will think that many boys and girls the world over are using the same products and that a large part of the world's supply of these useful articles comes from the pampas of the Argentine Republic.

TOPICS FOR STUDY

I

1. The wheat industry of the Argentine Republic.

2. Immigrants and their work.

3. Flax fields of the South.

4. The corn production.

5. Flights of locusts.

6. The cattle industry.

7. Life on an estancia.

8. Scenes in Patagonia.

9. Sheep ranching.

10. Cattle and sheep products.

II

1. Where in the United States would you expect to find large truck farms? What is raised on them? To what great cities are the products sent?

2. Write in a column the names of the great wheat-producing countries of the world. In another column write their capitals. In a third column write the chief seaport of each.

3. What things are necessary for the production of wheat? Compare the advantages of the United States and the Argentine Republic for raising wheat; for raising cattle. What countries in the eastern hemisphere possess similar advantages?

4. What country of the world ranks first in linen manufacturing? in the production of wheat? corn? cattle? sheep? flax?

5. Make a list of the places mentioned in Topic III which you think are so important that you should always remember them.

III

Be able to spell and pronounce the following names. Locate each place and tell what was said of it in this and in any previous chapter. Add other facts if possible.

Brazil	United States
Bolivia	Kansas
Uruguay	Dakota
Chile	Texas
Patagonia	Rhode Island
Italy	Andes Mountains
Ireland	Parana River
France	Buenos Aires
Belgium	Bahia Blanca
England	Rosario
Scotland	Chicago
Germany	

CHAPTER XI

A SAIL UP THE PARANA AND PARAGUAY RIVERS

AFTER our journey across the dusty plains of the Argentine Republic a trip by water will be refreshing. At Buenos Aires we go on board a large comfortable steamer for a sail up the Parana and Paraguay rivers, through the Argentine plains, and into the center of the inland country of Paraguay.

The lower Parana is wide and deep, and ocean-going vessels can go upstream as far as Rosario, a day's sail from Buenos Aires. In our trip between the two cities we see many signs of the cattle industry, which is so important in this part of South America. On the banks of the river are sheep and cattle pens covering many acres and filled with animals which were raised on the grassy pastures around. We pass large slaughterhouses and immense establishments for drying, salting, and chilling meat. On the fertile plains, which stretch for miles in every direction, thousands of cattle are feeding. At the wharves vessels are being loaded with animal products of every description.

Rosario is called the Chicago of the Argentine Republic. Judging by the number and size of the stockyards, the slaughterhouses, and the meat-packing establishments near the city, we should think that the whole world might be supplied with meat from this part of the La Plata basin. There are millions of cattle grazing in the pastures of Paraguay, Uruguay, and the Argentine Republic, but the plains are so vast, the grass so nourishing, and the climate so favorable, that in the future the industry will be much more important than it is today.

Not all the plains of the region are used for pastures. Here, as well as in other parts of the pampas, there are miles of wheat fields. As we approach Rosario we notice the great grain elevators and the tall warehouses along the edge of the bluff on which the city is situated. These are filled with wheat from the vast plains which stretch

*Figure 89—In this great slaughtering establishment
hundreds of cattle and sheep are killed daily.*

away for miles on every side. How easy it is to load the ships! Long chutes lead from the elevators down to the vessels waiting at the docks below, and the wheat slides down in a continuous stream into the deep, dark holds. A single elevator may have several chutes, so that more than one vessel can be loaded at once.

With the spread of the wheat industry Rosario has grown rapidly and has doubled its population in ten years. It is today a city larger than Omaha, Nebraska. Most of the buildings, whether dwellings or stores, are low, one-story structures, and most of the houses are built in the old Spanish style around a courtyard. The city is laid out in broad straight streets, parks, and squares, and has electric cars and lights and other conveniences of an up-to-date city.

The Parana is a large river twice as long as the Ohio. With its many branches it opens a way into the interior of the continent and connects the great inland pasture plains with the river and ocean ports. It rises in the highlands of Brazil and brings down annually to the La Plata an immense quantity of soil—enough, it is estimated, to make in a little more than twenty years an island a mile long, a mile wide, and a mile deep. Much of this soil is deposited in the La Plata near Buenos Aires, and constant dredging is necessary to keep the harbor of that city deep enough to accommodate its traffic.

During the rainy season the Parana overflows its banks in its lower course and spreads for miles over the land on either side. Sailing up the river at this time of the year we might easily imagine that we were sailing on a vast inland sea. Above Rosario the river narrows and flows between high banks, behind which are some of the richest wheatlands of the world. The country along the Parana and Paraguay rivers is very beautiful. On both sides of these streams the flat or gently rolling land is covered with fields of wheat, corn, and flax, or with grassy pastures dotted here and there with tall palm trees. Sitting on their horses among the flocks and herds we see many gauchos, who are every bit as fine riders as can be found on our Western plains. Each one is dressed in a wide hat, baggy trousers, and a poncho—a kind of blanket with a hole in the center through which it is slipped on over the head. On the wide level roads high two-wheeled wagons piled with wool, hides, grain, or vegetables creep along through the clouds of dust.

Figure 90—There are large stockyards near the Parana River.

Figure 91—An Argentine Gaucho

Now and then we pass unattractive little towns of low houses surrounded on all sides by the rich wheat fields to which they owe their existence. Out in the open country the house of the ranch owner sits in the midst of his thousands of acres far away from any neighbors, while scattered here and there over the wide treeless plain are the little thatch-roofed huts of the gauchos.

The day wears on as our boat makes its way northward. At night the cattle gather closer in the pastures, the gauchos come galloping home, and the fires to cook the suppers are kindled outside of the houses, making spots of light on the darkening plain.

In sailing up the Parana we have met many boats filled with logs. We think of the lumber industry in the United States and the great rafts that float down the streams to the mills, and we wonder why the people of Paraguay carry the logs in boats instead of letting the current of the river do their work for them. The reason is that these logs from the Paraguayan forests are so heavy that they would sink in the water. They come from the quebracho trees which grow in the northern part of the Argentine Republic, in Paraguay, and in southern Brazil. The word *quebracho* means "axbreaker," and the trees were so named because of the hardness of the wood. For this reason it is valuable for railroad ties, telegraph poles, and fence posts, and when put to such uses lasts for many years. Recently a much more important use has been found for one of the varieties of the quebracho tree. This is the making of tannin extract to be used in the tanneries of the world for changing the hard, hair-covered hides into soft, smooth leather.

A large part of the world's supply of tannin was formerly obtained from the bark of the oak, hemlock, and other common trees. It has now been successfully proved that not only the bark of the quebracho tree but the wood as well yields more tannin, of a better quality, and more cheaply manufactured than that obtained from any other source.

To see something of this industry we must go into the Gran Chaco. This is a vast plain, most of it unsettled and undeveloped, which includes northern Argentina and western Paraguay and which stretches northward into Brazil and eastern Bolivia. The Chaco is larger than our largest state, Texas. Thousands of Indians, some of them the remotest tribes of South America, live in its unexplored portions. Parts of it consist of swampy lowlands and tropical jungles, where alligators, peccaries, tapirs, jaguars, and huge snakes abound and where the mosquitoes would make life unbearable for the white man.

In other portions of the Chaco there are grassy plains where in the future millions of cattle will feed. Already a beginning has been made in this industry, and several large ranches have been started. One of the largest of these is owned and run by a man from the United States.

Figure 92—South American Indians of the Chaco

The greatest difficulty of the ranch owners is in getting their cattle to market, for it is a long, expensive trip by river and rail to Buenos Aires. When railroads are built from the large cities at the mouth of the La Plata to eastern Bolivia, and from Sao Paulo and Rio de Janeiro into northern Paraguay, we shall see a great growth in the cattle industry and other occupations of the Gran Chaco.

We are more interested in the forests of the Chaco than in its swamps or its pastures. These forests are made up of several hundred kinds of trees which in the future will serve many uses. At present the quebracho tree is the most valuable of them all. It does not grow by itself in continuous forests like our pine or hemlock woods, but is scattered in single trees or in groups throughout large areas. The cost of carrying heavy logs for long distances through a country with no roads or railroads is so great that it is much cheaper to take machinery and skilled labor from Europe and the United States into the Chaco and make the tannin extract there than it is to transport the lumber out of the country to manufacturing establishments in other continents. So into this far-off wilderness in central South America several large companies have brought men, machinery, oxen, building material, food supplies, and all the other necessities for life and work in such a place. Each company has built between fifty and a hundred miles of railroad from its section of the Chaco forest to the nearest river, and has placed a fleet of boats there to carry the products to the shipping ports. These companies have put thousands of men and oxen at work in the woods, and hundreds of workmen into the extract factories which they have built, and are making thousands of tons of quebracho extract every year. One of the largest of these companies employs more than ten thousand men in its great factories and its lumber camps. From the two million acres of forest land owned by this concern, thousands of horses and oxen draw the logs to the railroad or river. On some of the Argentine

Figure 93—In portions of the Chaco there are grassy plains where in the future millions of cattle will feed.

railroads you could walk for miles on the quebracho ties which have been supplied by this one great company.

To make the tannin extract the wood is cut by machinery into small shavings or chips. These are boiled in immense kettles and treated with different substances until the tannin is extracted, after which the water is evaporated and the tannin pressed into cakes and shipped down the river to Rosario, Buenos Aires, and other ports. It is then sent to European countries and the United States to be used in the leather tanneries. Many of you today are walking on leather that was tanned with quebracho extract. This is only a single instance of the new, important products which may come to the industrial world from the great forests of South America.

About twenty miles above the city of Corrientes the river bends to the east and forms the southern boundary of Paraguay. We will leave the Parana at this point and continue our trip northward by the Paraguay River. Few people realize the size of these great waterways of South America. We shall travel three hundred miles above the point where the Paraguay River enters the Parana before we arrive at Asuncion, the capital of Paraguay. Beyond that city we could continue our river trip for a thousand miles northward into the heart of Brazil. With the exception of Bolivia, Paraguay is the only country of South America which has no seacoast. It has an advantage over Bolivia, however, by being connected with the coast by the mighty Parana and by having other long navigable rivers running through the interior and on the southern, eastern, and western boundaries.

Paraguay is a third larger than Missouri, but it contains no more people than the city of St. Louis. The Paraguay River divides the country into two parts which are very different from each other. On the west is the Chaco, a region of grassy pastures, forests of valuable woods, swampy lakes, mosquitoes, and South American Indians unreached by civilization. It is in this part of Paraguay that the quebracho industry is carried on. We should not enjoy a trip into the Chaco. Mosquitoes are such a plague that in spite of netting we should carry on our bodies for some time the signs of their attacks. The mosquito netting would be no protection against the fleas which are so small that they could crawl through the meshes. Besides these pests there are swarms of flies and other insects that bite and sting. We might travel for miles without seeing a city, a village, or even a person, for there are millions of acres of land in western

Paraguay where no white man has ever set foot. Let us go instead into the eastern part of the country, where most of the people live and where most of the cities and towns are located. Here we shall see something of a product that does not grow in the United States but that yields a drink which is used by millions of people in South America.

Perhaps you are thinking that we shall visit coffee or cocoa plantations or tea orchards. Most of the people of Argentina, Chile, Paraguay, Uruguay, Bolivia, and parts of Brazil do not like beverages made from these plants as well as they do Paraguay tea, or yerba maté. Not only the natives, but the Englishman accustomed to his tea, the Italian to his wine, the German to his beer, and the Brazilian to his coffee, all like and use maté. It is said to be a more healthful drink than tea or coffee. Like

Figure 94—Workmen Enjoying a Drink of Yerba Maté

these it is a stimulant, but it leaves no bad effects. It enables people to do their work and to endure hardships without fatigue. In her great war the soldiers of Paraguay, provided with maté, could go on long marches and do hard fighting without being exhausted even if the food supply were short at times. Thousands of tons of maté have been shipped to European countries during the long war there, to supply the soldiers.

The tree from which the maté is obtained is somewhat like the holly and has similar glossy green leaves. Its size varies from that of a shrub to that of a full-grown orange tree. The smaller the shrub the better the tea made from its leaves. In some places the plants are scattered through woods of many different kinds of trees, while in other districts they grow by themselves in forests called yerbales. Thousands of people, both South American Indians and whites, are employed in gathering the leaves. Each workman takes with him into the woods a small ax, a few provisions, and some drinking water, as he may be gone for some days. He cuts the twigs and smaller branches and collects them in piles. He ties these up in bundles which he carries on his back to his camp in the forest and later to the nearest village. The leaves may be cured here or they may be packed in rawhides to be sent to some larger centers. If the village is near some stream they are sent by water; from the inland towns they are taken in great two-wheeled wagons drawn by oxen.

The leaves are dried over a fire and then ground into powder. The natives used to crush the leaves by pounding them with wooden clubs. They still do this in some regions, but most of the work today is done by machinery. In some parts of Paraguay the powder is put into green hides just as they are taken from the cattle. When the rude hide bags are full they are sewed up and put out in the sun to dry. As the skin dries it shrinks, and the contents becomes as solid as a rock. This is the old way of packing, but at the present time much of the maté is shipped in cloth bags.

Figure 95—Yerba maté is shipped away in bags.

The maté is a greenish-gray powder and makes a lighter-colored drink than the tea which we use in the United States. The people of South America pour boiling water over the powder much as we do in making tea. Instead of teapots and cups they use bowls or gourds and drink the maté through a brass or silver tube.

Some writers have called the eastern part of Paraguay the garden of South America. Fruits like the orange, flowers like the rose, plants like the cotton and tobacco grow well in the rich soil. In addition to these products the immense stretches of pasture land along and between the rivers support thousands of cattle and will in the future support many millions.

Asuncion, the capital of Paraguay and its only city of any size, is situated near where the Pilcomayo River, which forms part of the boundary of the country, enters the Paraguay River. It is more than a thousand miles by water from Buenos Aires to Asuncion. It takes four or five days to make the trip by the river and between two and three days by the railroad which connects the two cities. Asuncion is a quaint city. In some sections where there are large business blocks, fine public buildings, and modern stores, and where automobiles and electric cars fill the streets, we are reminded of some up-to-date city of the United States. In other parts the narrow streets, the oxcarts, the low one-story houses sitting close to the sidewalks, the flat roofs, and the iron-barred windows make us think of the cities of old Spain from which the early settlers of Paraguay came.

The muddy Paraguay River winds northward from Asuncion for more than a thousand miles through what is for the most part a great wilderness. In places the jungle comes down close to the water. If you were to leave the boat and go a mile

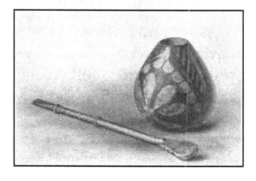

Figure 96—The people drink maté from a bowl or gourd through a brass or silver tube.

213

or two into the forest you would find jaguars, tapirs, snakes, chattering monkeys, and bright-colored birds nearly as numerous as they are in the deep forests of the Amazon valley.

Every now and then in the open places we see cattle feeding in green pastures, and once in a while the steamer stops at a small town or a hamlet. The low houses roofed with red tiles and painted in bright colors stand out boldly against the background of dense green woods. The little huts are dark and dirty. The earth floor, the hammock bed, the unwashed people, the grass-grown streets, and the lack of all comforts and conveniences make us glad that our stay is a short one. The people in these Paraguayan towns, most of them South American Indians or mestizos, shut away as they are from the world around, are unfamilar with modern ways. When railroads take the place of the long river trip, when settlers begin to fill up the empty lands, when people become better acquainted with the riches of this inland country of South America, the condition of its people will be greatly improved.

As we travel nearer the boundaries of Brazil and Bolivia the river grows narrower, and far away to the north we see green hills rising into low mountains. For several days the air has been growing warmer. The sun shines hotter, the trees are larger, and the vines clamber higher and thicker than in the lands to the south. By these and other signs we know that we have passed from the temperate into the torrid zone. We see clumps of bamboos and groups of palm trees, and in the scattered villages that we pass there are orange, lemon, and banana trees. On both sides of the river the forests alternate with rich rolling pasture land where millions of cattle might find food the year round. Now and then we pass a comfortable ranch house surrounded by its acres of grassy plain, and again we catch a glimpse of a little village of mud huts where unclad children stop their play to watch the boat as it passes by, while the women continue their work of washing clothes in the river.

Figure 97—The Paraguay River winds northward from Asuncion for many miles.

Both in the cities and in the villages we see more women than men. The only war in which Paraguay has engaged since her Spanish war for independence was against the combined armies of Argentina, Brazil, and Uruguay. So fierce was this conflict and so long drawn out that during the five years that it continued the population was greatly decreased. Nearly all the able-bodied men of military age were killed. Even today, half a century or more later, the women far outnumber the men, and we see them much more often at work in the fields than we did in Argentina or Uruguay.

Figure 98—Now and then we pass a little village.

Besides the cattle ranches and wheat fields similar to those that we have seen in other countries of the La Plata basin, we notice now in each village fields of manioc such as we saw in Brazil and Guiana. If we should stop in one of the little hamlets along the river we might be offered some bread made from manioc flour. We should not like it as well as the wheat bread to which we are accustomed. We should enjoy, however, the delicious oranges which grow so abundantly in nearly all parts of Paraguay. For a cent we could buy all that we could eat. Most of the boats which we meet are carrying quantities of oranges down to Asuncion, Buenos Aires, and other cities. The yellow balls lie in piles on the wharves, and in one village we see cart loads being dumped on the ground near the river. In some places large quantities of delicious fruit lie rotting under the trees. As Paraguay develops, as railroads are built and quicker means of transportation are provided, oranges will form an important product of the country.

In the northern part of Paraguay we see, taking the place of wheat fields and cornfields, large tobacco and cotton plantations. Maté is the principal vegetable product of Paraguay, but both tobacco and cotton are important crops. Large quantities of tobacco are used in the country, as not only the men but many of the women smoke, but so much is raised that still larger quantities are exported. The soil and climate in the North are very favorable to the production of cotton. In some places the plants are much larger than those that grow in our Southern states, more like small trees, and the fiber produced is long and silky and excellent for manufacturing.

Ranching is and for many years will be the most important industry of Paraguay. The number of animals is increasing every year, and wealthy men from both the Argentine Republic and Brazil are investing more and more money in cattle and land. Now and then in our trip we have seen tanneries and establishments for drying and salting meat. The frozen-meat plants will in time be built farther and farther up the rivers, so that fresh beef and mutton can be sent easily and cheaply from this inland country to Europe.

TOPICS FOR STUDY

I

1. The Parana River.

2. The cattle industry of Paraguay.

3. The city of Rosario.

4. The wheat industry of Paraguay.

5. Quebracho trees and tannin.

6. The Gran Chaco.

7. Size and situation of Paraguay.

8. The Paraguay River.

9. The maté industry.

10. Asuncion, the capital of Paraguay.

11. Northern Paraguay.

12. Orange groves of Paraguay.

13. Tobacco and cotton plantations.

II

1. Find the length of the Parana River. Use the scale given on the map of the United States and see how far the river would stretch in a straight line across our country.

2. Find the names of some of the great packing-house companies in the United States. Make a list of all the products sold by these concerns.

3. Make a list of the contrasts between Paraguayan cities and those of the United States.

4. Find a description of tanning leather and tell the class something of the way in which it is done.

5. Make a set of topics about the Paraguay River from which you could give a lecture to your classmates.

6. What countries of the world produce tea? coffee? cocoa? maté? What part of the plant is used in each case?

7. Imagine yourself a country boy or girl of Paraguay and write a letter to one of your schoolmates here telling of your life.

8. What is the boundary between the torrid and the south temperate zones? How far is this line from the equator?

9. What countries of South America lie in the temperate zone? in the torrid zone?

10. Write in sentences the words *quebracho, tannin, maté, manioc, gaucho, poncho.*

11. Make a list of the places mentioned in Topic III which you think are so important that you should always remember them.

III

Be able to spell and pronounce the following names. Locate each place and tell what was said about it in this and in any previous chapter. Add other facts if possible.

Argentine Republic	Pilcomayo River
Uruguay	Ohio River
Brazil	Gran Chaco
Bolivia	Pampas
Chile	Buenos Aires
Guiana	Rosario
Spain	Sao Paulo
Texas	Rio de Janeiro
Missouri	Corrientes
Parana River	Asuncion
Paraguay River	Chicago
Uruguay River	Omaha
La Plata River	St. Louis
Amazon River	

CHAPTER XII

THE SOUTHERNMOST
TOWN IN THE WORLD

OUR trip through Paraguay has taken us through the tropical and semitropical regions of South America. The air has been hot, the vegetation luxuriant, and the forests dense. Now let us turn our faces southward to the cool ocean breezes of the temperate zone and the chill winds that blow around the southern tip of the continent. The great highland of the western hemisphere extends from Alaska to the extreme southern end of South America. In this southern part of the highland the deep valleys between the low mountains are below the level of the ocean and are filled with water, thus making the peaks into innumerable islands. At the very tip of the most southern of these islands stands Cape Horn. This much-dreaded cape, swept by fierce winds and awful storms, is a giant rock fourteen hundred feet high jutting out into the southern ocean. The waters around, which lash themselves continually into giant waves, are more dreaded by sailors than those on any other trade route of the world. Strewn around on all sides are the wrecks of vessels, making the huge rock appear, as one writer says, like a giant headstone in a sailors' graveyard.

Figure 99—Cape Horn

It is possible for us to take a trip around South America, however, without passing this dangerous spot. Two hundred miles north of Cape Horn there is a channel which will take us from the Atlantic to the Pacific Ocean in less time and with much less risk than by rounding the cape. This waterway which separates the large island of Tierra del Fuego from the mainland is the Strait of Magellan. It is more than three hundred miles long and was discovered by the famous explorer Ferdinand Magellan, in his wonderful voyage around the world in 1519–1522.

We must remember that to the day of his death Columbus did not know that he had discovered a new world. He believed that the earth was round and that by sailing westward he would arrive at the eastern coast of Asia. This was a very reasonable belief, as he knew nothing of the great continents of North America and South America which lay in his way. Consequently when, after his long voyage, he finally sighted land, he supposed that it was a part of India or islands off the coast.

In 1513 Balboa, a Spanish explorer, from the top of a mountain in the Isthmus of Panama, discovered a great ocean to the west of the Americas, which he called the South Sea. It then became known that a wide stretch of waters must be crossed before the rich countries of India and China could be reached. The rulers of several European countries sent daring navigators to explore the waters around this great western world and find a water route to Asia. This was what Magellan set out to do. With his five small ships he skirted the eastern coast of South America, hoping to find a passage through to the Pacific Ocean. Magellan succeeded in sailing through the strait that now bears his name and continued his voyage across the Pacific to the Philippine Islands, where he was killed by the natives. One of his vessels continued on its western journey, rounded the Cape of Good Hope on the southern point of Africa, and so reached Europe and the port from which the expedition had set out. This was the first time that anyone had ever sailed entirely around the earth. Even today such a voyage is a wonderful trip, but it seems more wonderful to think of its being done in Magellan's time. The journey was made in ships smaller than we should think safe for such a voyage; the knowledge of the sailors was scanty compared with that of the captains of our great liners; and it took as many months to complete the voyage as it would take weeks at the present time. There was no wireless apparatus in those days, no lighthouses, no lifeboats, no water-tight compartments such as safeguard the passengers who journey on the water today, and for months and even years the bold sailors were out of touch with the civilized world. All hail to Magellan and his brave crew! The strait bearing his name will always be to us something more than a narrow passage of water connecting two oceans, when we think of the courage, the daring, and the perseverance of the man who discovered it.

The passage through the Strait of Magellan is safer than the route around Cape Horn, yet the names which some of the early explorers who tried to follow

Figure 100—The snow-covered peaks make the scenery in the Strait of Magellan very beautiful.

Magellan's route to the Pacific gave to different points in the narrow waterway tell their story of shipwreck, of hunger, of suffering, and of despair. Among others we notice such names as Fury Island, Famine Reach, Fatal Bay, Last Wreck Point, Desolation Harbor, and Hope Inlet.

If one of you should sail down the Atlantic shore of South America and enter the Strait of Magellan from the eastern end, and another should sail a few miles into the Strait from the western entrance, your descriptions would be very different, and it would seem hardly possible that both of you were speaking of the same body of water. The eastern half of the strait is a broad channel dividing the southern part of the great Argentine plain. The low level land stretches away to meet the sky on the mainland to the north and on the island of Tierra del Fuego to the south. The western half of the strait is very different. Here it is a deep narrow gorge which cuts in two the Andes Highland. For much of the year the plains in the east are bare and brown, for that region lies in the path of the westerly winds and little rain falls east of the mountains. The peaks in the west are drenched with rain, and the steep cliffs, the wooded slopes, the beds waist-deep of moss and ferns, the blue-white glaciers in the passes, and the gray or snow-capped mountain tops make the scenery in this part of the strait very beautiful.

There is one way and only one in which the two ends of the strait are alike. From your steamer you can look as far as the eye can see over the broad plains in the east or gaze on the glacier-covered peaks and deep gorges in the wild lands of the west, but in neither part will you see any sign of human life. A few Indians inhabit these desolate regions, but their tents and huts are farther inland and they seldom come in their canoes to the more open stretches of water. It was doubtless the signal fires and camp smoke of some of these South American tribes of Indians that caused Magellan to give to the group of islands south of the narrow strait the name Tierra del Fuego (land of fire).

These Indians live in some of the most primitive conditions. During the day in their rude dug-outs they roam the wind-swept channels in search of whales, seals, or fish. At night they seek the shelter of their comfortless tents of skin or branches of trees. In your passage through the strait you will wear your thickest clothes, and even then you will be none too warm. Formerly the natives wore little or no clothing even in the winter season to protect them from the fierce gales and chilling

Figure 101—Some of the Indians of Tierra del Fuego wear the skins of animals.

dampness. Now they wear the skins of animals, and in

some cases cast-off garments which they obtain from wrecks or from the white people who pass through these regions.

On the Chilean side of the strait, about halfway between the Atlantic and Pacific oceans, stands the town of Punta Arenas, or Sandy Point. We shall surely wish to visit here, because Punta Arenas is the most southerly town in the world. By looking at a map you will find that it is directly south of Boston and as far below the equator as Edmonton, Canada, is north of it. If you were to draw a circle around the globe passing through Punta Arenas you would find that it touched very little other land, for the town is hundreds of miles farther south than Cape Town in southern Africa.

The houses in Punta Arenas are little one-story buildings, many of them built, roof and all, of corrugated iron. There are only about a thousand people living here, but we are surprised that there are so many in such a dreary place. The wind blows constantly and much of the time so fiercely that little vegetation is possible. But though it is cold and damp, Punta Arenas is not a sickly town, for the very wind that we find so disagreeable helps to make it healthful. The people are made up of many different nations—Chinese, Scotch, Italians, Spaniards, Indians, and Germans. Many of them are rough characters, and it is safer, so it is said, not to inquire too closely into the life history of most of them. The Scotch people who have settled here seem to be the most industrious and make the best shepherds.

There are millions of sheep in this bleak southern

Figure 102—About halfway between the Atlantic and Pacific Oceans stands the town of Punta Arenas.

land both on the mainland of the continent and on the island of Tierra del Fuego, and, although it is situated in such an out-of-the-way place, the town of Punta Arenas is an important wool-shipping port. The sheep, as well as the shepherds who care for them, suffer a good deal during the winter storms, but the coarse tufted grass is nourishing and the cold weather makes necessary a heavy coat which adds to the value of the wool. The sheep are divided into flocks of two or three thousand, each in the care of a shepherd who for weeks at a time lives on the open plains with no other company than his dogs. The wool is brought in heavy oxcarts for long distances to Punta Arenas, which is the only port within a thousand miles.

There are some gold mines in this bleak southern land, and the men who work in them live hard lives, with few comforts or enjoyments. At one time it was thought that great quantities of gold would be mined here, but the industry is of little importance today. The real wealth of the region is in the stretches of coarse grass and the thick coats of the animals which feed on it.

Vessels passing through the strait leave the mails and the supplies that are needed in this desolate region. All clothing, building material, foods, machinery, iron and steel, and all those numberless things that make for the comfort and convenience of life come to Punta Arenas from the outside world. For their return voyage to northern countries the ships load with frozen, salted, and canned meats, wool, skins, hides, furs, whale oil, and whalebone. Punta Arenas is an important coaling station also, and many vessels take on coal which has been stored here; for the long voyage to the nearest Chilean port on the Pacific or the nearest Argentine town on the Atlantic where fuel can be obtained takes several days.

As the southern part of South America develops it was thought that Punta Arenas would grow in importance as the chief shipping port of that part of the continent. But the opening of the Panama Canal and the increasing trade of the Trans-Andine Railroad may lessen the number of vessels passing through the Strait of Magellan, and many of the products of these southern lands may in time be shipped more largely through northern cities.

In the Falkland Islands off the southeastern coast of South America whaling and sheep raising are important occupations. These islands belong to Great Britain, and few vessels call there except English ships bound around the cape or through the Strait of Magellan.

South of the strait is the Fuegian Archipelago. It consists of many bleak, wind-swept islands, large and small, separated from one another by winding, stormy passages and comprising altogether an area nearly as large as the state of Kansas. The name Tierra del Fuego, which Magellan gave to the entire group of islands, is now applied usually only to the largest one, which is about half the size of the state of Iowa. When the boundary line between Chile and Argentina was finally decided on to the very tip of South America, the larger and the more valuable part of Tierra del Fuego was given to Chile. The eastern part of the island, which belongs to Argentina, is about as large as the state of Massachusetts.

The most of Tierra del Fuego is a plain, a continuation of the great level stretches of Argentina. The climate is cold, and parts of the island are dry, but most of it is covered with a coarse grass on which sheep thrive well. The Andes Mountains continue down the coast of Chile and curve into the southern part of Tierra del Fuego. The lower slopes are covered with evergreen trees, which stand out in sharp contrast to the snowy peaks and white glaciers above. During long ages this mountainous coast of South America has been sinking so that now the ocean fills the valleys between the peaks, thus making thousands of islands along the Chilean border separated by deep, narrow inlets or fiords similar to those of Norway. These islands are drenched with

Figure 103—There are great glaciers on the mountains that border the Strait of Magellan.

rain brought by the westerly winds and are covered with a rich forest growth. Tierra del Fuego is the only island of the group which is inhabited by white people or has as yet been at all developed.

The coasts of few countries offer such sharp contrasts as are found between the northern and the southern parts of Chile. Nowhere in the world can one find drier and more barren regions than lie on the Peruvian and north Chilean coasts. On the other hand there are few places in the temperate zone where greener, richer, more luxuriant vegetation exists than on the western slopes of the Andes Mountains in southern Chile. Such contrasts have a great effect on the people and the industries of Chile, and in a later chapter we shall enjoy a visit to this narrow ribbon-like country.

TOPICS FOR STUDY

I

1. Cape Horn.

2. The Strait of Magellan.

3. Magellan and the first voyage around the world.

4. Indians of the Fuegian Archipelago.

5. Punta Arenas.

6. Sheep ranching.

7. The Fuegian Archipelago and Tierra del Fuego.

II

1. Sketch a map of South America showing Tierra del Fuego, Strait of Magellan, and Cape Horn.

2. Trace the route of Magellan's ship around the world.

3. Find in your history the names of some Spanish explorers. What did each one discover or explore?

4. Name the islands in the western hemisphere that belong to Great Britain.

5. What are the most important sheep-raising countries of the world? Which one ranks first in this industry?

6. What is an archipelago? Name any of which you have ever heard.

7. Study a map of the winds and find why northern Chile is a desert and southern Chile so well watered.

8. Make a list of the places mentioned in Topic III that you think are so important that you should always remember them.

III

Be able to spell and pronounce the following names. Locate each place and tell what was said of it in this and in any previous chapter. Add other facts if possible.

Paraguay	Strait of Magellan
Chile	Tierra del Fuego
Peru	Fuegian Archipelago
Argentine Republic	Falkland Islands
Great Britain	Philippine Islands
Norway	Isthmus of Panama
India	Panama Canal
China	Cape of Good Hope
Kansas	Punta Arenas
Iowa	Boston
Massachusetts	Cape Town
Andes Mountains	Edmonton
Cape Horn	

CHAPTER XIII

OVER THE ANDES TO CHILE

IN order to get from Argentina to Chile by land we shall have to cross the Andes Highland. Perhaps you are thinking that we shall have a long, hard trip on horseback or muleback over the high, cold passes of the mountains. Not very many years ago people did travel in this way over the highlands, but today we can ride the entire distance in comfortable cars.

There are many wonderful railroads in the different countries of the world. There are those in the United States which cross great deserts and high mountains; there is the Trans-Siberian road thousands of miles long which connects the Baltic Sea and the Pacific Ocean and runs for miles in a straight line across the plains of Siberia; there is the Cape-to-Cairo Railroad in Africa which, when completed, will extend entirely across that continent from Cape Town in the extreme south to Cairo on the northern shore. The railroads of Alaska have been built over the desolate snow-clad passes at great expense and at the cost of many lives. In South America we shall find railroads as wonderful as any in the world, roads which run through tropical forests, climb high mountains, bridge deep canyons, and cross vast deserts. Traveling on some of them may not be very comfortable because of cold or heat or dust or the mountain sickness which many people suffer in ascending great heights. We shall not wish to leave South America, however, without knowing more of its railroads and seeing the countries and the industries which are served by them.

Not many years ago the only routes from Buenos Aires on the Atlantic coast to Valparaiso, the seaport of Chile on the Pacific, were by water around the southern end of South America or by a slow tiresome horseback trip across the plains of Argentina and over the Andes Mountains. The ocean trip around Cape Horn or through the Strait of Magellan was long and dangerous. The overland journey was so hard and the dangers were so many that few had the courage to undertake it or the strength to endure it.

In opening up her great plains Argentina built a road to Mendoza on the eastern slope of the Andes. On the other side of the mountains, Chile, in developing her resources, constructed a railroad which climbed the western slopes. These roads were in operation for some years before they were connected across the mountains, and travelers could journey over the heights only at certain times of the year and then at great risk. Today we can go in three days from the fine railroad station in Buenos Aires for a distance of nearly nine hundred miles to Valparaiso on the Pacific. We race across the maize-covered plain, on between acres of purple alfalfa, waving wheat, and fields of flax covered with its pretty

235

blue flowers, past remote, little mud huts of Italian laborers and large, low buildings of great estancias. Thousands of cattle, sheep, and horses dot the plains, and the straight figure of the solitary gaucho sitting astride his motionless horse or loping easily along over the level land gives a touch of life to the landscape. Once in a while we catch a glimpse of a long-legged flamingo or some ostriches feeding near a flock of sheep. These ostriches—rheas if we call them by their right name— are common in this part of South America. They are similar to the African species, but their feathers are not so valuable.

On we go over the track which for many miles is without a curve. The dust sifts in at the doors and windows, and over a moving herd which we see in the distance it flies in clouds. As far as we can see there are no hills larger than those built by ants and no valleys deeper than the ruts worn by the heavy cart wheels. In

Figure 104—An Argentine Corncrib

Figure 105—Lining either side of a broad dusty street are odd-looking buildings one story high.

the distance a line of high two-wheeled wagons filled with bags of wheat is lumbering slowly over the plains. The wagons are very heavy and are large enough to hold so much grain that it takes several pairs of oxen to draw one of them. As we watch the long dusty line we are reminded of the curious old prairie schooners in which the pioneers crossed the United States to new homes in the unsettled West.

We stop at intervals at some camp towns separated from their nearest neighbors by many miles of dusty plain. We would far rather live on some remote ranch than in one of these unattractive places. Lining either side of the broad dusty street that extends the length of the town are strange-looking brick buildings one story high. They look to us more like huge boxes than comfortable homes. The front wall is higher than the others and rises above the flat roof, making the house from the street in front look taller than it really is. At the station many horses are standing, while groups of cowboys and Spanish and Italian laborers loiter about, looking at the train and the passengers. Little of importance happens in these remote towns, and the arrival of the express train bound from ocean to ocean is the event of the day.

At the foot of the Andes Mountains, six hundred and fifty miles from Buenos Aires, is Mendoza, the most western city and one of the prettiest in the republic. We have grown so tired of the bare, flat plains that this place, with its background of mountains, its hills, its trees, and its trickling brooks, is a pleasant sight.

In the southern part of South America the great highland shuts out the moist westerly winds from the eastern slopes of the Andes, and the climate of Mendoza is therefore very dry. Nothing grows here except where irrigation is used. On the sides of the streets and in the orchards and gardens and vineyards we see the little streams which have been led in canals and ditches from the river that comes tumbling down from the mountains. The river is thick with the mud that it carries, and so enriches the soil as well as furnishes the water needed for cultivation.

The low mud and brick houses with their thick walls give the town a peculiar appearance. Mendoza was once destroyed by an earthquake, and since that time few houses more than one story high have been built. The bricks of which many of the buildings are made are manufactured in a curious way. In places where the soil is of the proper kind water is poured over the

Figure 106—The vineyards stretch for miles around Mendoza.

earth. Horses are then driven round and round in a circle until the soil is churned into a thick mud. This is mixed with straw, molded into the form of bricks, and dried in the sun.

All around Mendoza are vineyards and farms shaded by rows of poplar trees which have been planted by millions to supply the lumber which is needed in this treeless country. The vineyards interest us more than anything else, for we had not expected to find such a great industry in this rainless region of Argentina. They stretch for miles around the city, each vineyard watered by the little streams which spread themselves in a network among the vines. Let us ride out among them. The vines, pruned back and fastened to wire and posts, grow close to the railroad on either side. They are planted so evenly that we can look for long distances down the straight rows. How dark and rich the soil is!

*Figure 107—We see high carts filled with casks
on their way to the railroad station.*

It is cultivated so carefully that there is not a weed in sight. In every row we can see the little stream of muddy water that makes these great vineyards possible. How thick the clusters of grapes hang on the vines. Millions of pounds of this fine fruit are pressed into wine. We see piles of grapes being brought to the presses and high carts filled with casks on their way to the railroad station. There are between two and three thousand wineries in Argentina, most of them in Mendoza. These are fitted with presses, vats, and machinery as modern as any that you might find on the banks of the Rhine in Germany or on the Rhone in France.

Not all the luscious grapes of Mendoza are made into wine. Great quantities of the fruit are sent in special trains down the steep slopes and across the wide plains to Buenos Aires to supply the city and the surrounding regions. Some of the fruit is loaded onto refrigerator ships and sent to New York, where it arrives in as good shape as that which comes from California. Now that the Panama Canal is opened, a great deal of this fruit, and some from the vineyards of Chile also, will in the future be taken to Valparaiso on the Pacific and thence by the shorter route to New York.

Leaving Mendoza, we continue our trip over the mountains. From the car windows as we ascend the slopes we can see vineyards, peach orchards, and fig trees watered by canals from the Mendoza River, which is fed by the snows above. As we rise higher we leave the cultivated lands. The air grows cooler and the vegetation scarcer. We pass small, isolated stations, each with a huge pile of fuel near and a few goats feeding on the stunted shrubs and grass around. Always ahead of us loom the snow peaks of the Andes, which we must

Figure 108—From here to the Chilean side of the mountains a wonderful tunnel has been built.

241

cross before we can get into Chile. Now we are so high that the mountains are bare, with hard, stony faces down which pour foaming cascades into deep gorges far below us. The scene is wild and desolate. There are no trees, and only a few blades of grass grow in the clefts of the rocks. Higher still we climb until, a little more than a hundred miles from Mendoza, we come to our last station in Argentine territory. From here to the Chilean side of the mountains, ten thousand feet above the level of the sea, a wonderful tunnel two and a half miles long has been built.

Before this tunnel was made all travelers from the Atlantic to the Pacific were obliged to take a cold, dangerous trip on muleback up over the high pass. Now, for those who choose this route, comfortable four-horse coaches have been provided. We do not wish to lose

Figure 109—Before the tunnel was made travelers were obliged to take a dangerous trip on muleback over a trail that zigzagged across the high pass.

any of the grand mountain scenery, so with extra wraps to protect us from the cold we take our places in one of the carriages. We zigzag back and forth up the trail, enjoying the view of the distant mountains outlined against the clear blue sky. All vegetation has long since disappeared. Rocky slopes, snowy peaks, and bluish-white glaciers meet the eye on every side. One more sharp turn. Our carriage stops, and we hold our breath in sudden wonder. There before us, almost thirteen thousand feet above the waters of the Pacific Ocean stands a massive statue of Christ. With a large cross supported in one hand and with the other uplifted in blessing, the great figure stands silent and serene amid the storm-swept rocks and peaks of the mountains. On the granite base of the monument are inscribed these words, "Sooner shall these mountains crumble into dust than the people of Argentina and Chile break the peace to which they have pledged themselves at the feet of Christ the Redeemer."

This statue on the boundary line of these two South American countries is the famous Christ of the Andes. It was cast from the melted cannon of Argentina and Chile and was here erected as a symbol of perpetual peace between the two nations. They had had trouble over their boundary line and war had threatened, but the question was finally decided by arbitration, and in 1904 this beautiful statue was set up to commemorate the peaceful settlement. Near by we see the boundary posts with the word *Argentina* on one side and *Chile* on the other. Passing these we begin our downward course on the Chilean side amid rocks, foaming streams, and

Figure 110—Christ of the Andes

deep gorges similar to those on the eastern slopes.

Gradually the air grows milder, a few blades of grass and stunted shrubs appear, and hardy mountain flowers carpet the rocks. We have left the snow sheets, the glaciers, the keen frosty air, and the bare rocky peaks behind. Before lies a new country, by us as yet unexplored, and with thoughts of the pleasure in store for us we leave our coaches for comfortable cars and speed down the slope into Chile.

TOPICS FOR STUDY

I

1. Railroads of South America.

2. Routes from Buenos Aires to Valparaiso.

3. The Trans-Andine Railroad.

4. Scenes on the pampas.

5. Mendoza and its vineyards.

6. The Christ of the Andes.

II

1. What great railroads of North America do you know? Where do they run? What large cities are located on them?

2. From the railroad station get some folders which will give you the route of some of these important railroads.

3. On a map of Eurasia trace the Trans-Siberian Railroad. On a map of Africa trace the route of the Cape-to-Cairo Railroad.

4. On a map of South America trace the Trans-Andine Railroad. Show Valparaiso and Buenos Aires.

5. In what parts of the United States is irrigation necessary? Explain the cause of the lack of rainfall in this region.

6. Read in your geography or in some other book about the grape and wine industry of Europe. What countries, cities, and rivers are especially noted for this industry? On an outline map of Europe show these places.

7. Make a list of the places mentioned in Topic III which you think are so important that you should always remember them.

III

Be able to spell and pronounce the following names. Locate each place and tell what was said of it in this and in any previous chapter. Add other facts if possible.

Germany	Cape-to-Cairo Railroad
France	Trans-Siberian Railroad
Alaska	Trans-Andine Railroad
California	Buenos Aires
Rhine River	Valparaiso
Rhone River	Mendoza
Mendoza River	Denver
Andes Mountains	San Francisco
Panama Canal	New York
Strait of Magellan	Cape Town
Cape Horn	Cairo
Baltic Sea	

CHAPTER XIV

CHILE AND THE CHILEANS

AFTER our cold ride over the Andes we are glad to get into a comfortable train once more. At Caracoles, ten thousand feet above the level of the sea, where the Chilean end of the long tunnel begins, we take a train on the narrow cogwheel railroad and begin our ride down the western slope of the mountains into the valley of Chile. We rush down steep grades, through short tunnels, over bridges, past deep gorges, and beside mountain rivers whose waters are broken by falls and rapids.

We pass the little station of Juncal, for several years the terminus of the railroad. Near here is a deep gorge called "Salto del Soldado," or the Soldier's Leap. A Chilean in the seat beside us tells us that the place received its name from a soldier who, when pursued by an enemy, leaped across the chasm and was saved. The story-teller is so kind and polite that we do not like to contradict him even though the width of the gorge makes his tale seem impossible.

In the sky above us, so far away that they look no larger than swallows, are some great birds wheeling, circling, and floating in the thin blue air. They are condors, birds as large as the largest eagles. In our travels through Chile we shall see the condor pictured and mounted many times, for it is the national emblem of that country, as the eagle is of the United States. You can imagine how large these great birds are when I tell you that the outstretched wings from tip to tip measure from nine to twelve feet. Those that

Figure 111—The Condor is the national emblem of Chile.

we see are so far above us that it seems as if they could distinguish nothing on earth, yet their sight is so keen that if a sheep or a goat should die in the high pastures, it would not be long unnoticed by these condors, which look so small to us now. They would swoop down and, circling nearer and nearer the earth, would finally alight on their prey.

Since we left the coaches for the train we have been steadily descending the steep slopes. Before we come to the station of Los Andes the air grows milder and the gray rocks begin to have a thin covering of green. At this town we leave the little narrow-gauge railroad and change to one of greater width. Before we take the train into the valley we have time to look about a little in Los Andes, our first Chilean town. Let us walk down the street from the station. Like the other streets of the place it is very wide and straight. On either side are little trickling canals of clear mountain water. Rain seldom falls here, but the brooks are kept full from the melting snows above. Beyond the canals on either side of the street are low houses built of stone. This is the cheapest building material in the region and there is an inexhaustible supply of it in the hills around. Near by are large fruit orchards, and if we were to peep into some of the houses we might find the women canning and preserving pears, peaches, and other fruit, for this is an important industry here. Beyond the orchards lie fields of wheat, and higher on the slopes are flocks and herds of cattle and sheep.

Figure 112—On the Chilean Andes

Figure 113—The streets of Los Andes are wide and straight.

See the line of small gray donkeys coming up the steep trail into the town. Each one is so loaded with firewood that little but his legs is visible. Wood is the only fuel used here, and every day long lines of donkeys with their drivers plod along the mountain paths to collect and bring in the wood. Donkeys are very useful animals in these mountain towns of Chile. There are some stopping in the street. Each one has a large can hanging on either side, from which the milkman measures out to his customer the quantity of milk that he wishes.

The ride down from Los Andes to Santiago is very interesting, and we enjoy every minute of it. The railroad follows the Aconcagua River, a stream named from the great peak from which it comes. The swift mountain river plunges in waterfalls down high cliffs and dashes in cascades over the rocks as it hurries down the slope. From time to time we catch glimpses of the great white head of Mount Aconcagua, the highest mountain of South America, rising above all the other giants of the Andes.

Now we are passing between fields inclosed by low mud walls. A network of canals from the river extends through each field and furnishes the water for the wheat and corn and the vegetables and fruit that are growing there. Some of these products are sent to Santiago to supply its markets, and some are shipped away from Valparaiso to other countries. In the distance we can see dry, cactus-covered hills and large fields inclosed by stone walls, where cattle, horses, and sheep are feeding. Now the train flies by scattered mud huts, the homes of laborers on some great estate which stretches for miles along the track. We catch glimpses of heavy, two-wheeled oxcarts loaded with wheat from some distant hacienda, as the Chileans call their large estates. Off in a field to the right some men are plowing with a yoke of oxen. The ox is the common farm animal in Chile and for all heavy work takes the place of the horse and mule.

Here we are at last at Santiago, the capital of Chile. It is not so modern as Montevideo, nor so rich as Buenos Aires, but it has what no city on the plains of Uruguay or Argentina can ever have, and that is the beautiful view of the high mountains which tower on either side. The lofty, snow-capped Andes lie on the east and the lower coast ranges to the west. With its wonderful scenery, its delightful climate, and all the conveniences of a modern city, we do not wonder that the Chileans love their capital.

The easiest way for us to see something of Santiago is from the top of a street car. The seats on the top of the "double-deckers" are cheaper than those inside and we can ride a long way for less than two cents. Who is the woman in cap, dark-blue dress, and neat apron, who stands on the rear platform and looks at us as we get on? She is the conductor. Many of the street-car conductors in Chile are women. When the country was at war with Peru and Bolivia and the men were needed in the army, the women took their places on the cars. They did the work so well that when the war was over, the officials of the roads saw no reason for removing them, and women have done some of this work ever since.

Figure 114—We find that many of the street-car conductors in Chile are women.

What a beautiful street it is on which we are riding! It is the Alameda de las Delicias. This long musical Spanish name means the "delicious walk" or "delicious avenue." The Alameda de las Delicias is the finest avenue in the city. It is more than three hundred feet wide. Measure the width of the widest street in your home town or city and see how it compares with the Alameda. The driveway on either side accommodates teams and street cars. In the center, shaded by large trees, is a wide promenade. Under each row of trees a little stream of clear water flows in a neat, walled channel. Scattered here and there along the avenue are statues of Chilean heroes, while stone seats under the trees make comfortable resting places for the promenaders. In the evening these seats are sure to be full of people who are enjoying the music of the bands which play in the band-stands.

Let us remain on the car and ride out to Cousiño Park. This is the "Coney Island of Santiago" and has all the amusements of such a place. We can shoot the chutes, enjoy the skating-rink and the merry-go-round, visit the cafés, and watch the dancers. There are many dance halls in the park, which are especially crowded every Sunday afternoon. Dancing is very popular among the Chileans, and on Sundays they go in crowds to the parks to enjoy this and other amusements. Chile has banished the bull-fight, which is the chief Sunday-afternoon entertainment in many South American cities, but dancing and horse racing are the weekly pleasures of hundreds of people.

Señora Cousiño, who gave the park to Santiago and who built the finest residence in the city, was called at one time the richest woman in South America, if not in the world. In a trip to the southern part of Chile we shall stop at Lota, a mining town founded by Señor Cousiño, and see the beautiful white marble palace built there by his wife. It is the show place of the town, and stands in the midst of green lawns adorned with terraces, statues, arbors, fountains, and artificial lakes scattered among lovely gardens and widespreading shade trees.

Returning from Cousiño Park we will take a trip to the top of Santa Lucia. This rocky hill, more than two hundred feet high, stands in the center of Santiago. The early Spanish explorer who founded the capital built a fortress on the rock and laid out the town at its feet. Today we walk down the long, straight streets which he planned hundreds of years ago, and which divide the city into squares like a checkerboard. Old cities in Spain were often laid out in this way, and the Spanish discoverers in the New World followed the same plan.

Santa Lucia was first a fort, built to defend the city at its base. After this it was used as a cemetery. In more recent years it has been made into a beautiful park. It has winding paths and roads, grottoes and gardens, cafés and fountains. In odd little nooks and corners ferns, plants, and shrubs have been planted, and comfortable seats invite one to rest on the way to the summit. Bright flowers peep out from every cranny, beautiful statues stand in unexpected corners, creeping vines cover the rocks, and splashing brooks come leaping down over the steep cliffs. At night the hill, as well as the city below, is brilliantly illuminated with electric lights.

Beautiful as the climb is, the view from the top of Santa Lucia is even more lovely. Below us lies the capital, hemmed in by the mountains around and divided into squares by its long, straight streets. Through the heart of the city runs the Alameda. In its walled channel lies a little river spanned by several bridges. The towers of numerous churches rise far above the low flat roofs of the houses. It seems odd to be in a city nearly as large as San Francisco and see no chimneys rising from the roofs. Santiago is as far south of the equator as Birmingham, Alabama, is north of it. Though the winters are short, the temperature sometimes falls below the freezing point. The houses, many of which have no furnaces or stoves for heating, are often chilly, though the sun warms them in the middle of the day. Most of the people prefer to do without heating arrangements and trust for warmth to extra clothes, which are needed fully as much in the houses as they are out of doors. Some of the newer buildings are provided with furnaces and stoves, but these are lacking in most of the houses.

Another odd thing that we notice as we look down on the capital is the fact that the trees seem to rise from out the middle of the buildings. As in many other South American cities, most of the houses of Santiago are built around a patio, and in many of these there are trees and gardens. A large wooden door, which is closed and locked at night, opens onto the street. If the house is of one story all the rooms open onto the courtyard. If the building is of two stories the upper rooms open onto a gallery which runs around the inner square. Some of the houses of the wealthier people are very large and often contain forty or fifty rooms. It is a custom in Chile for a son to bring his wife to his father's house and make his home there; so it is necessary to have more rooms than in our country, where the young couple usually set up housekeeping by themselves.

Now let us look at the part of the city on the other side of the little river. That is where the poor people live. In this section the houses are small and mean, and whole families live in one room and sleep on the floor. These rooms are often below the street level, and in the rainy season they are sometimes flooded. At such times the people suffer dreadfully, as the poor families do in the large tenement blocks in our great cities during the very hot or the very cold weather.

The poor class of people in Chile work hard and have few comforts. Their wages are small, so that they are obliged to live in poverty. Many of them drink a great deal, especially on Sundays and holidays. On the day following no one expects that much work will be done. Few factory hands are ready at their machines, few farm laborers appear in the morning to do a hard day's work, and even many of the house servants are not able to attend to their duties. All this must be changed before Chile can make the most of her resources and industries.

We shall always remember the sunset from the top of Santa Lucia. The darkening city, the green plain beyond, the fleecy clouds touched with rainbow colors, the mountains, now snow-white, now slowly changing to a delicate rose-pink, and the purple shadows falling over peaks and valleys as the sun sinks lower—all this is a sight which once seen can never be forgotten.

Before leaving Santiago we will make a trip to the Zoo, where we may become acquainted with some of the animals which we shall see on the great highland of South America. This is our first sight of the llama, the chief burden-bearer of Peru and Bolivia. As we go into the mountainous portions of those countries we shall see great numbers of these animals and their South American Indian drivers.

Figure 115—The Llama is the chief burden-bearer in the countries of Peru and Bolivia.

Here are some other animals that look somewhat like the llamas. They belong to the same family and are called vicuñas. Their fur is very fine and silky and makes excellent cloth. These animals are not so common now as they once were, and the goods made of their hair is very valuable.

Figure 116—Alpacas are raised for their long fine wool.

Those are alpacas standing near. How much they look like the llamas. Alpacas are raised for their long, fine wool, but the cloth which we call alpaca usually contains little, if any, of this material. Fabrics woven of the real alpaca wool are very expensive and are seldom seen in our stores.

Figure 117—Another South American animal is the guanaco.

Another South American animal of the same family as these which we have mentioned is the guanaco. It is found chiefly in southern Chile and Argentina and in the island of Tierra del Fuego. The guanaco furnishes the Indians with flesh for food, wool for clothing, and skins for tents. It would be as hard for some of the tribes to live without the guanaco as for the Eskimo or the Laplander to do without the reindeer.

In the Zoo we discover still another animal, much smaller than any of these mentioned, which we are very glad to see. This is the chinchilla. Have you ever seen anything that was made of its soft gray fur? It is very expensive and therefore not very common. The chinchilla is a small animal, not much larger than a gray squirrel. It lives in the mountains of Chile and Peru, and is caught in traps by the natives. It is a shy animal, but in spite of this fact many skins are exported from Chile each year, though the number is constantly decreasing.

To-night we will go to the plaza in Santiago. It is brilliantly lighted with electricity, and a band is playing. Crowds of young people are promenading, while the older ones rest on the scattered seats and chat with friends. The young ladies and girls are walking around the plaza in one direction and the men and boys in the other, but you see no couples strolling off by themselves. No young lady would ever think of doing such a thing as coming to the plaza without having the company of her mother or some other older person. These older people often occupy seats while the young ladies stroll along, but the eyes of the chaperons rarely wander far from their charges. If any young man sees a young lady whom he thinks attractive he finds out who she is and perhaps later calls at her home. But until their engagement he sees little, if anything, of her alone. Her people always receive him when he calls, and someone always accompanies her when she goes out. This is the custom not only in Chile but in all South American countries. Few young ladies who live there know any such freedom as the girls of the United States enjoy.

The hotel at which we are stopping is on one side of the plaza. We retire early, but the music of the band keeps up until a late hour. In the morning business starts a little later than is usual with us, so that, after all, the Chileans get in their needed sleep.

Today we will take a ride into the country around Santiago. The long, narrow valley in which the capital is situated may well be called the "Garden of South America." It is six or seven hundred miles long, but the coast ranges rising in the west and the high snow-capped Andes on the east make it so narrow that its entire area is but little more than twice that of Massachusetts. This long, narrow valley is the real Chile. Here are most of the cities and towns, here most of the people live, and here are the farms that supply the Chileans with food and the ships in the harbor of Valparaiso with their cargoes.

On the slopes of the mountains on either side are pastures, where large herds of cattle and sheep are feeding. Below the pasture lands are fields of alfalfa and vineyards. The climate of this central valley is as favorable for the production of good grapes as is the valley of California, and Chile is noted for its fine wines. The railroad which runs the length of the valley takes us past fields of wheat and corn, peach and pear orchards,

Figure 118—On the slopes of the mountains are pasture lands where large herds of sheep feed.

and flourishing gardens where beans, onions, squashes, tomatoes, strawberries, and melons look as familiar as if growing on our farms at home. The seasons in Chile are the opposite of ours, and these crops are raised during our winter. Vessels carrying these fruits and vegetables can run from Valparaiso to New York by way of the Panama Canal in two weeks, and thus supply our winter markets.

Many of the fields where cattle and sheep are feeding are surrounded by stone walls, and those where the crops are being raised are inclosed by low mud banks. There is little rain during the summer in the valley of Chile, and the crops which are raised here must be irrigated. The water is taken from the swift mountain rivers, which give to the plants not only the moisture that they need but much of their food as well. Rushing down the steep slopes the streams bring large

261

Figure 119—Many of the fields are inclosed by stone walls.

quantities of silt. This is dropped in the valley, and every year adds to the fertility of the soil. The valley of Chile has been built up in this way by the wash from the mountains on either side, and consequently it contains some of the richest farming land in the world. As we ride through it, we see the great estates, the laborers and their huts, the heavy ox-teams, the women at the stations with all kinds of fruit for sale, the fertile fields with their irrigating streams, and the flocks and herds in the stone-walled pastures.

The few wealthy farmers who own most of the land in the valley reckon the size of their estates in miles rather than in acres. The owners usually live, for a part of the time at least, in Santiago and leave the care of their farms to overseers. The Indian or mestizo laborer is given his home on the estate, usually a mud hut of one or two rooms; he has some land on which to raise his beans, onions, wheat, corn, and what not, and he is paid a little money. In return he must work in the fields of the owner, cultivate his land, and tend his crops. There is usually a store on the estate where the laborers can buy provisions at prices which the proprietor may fix to suit himself.

Chile is one of the most progressive countries of South America. Her progress will be more rapid when once she begins to cut up these estates in her rich valley so that more people can work their own land. In Chile, as in other countries of South America, the wealth and power are in the hands of a few people, and the poorer working classes own little land or other property. The real strength of any nation lies in the hard-working, independent middle classes, which today these countries lack.

From what we have seen of the farms we can guess what are some of the products that Chile exports. Many of the live cattle and sheep and much of the dried meat go to Bolivia and Peru; while the frozen and canned meats, the bones, hoofs, skins, wool, and hides are sent across the ocean to Germany, England, and other foreign lands. The grains, wheat and barley, go to South American countries and to lands in the eastern hemisphere. Most of our imports from Chile are the minerals, of which we shall read in another chapter.

If the central valley is the Chile of today, the southern part of the country may well be called the Chile of the future. The enormous amount of timber there will prove to be one of the treasures of South America, the rapid rivers will provide the power to turn the wheels of as many mills as may be built, and the grassy pastures will furnish food for millions of cattle and sheep.

One fourth of Chile is made up of islands. Notice how many there are near the coast in the southern part of the country. Here we find the high cliffs, the abrupt shores, the winding fiords, the deep inlets, the blue glaciers filling the passes, the waterfalls, and the wooded slopes all very much like the coast of Norway, where similar ranges of mountains come close to the sea.

The United States is situated in the north temperate zone, where the wind from the west blows more than from any other quarter. Ever since we came far enough south to enter the south temperate zone we have been also in a region of westerly winds. These are full of moisture which they have taken from the Pacific Ocean as they blew over it. As they pass over the mountains they become chilled and drop their moisture on the westerly slopes. You can see the same thing happen, in a smaller way, when you hold a cold plate against the moisture-laden air coming from the nose of a teakettle. In temperate Chile, therefore, we find a heavy rainfall on the western slopes of the mountains, while the Argentine side is dry. Later in our trip, as we go farther north toward the torrid zone, we shall find things very different.

The rainfall in southern Chile causes a heavy forest growth on the scattered islands and the western mountain slopes. If we were to try to walk through the forests we should find ourselves waist-deep in wet ferns, moss, and grass. When once the land is settled, sawmills built, and coast towns started where commerce may be carried on, there will be enough timber in southern Chile to supply the country with all that she will need for hundreds of years. Little of the forest is being used at present. Forest fires destroy large areas annually, and where the land is cleared for ranching, the lumber is burned or left to rot. As Chile becomes more thickly settled and the value of the forests more widely known, more careful methods of lumbering will prevail.

This cold, damp southern Chile seems a dreary place in which to make one's home. But, as in southern Argentina, shepherds are taking up land, living in their isolated huts, and, with no company for miles around except their faithful dogs, are caring for their large flocks. So rapidly has the sheep industry spread in the last few years that today in the southern part of Chile there are more than two million sheep besides several thousand cattle. Much of the wool, skins, and hides are shipped from the Chilean town of Punta Arenas, of which you read in Chapter XII.

We notice that the people in the southern part of the Chilean valley differ in their appearance from those who live farther north. Their features show clearly their South American Indian ancestry. Their complexion is darker, their cheek bones are higher, and their hair is straighter and blacker. Besides these mestizos, we see also in the southern towns many full-blooded Indians who have come, some on horseback and some in clumsy oxcarts, to trade their wheat or corn for a new blanket, a gay handkerchief, or a bright silver buckle.

These people are the Araucanians, one of the bravest of the Indian tribes in the Western Hemisphere. That the Chileans are splendid fighters is due partly to the fact that many of the people are descended from the brave Araucanian Indians.

Figure 120—These people are the Araucanians.

In the sixteenth century the Spaniards conquered much of the west coast of South America. Gradually they ventured farther and farther south and waged many fierce battles with the South Americans Indians. The Spaniards had an advantage in being mounted, and the Indians were terrified at the horses, which they had never seen before. They thought that the animal and the rider were one person and that these strange beings were much more powerful than ordinary people. The Spaniards, too, had the advantage of firearms, while the Indians had only wooden lances, bows and arrows, and clubs. In spite of these handicaps, the numbers of the Araucanians were so great compared with the numbers of the Spaniards and they fought with such fierceness that the Spaniards were unable to conquer them as they had the tribes farther to the north.

For many years the Biobio River, one of the important streams of Chile, was the boundary between the Spanish settlements in the North and those of the Indians in the South, who lived in freedom in their wet, forested lands. Their descendants still live in this part of the country. Their homes are low, thatched huts, with earth floors and a skin hung for a door. Some of the South American Indians have become farmers, some of them are laborers on the large estates of the Chileans, while still others in the more remote places live much as their ancestors did centuries ago.

We have visited central and southern Chile. Now we will sail up the coast and see what the northern part of the country is like. We shall find it very different from the portions that we have seen. Southern Chile is heavily forested, but the northern part is bare. In the north of Chile it is always hot; in the south it is always cool or cold. In the central part, during the hot summer, we can swelter in the hot valleys, with cold, snow-capped peaks within a few hours' ride of us. The southern part of the country is well watered, while the North is dry. The cooler sections are fertile and are covered with a luxuriant vegetation; the hot region of the North is one of the most barren, desolate parts of the earth. To understand why these things are so we must learn something of the country as a whole.

There is no country in the world as long and narrow as Chile. A map of it, if laid on one of North America made on the same scale, would stretch almost the entire distance from Sitka, Alaska, to the southern tip of the Peninsula of California. Nowhere in all its great length is the country wider than the state of California, and much of it is considerably narrower. If it were of a different shape it would cover quite a slice of the United States. If we painted over a part of our country the size of Chile, it would blot out all of the New England States, the Middle Atlantic States, Maryland, Virginia, North Carolina, and nearly all of South Carolina.

The length and surface of Chile give it a great variety of climate. The southern part lies in the temperate zone, where westerly winds prevail; while the northern portion lies in the torrid zone, where east winds blow. These come from the Atlantic Ocean, cross South America, and lose their moisture on the great plains and on the eastern slopes of the Andes Mountains. Therefore on the western slopes of the mountains in northern Chile and Peru we find a great desert. Farther south in the temperate zone, where the westerly winds prevail, the western side of the highland is well watered and the Argentine slopes are dry.

A sail up the western coast from Cape Horn to Peru will take between two and three weeks. Our first stop is at Valdivia, one of the most important places in the southern part of Chile. This town and the region around it are peopled largely by Germans. They are thrifty, hardworking settlers, and have built up a prosperous colony in this part of Chile. They have not adopted many of the Chilean ways, but live much as they did in their home country and speak the German language. In southern Brazil there are large and prosperous settlements of Germans, who follow the customs of their homeland and have little to do with the Brazilians.

Our next stop is at Lota, a mining town founded by the Cousiño family, who opened up the coal mines there. Many of the vessels which round the southern coast of South America stop at Lota for coal. Some of the mines are so near the coast that the gangways run out under the ocean and the miners work hundreds of feet beneath the blue waters of the bay. As we entered the harbor we must have sailed directly over their heads. There is little difference between the mines here and those in our country. Everything is carried on in the most modern way, and the machinery is as good as that in a Pennsylvania mine. The gangways are lighted by electricity, and electric cars run far out through the tunnels to bring the coal to the shafts, where it is hoisted to the surface.

The chief city of southern Chile is Concepcion. It is situated on the banks of the Biobio River and has a splendid harbor at its mouth. As ranching and farming spread farther and farther south a great future as a shipping port lies before Concepcion, and it will pay us to make a short visit there.

269

See those whaling vessels just returned from the Antarctic Ocean. They had a successful year and brought back whalebone and a large quantity of oil, which will be refined here at Concepcion before it is sent away.

The plentiful rainfall in the region around Concepcion makes irrigation unnecessary. Had we time to go out into the country we should see prosperous farms, where vegetables and wheat are growing and where cattle and sheep are feeding in green pastures. Some of the farms are on land where the forests have but recently been cleared away, and in some places the stumps are still seen in the fields. Stretching southward from here for some three hundred miles is some of the best farming land in Chile, well watered and fertile, and it is in this region that large quantities of wheat are produced.

Our next stop will be at Valparaiso, the chief seaport of Chile and the door to Santiago, the capital, which lies over the mountains a five hours' ride away. Valparaiso is one of the largest cities on the Pacific coast of the two Americas, yet its harbor is one of the poorest. It is exposed to severe storms which during the winter often blow down from the north and cause much damage to shipping. The mountains here run very close to the ocean and their steep cliffs extend under the water. Therefore the harbor is very deep and vessels can find anchorage only near the land. During the northers, as the winter storms are called, ships often put out to sea to avoid being blown onto the rocks. Were it not for the great depth of the harbor, a breakwater to protect the shipping would have been built years ago. It will cost millions of dollars to build the wall even up to the level of the water, and many millions more to complete it. This great task might not have been completed for many years to come if it had not been for the building of the Panama Canal. The ocean route through the Canal will bring Valparaiso nearer to European ports and to those on the eastern and southern coasts of the United States, and for this reason the trade of the Chilean city is increasing rapidly. This increased trade has made it necessary to improve the harbor and to make shipping safer and easier. Consequently the Chilean government has appropriated millions of dollars to be spent in building new docks and a breakwater and in improving the harbor in other ways.

There are many vessels in the harbor of Valparaiso flying the flags of many nations. Near the shore are the smaller vessels which run up and down the west coast of South America. Farther out are the large sailing vessels from far-away ports and great ocean steamers from foreign cities. Small boats ply between them and the wharves, carrying to shore the passengers and freight. What a variety of merchandise there is! There are bales of cotton and woolen goods from England, silk and wine from France, jute bags and bagging from India, coal from England and Australia, iron and steel manufactures and petroleum from the United States, Germany, and England. There are many other goods brought to Chile such as a country that does comparatively little manufacturing must import.

The word *Valparaiso* means the "vale of paradise," but the place is not so beautiful as the name would

*Figure 121—Valparaiso lies in a half circle
between the mountains and the sea.*

lead one to suppose. It was named not from its beauty but because the homesick explorer who captured the South American Indian village which stood on the site wished to have something to remind him of his home, the sunny town of Valparaiso in Spain.

The city lies in a half circle around the bay on a narrow plain between the mountains and the sea. In places this plain is only wide enough for two or three streets. In other parts it stretches out to half a mile or more. The business part of the city lies along the water front, and the houses rise one above another, while the streets zigzag up the steep slopes.

We should like to spend the first night of our visit to Valparaiso on board the vessel in the harbor. The sun drops down into the ocean in the west and the full moon rises over the mountains to the east, flooding the city and the sea with its silvery light. As the darkness gathers, the electric lights twinkle out one by one, and soon the whole slope is ablaze, looking, as one writer says, as if the city was tipped up on end. In the morning we are up in good season to see the sun rise over the mountain wall and drive away the mists and shadows in the valleys.

Now we will go on shore and take a trip through the city. As we walk up from the wharves we are told that much of this land where now stand large business blocks, warehouses, shipping offices, and public buildings has been built up above the water to make the narrow plain a little wider. A walk up Victoria Street makes us realize what a large commercial city Valparaiso is. The shops are much larger and finer than those of Atlanta, Georgia, a city of about the same size. The street is full of heavy trucks, automobiles, and the high two-wheeled oxcarts similar to those which we saw in Argentina. These are filled with fruits and vegetables and produce of all kinds for the market, which during the morning hours is crowded with customers buying the supplies for the day. We see also loaded carts drawn by three horses harnessed side by side and driven by a man who rides one of them.

We meet so many Chilean ladies in the street dressed in black and with black shawls draped over their heads that we wonder if the whole city is in mourning. The women are on their way to church, and the black dress and the manto, as the head drapery is called, are not a sign of mourning. All ladies in Chile wear this costume to church, and a very becoming one it is to the oval faces, clear complexions, and dark eyes of the

Figure 122—All ladies in Chile wear this costume to church.

wearers. Every woman in Chile, rich and poor, old and young, wears the manto. Sometimes it is of fine material and beautifully embroidered, sometimes it is coarse and ragged. It is the only head-covering allowed in the churches, and it is worn commonly on the streets during the morning hours. These same black-draped ladies may be seen in the afternoon driving in the parks, wearing the most fashionable Parisian dresses and hats.

Most of the business blocks and homes of the poorer people are in the lower town, while the wealthier class live on the cliffs. What a climb it will be to get up there, you think. We can go very easily by taking an elevator which will lift us up without loss of time, or we can go in a cable car. It is pleasant and cool on the height, and the view of the lower city and the bay is lovely. Yet even here among the fine houses and beautiful gardens there are sights which seem odd to us.

See the peddler carrying his vegetables on the back

Figure 123—A Chilean Milk Cart

of a donkey. And look, there on the other side of the street is a milkman carrying his milk in the same way. It is easier for the animals to carry their loads on their backs up the very steep hills than it is to pull heavy wagons. In some parts of the city it would be possible for us to get our milk fresh from the donkey or the cow, for the merchant drives them from door to door and milks them in the sight of his customers.

If we lived in Valparaiso we should be in constant dread of an earthquake. The Chileans, however, get so used to the slight shocks which come every few days that they pay little or no attention to them. In 1906, the same year that San Francisco suffered so terribly from a shock, an awful earthquake visited Chile. The whole city of Valparaiso trembled, houses shook and fell, electric-light poles crashed to the ground, and gas pipes and water pipes broke. The whole city was in darkness, and there was no water to fight the awful fire which raged through the night. Hundreds were killed, thousands lost their homes, and millions of dollars' worth of damage was caused. Though the disaster was a terrible one, Valparaiso is a better city today because of it. The lower town, where the poorer buildings are, suffered the most. In rebuilding this part of the city the streets have been widened, better buildings put up, and the people who occupy them live in a more healthful way.

Much as we have enjoyed our visit to Valparaiso, we must leave it and continue our way northward. So with a farewell look from our steamer at the "Vale of Paradise," we leave the harbor and steam toward the north.

TOPICS FOR STUDY

I

1. Scenes on the Trans-Andine Railroad.

2. The condor, national emblem of Chile.

3. Santiago, the capital of Chile.

4. Animals of western South America.

5. The valley of Chile.

6. Resources and industries of southern Chile.

7. The Araucanian Indians.

8. The climate and rainfall of Chile.

9. Size and shape of Chile.

10. Lota, Valdivia, and Concepcion.

11. The seaport of Valparaiso.

II

1. Sketch a map of South America. Show in it the country of Chile. Draw the equator; the tropic of Capricorn. Indicate the places mentioned in the chapter. Draw a dotted line to indicate the Trans-Andine Railroad. Write the names of the cities situated on it.

2. Write a list of the animals spoken of in the chapter. In a sentence describe each one.

3. Write a list of the animals in the world which yield a fiber from which cloth is made.

4. Make a list of the capitals of the world which are situated in the mountains; those which are built on plains.

5. Why have Chile and Norway irregular coast lines with deep inlets and many islands? Do you know what is meant by a drowned valley?

6. What advantage is it to a nation to have the farmers own the land which they till rather than work on large estates of other people?

7. Write a list of the products of Chile.

8. What part of Chile has a heavy rainfall? Why? Where in the United States is irrigation necessary? Why?

9. What effects does its great length from north to south have on Chile?

10. Make a list of the places mentioned in Topic III which you think are so important that you should always remember them.

III

Be able to spell and pronounce the following names. Locate each place and tell what was said of it in this and in any previous chapters. Add other facts if possible.

Germany	Peninsula of California
France	Panama Canal
Spain	Cape Horn
England	Buenos Aires
Norway	Montevideo
Australia	Santiago
United States	Valparaiso
India	Lota
California	Valdivia
Pennsylvania	Concepcion
Peru	Punta Arenas
Bolivia	San Francisco
Argentine Republic	Birmingham
Uruguay	New York
Tierra del Fuego	Sitka
Mount Aconcagua	Atlanta
Andes Mountains	Paris
Aconcagua River	Juncal
Biobio River	Los Andes

CHAPTER XV

DESERTS AND DESERT PRODUCTS

IT is a sail of several days from Valparaiso to the boundary of Peru. As we go northward along the Chilean coast, first the trees, then the lower growth, the shrubs and the bushes,—then the grass and every bit of green disappear, and a long narrow strip of rock and sand, known as the desert of Atacama, rises from the water. One writer says that in comparison with this awful region the Desert of Sahara is a botanical garden. For hundreds of miles on the western slopes of the Andes in northern Chile, Bolivia, and Peru, this bare, dreary landscape, scorched by the tropical sun, is all that can be seen. Chile seems to us a wonderful country. The southern portion is covered with thick, water-soaked forests, the northern part is a forbidding desert, and much of the central region is too mountainous for cultivation. Yet out of the fertile strip left her, Chile has made herself a name in the world as a strong, progressive nation.

A visit to northern Chile will not be an easy one. We are on the edge of the tropics, and the country is hot. It never rains here, and the dust which blows everywhere and penetrates every crevice is irritating. The trip on some of the railroads will take us so high that we shall be troubled with mountain sickness. Yet in this bare, unpleasant region there is carried on an industry so important, and from the rocky soil there is obtained a product of such great value, that we must not think of leaving Chile without seeing something of this part of the country.

You are probably wondering what this product can be which is so valuable, which is found in a desert, and which has induced people to invest so much money in such a barren place. No plants grow in the Chilean desert, yet from it is obtained a product which farmers all over the world use to improve their crops.

Plants, like people, need food to make them live and thrive. They obtain this food from the earth, and in time they take much of the goodness out of the soil. To insure good crops this plant food must be replaced by fertilizers. One of the foods that plants most need is nitrogen, but they can make use of it only when it is mixed in the soil with other substances, thus forming compounds known as nitrates. Nitrate of soda is the only fertilizer which contains this food in a suitable form, and Chile is the only country in the world that possesses large deposits of nitrate of soda. Many companies have invested enormous sums of money to build railroads, establish plants, and induce men to live in the nitrate region and get the plant food from the rocks, to separate it from the worthless material with which it is mixed, and to ship it to foreign ports.

We can get into the nitrate region from many ports in northern Chile from which short railroads lead up into the mountains. Many of these little seaports would not exist were it not for the nitrates, and the shipping of this one product is the sole business in these places.

Iquique is one of the most important of these coast towns. It is hard to imagine forty or fifty thousand people living in such a dreary place. The city is wedged in between the sea and the bare, desolate hills behind. It has street cars, electric lights, wide paved streets and sidewalks, good stores, clubs, and many other modern conveniences of a large city. Yet it has no green lawns, no trees, no shrubs and plants except in the public squares, where a few discouraged-looking ones manage to live if liberally supplied with the water which has to be brought from the mountains more than one hundred and fifty miles away. The houses are built chiefly of mud, bamboo, or corrugated iron. The population is for the most part a rough one. There is no leisure class, for no one lives in Iquique or in any other of the nitrate ports unless compelled by business to do so. The dust is irritating, and the heat of the sun is intense during the day. Every necessity of life—food, water, clothing, lumber for building, and coal and wood for fuel—must be brought here by water. Hundreds of vessels enter the harbor of Iquique every year, and no matter how varied may be the goods which they bring, they all leave the port with the same cargo—nitrates.

There are several short railroads on this part of the Chilean coast, connecting the ports with the wealth of the hills behind. For many years these northern coast towns were not connected with the cities farther south except by water. Now, however, Chile is building a long railroad from Arica, a nitrate port north of Iquique, to Puerto Montt in the south—a distance of more than two thousand miles.

Figure 124—Arica, a Nitrate Port

One can usually judge of the prosperity of a country by the length of its railroads. Chile is rapidly developing hers. Besides the Trans-Andine Railroad, by which we came from Argentina, two other mountain roads are planned, one to cross the Andes three or four hundred miles north of Santiago and the other about the same distance south of the capital. Railroads have already been built both from Arica and Antofagasta, important nitrate ports in northern Chile, to La Paz, the capital of Bolivia. On one of these, connections can be made by which one can go across Argentina to Buenos Aires. By means of these roads the products of coastless Bolivia reach the ocean.

We will leave our vessel at Antofagasta, a city almost on the tropic of Capricorn and a very important port in the shipping of nitrates. We will take the railroad which leads up into Bolivia and make our entrance into that country by this route, stopping on the way to see what nitrate of soda looks like and how it is obtained.

Brown seems to be the prevailing color in Antofagasta. The houses are brown, the streets are brown, and the hills that rise behind the town are brown and bare. It never rains in Antofagasta, and the water that is used in the place is brought from the mountains nearly two hundred miles away. Yet the plazas are green with trees, shrubs, and blossoming plants, and in the outskirts, by means of irrigation, the farmers raise fruits and vegetables.

The railroads from the interior bring down to Antofagasta not only nitrates but silver, tin, and copper from some of the richest mines in the world, which we shall visit later. Nitrates and copper are the two most important products of Chile. Much of the copper is mined in the northern part, though some deposits are worked in the south near Lota, where the rich coal beds are. At Chuquicamata in northern Chile there is a mountain of copper. The region is within a hundred miles of the ocean and the ore lies near the surface, so that it is easily mined and exported. A corporation from the United States has bought up the land, has built a railroad to the coast, and has erected smelters there.

*Figure 125—Antofagasta lies between
the bare, brown mountains and the sea.*

Copper will soon be produced in enormous quantities and shipped to northern countries.

Directly after leaving Antofagasta we begin to climb the slopes. Never before have we seen such a country. Great bare hills rise into bare mountains; bare plains and plateaus dip into bare valleys. Nowhere do we see a green thing—a tree, a shrub, or even a blade of grass. We pass gray salt plains large enough to supply the world with that much-needed article. We see white, glistening lakes covered not with hummocks of ice, as it looks to us from a distance, but with borax, and we see men at work digging it up and loading it onto cars. Farther on there are stretches of black lava, the result of awful eruptions of some old volcano now cold and silent. Alongside of the railroad are telegraph and telephone poles, and close beside the track there runs for miles a great iron pipe which supplies the railroad, the stations, and the town of Antofagasta with water.

As we ride along we cannot help thinking what a difference in the appearance of the country a few good rains would make. The slopes would be covered with green and the valleys with flowers, and it seems as if the people who live here would be much happier. This is not the case. This is one place in the world where the people do not want rain. If the climate should change and a large amount of rain should fall, the wealth of the people would disappear, for the water would gradually dissolve the nitrate and carry it away to the ocean.

The deposits of nitrates extend in a long, narrow strip about two and a half miles wide for nearly five hundred miles north and south. They do not lie close to the shore but are found from fifteen to fifty miles or more away from the ocean and not less than three thousand feet above its level. In the nitrate fields of the country the surface is all upheaved and looks as if some mountain giant had plowed it into huge furrows. Except for its tossed-up surface the land looks to us no different from that through which we have been passing and gives no evidence of the wealth hidden under its desolate-looking surface.

The largest deposits of nitrate lie in a high valley four or five thousand feet above sea level between the Andes Mountains and the coast ranges. Every now and then branch tracks put off from the main line and run out to where we can see long, low buildings with tall chimneys. These are the oficinas, where the nitrate rock, called caliche, is crushed and treated. On the sidings at the stations and on these branch lines we can see hundreds of trucks filled with bags waiting to be sent

*Figure 126—In the nitrate fields the surface
of the country is all upheaved.*

down to Antofagasta. The trains coming up the slopes
are as full as those going down. Thousands of men
work in the nitrate fields. Homes must be provided
for them and their families, and all articles of clothing,
food, and even the water which they drink must be
brought to them.

We will stop at one of the little stations on our way
and make a visit to an oficina, where we can learn more
of this important industry. There are a good many
buildings in the establishment. Those little cabins of
corrugated iron are the laborers' homes, and the larger,
better buildings are for the overseers, engineers, and
other skilled workmen from the United States and
European countries. We can see some tennis courts
and a little farther on a schoolhouse and a store. Before

us is a large building with tall chimneys, and at one side there are a number of big, open tanks. Men are shoveling up the grayish white material, filling bags, loading cars, and letting water into huge vats.

Did you hear that loud report? Look at the column of smoke rising in the field over there to the right. That is where the men have been blasting to get at the rock in which the nitrate is found. This rock lies usually from eight to ten or twelve feet below the surface of the ground. A hole is dug and a charge of dynamite or powder attached to a fuse is placed at the bottom. Sometimes this is done by a boy who is let down into the hole and who digs out a little space at one side so as to place the charge under the solid rock. He is then lifted up and the fuse lighted. When the explosion occurs, it loosens and breaks up tons of rock and soil which cover the nitrate deposits. With heavy hammers, pickaxes, and crowbars the men remove the loosened mass and load it onto two-wheeled carts drawn by mules. At some oficinas little branch tracks run out to the places where the blasting is going on, and the nitrate rock is loaded into the cars to be taken to the crushing mill.

Let us look at the great blocks of dull-gray rock in the carts. The superintendent tells us that it is nearly half pure nitrate of soda. In some places the deposit is not nearly so rich and does not yield more than a third or a fourth of its bulk in nitrate. Little as yet is mined where the rock yields less than a fifth. In time, however, when the deposits are nearly used up, these poorer beds will be worked also.

*Figure 127—An oficina where the nitrate rock
is crushed and treated.*

We will follow the carts to the oficina. Here great machines worked by steam or electricity crush the rock to a coarse powder. This is taken to the boiling kettles, immense tanks filled with water and fitted inside with steam pipes. What a steaming and a bubbling there is all around! We go nearer and peer into one of the huge vats at the yellowish-colored liquid in which the nitrate has dissolved. The boiling is kept up for some time, after which the liquid is drawn off into large shallow vats. Here it cools, and the nitrate forms in crystals on the sides and bottom. The water is then drawn off, and workmen shovel the white sparkling stuff onto the drying boards. Here it will remain exposed to the hot sun and dry air until every particle of moisture has disappeared. It is then graded according to quality and put into bags to be shipped away. The very best nitrate of soda is used in making powder and other explosives; some is used in different compounds, such as bleaching powders and dyestuffs; some is used in the manufacture of glass and steel; but the great bulk of the product is used in making fertilizers.

The liquid which is drawn off from the vats where the nitrate has crystallized yields another very valuable product. This is iodine, used in medicines, in photography, and in the making of dyes. The liquid is treated with different substances until the iodine forms into a black powder. This is heated and treated with still other chemicals until it turns to a vapor, which when cooled changes into pretty violet-colored crystals. In proportion to its bulk iodine is very much more valuable than nitrate of soda, and the small casks in which it is shipped are each worth several hundred dollars.

A large part of the territory which is now northern Chile formerly belonged to Bolivia. After the value of this desert land was known, many disputes arose between these countries concerning the boundary lines and the nitrate fields. Finally, in 1879, war was declared. Peru had sided with Bolivia in the quarrels, so Chile declared war against both of her northern neighbors. The struggle lasted for four years, and at the end of that time Chile was victorious. She took possession of the nitrate fields, made Bolivia an inland country, and deprived her of a great source of wealth. Today Chile owns about all of the nitrate deposits yet discovered. She exports millions of tons each year and levies a tax on every ton that leaves her ports. An immense sum thus comes annually to the Chilean government from this one industry. This is one reason why she has progressed so rapidly and has been able to build expensive railroads.

It has been found that fertilizers that contain nitrate of soda are especially good for the production of the sugar beet, and therefore nitrates are shipped from Chile to Germany and France for use on the beet farms. In ordinary years large quantities go to these two countries and to England. During the great European war much smaller amounts were shipped to these countries, and as a consequence there was much suffering in the nitrate towns, where all the people depend on this one industry. The United States uses thousands of tons of nitrates yearly, all of which comes from the beds of Chile. The building of the Panama Canal makes the voyage from northern Chile to our eastern ports much shorter than it was before the Western Hemisphere was cut in two. Some of our corporations engaged in the manufacture of explosives own large areas in Chile and import great quantities of nitrates to their own factories.

No one knows how long the deposits of Chile will last. Some authorities say that they will be exhausted in fifty years, while others think that they will last two or three centuries. Sooner or later the time will come when they will be gone. For years people have wondered where we shall get the plant food which the crops of the world demand.

The air contains large quantities of nitrogen. By taking it from the atmosphere, combining it with other substances, getting it into such a form that plants can use it, and doing all this cheaply enough to make the product commercially valuable, we should have plenty of plant food for all time. In the great laboratories of the world, chemists have worked for many years on this problem, and today artificial nitrates are made in large quantities. People who are familiar with this industry believe that it will not be very long before artificial nitrates will take the place of the natural product. This will be no more wonderful than the work of the scientists in extracting the sugar from the beet, in manufacturing artificial camphor, or in making from chemicals delightful perfumes which have the fragrance of real flowers.

TOPICS FOR STUDY

I

1. Contrast between northern and southern Chile.

2. Chilean railroads.

3. Iquique and Antofagasta.

4. The nitrate industry.

5. Manufacture of iodine.

6. Artificial nitrates.

II

1. Sketch a map of South America. Show the country of Chile. Write the names of all countries which it touches. Show the waters which border it.

2. On the map mentioned above show by arrows the direction of the wind in northern Chile; in southern Chile. What are the effects of the direction of the wind in the different parts of the country?

3. Make a set of topics from which you could write an essay of the nitrate industry.

4. Make a list of the great deserts of the world. Locate each one.

5. Deserts are caused by lack of heat, lack of water, and lack of good soil. Classify your list of deserts according to the cause.

6. Use in sentences the words *oficina, caliche, iodine, nitrate of soda, chemists, fertilizers, laboratories.*

7. Name the waters on which a vessel would sail in going from Antofagasta to the chief port of Germany; to an important seaport of England.

8. Make a list of places mentioned in Topic III which you think are so important that you should always remember them.

III

Be able to spell and pronounce the following names. Locate each place, and tell what was said of it in this and in any previous chapter. Add other facts if possible.

Peru	Tropic of Capricorn
Bolivia	Trans-Andine Railroad
Argentine Republic	Panama Canal
England	Iquique
Germany	Antofagasta
France	Puerto Montt
Norway	Santiago
United States	Valparaiso
Desert of Sahara	La Paz
Andes Mountains	Buenos Aires

CHAPTER XVI

BOLIVIA — ITS MINES AND ITS PEOPLE

No one stays long in northern Chile for pleasure, as it is too dreary and desolate a region. So after learning something of the great nitrate industry we are glad to go back to the main line of the railroad, which runs from Antofagasta to Bolivia, and continue our trip up into the clouds.

Anyone wishing to visit the plateau of Bolivia must enter it by rail, for other countries lie on all sides between it and the ocean. The only means of shipping goods to foreign countries is through Chilean and Peruvian ports or on the backs of llamas or mules over the mountain passes to ports on the Paraguay River or on branches of the Amazon. No country ever needed railroads more than Bolivia, and the money which she has invested in them during the last few years shows that the government fully realizes their importance.

Since we left the port on the Pacific Ocean our train has been steadily climbing the steep slopes of the Andes. When about one hundred and fifty miles from our starting point at Antofagasta we come to the Loa River. Thus far in our journey up the Andes the slopes have been brown and bare; not a tree, a shrub, or a blade of grass could be seen. Here in the valley of the Loa and irrigated by its waters are green pastures where cattle and sheep are feeding and patches where grain and vegetables are cultivated.

Figure 128—We cross the Loa River on one of the most wonderful bridges in the world.

After a ride of about two hours we cross the Loa River again on one of the most wonderful bridges in the world. We hold our breath as the train glides over it. Looking out of the window we can see, nearly four hundred feet below us, the little river rushing on its way to the sea.

Just beyond this point we catch a glimpse of the great reservoirs, blasted out of the solid rock, which the railroad company has built at great expense to collect the waters of some small mountain rivers. This is the only supply of Antofagasta, the nitrate fields, and the railroad itself, for no other water can be obtained in this region except by distilling that of the ocean. From

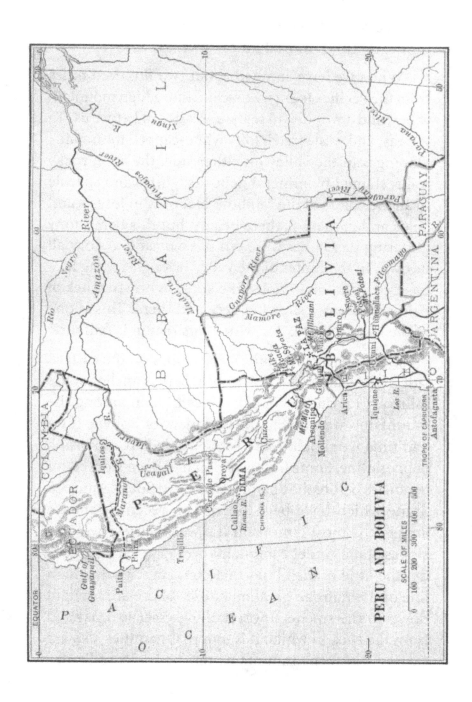

PERU AND BOLIVIA

SCALE OF MILES

0   100   200   300   400   500

the reservoirs the pure mountain water is led in pipes for nearly two hundred miles down to sea level.

When we have climbed about two hundred miles from the Pacific Ocean we descend into a high mountain valley, and a wonderful scene spreads out before us. To the east and west stretch lofty white-capped mountains. Sloping into the valley on either side, the bare, rocky walls, stained by mineral deposits, glitter and sparkle in all the colors of the rainbow. Not only in forests and fields and gardens is there beauty, but this bare, stony, glittering desert has a wealth of color and a glory all its own. In the center of the valley lies a glistening lake covered with what looks like snow, with stretches of pale-green water showing here and there. This is one of the lakes of borax for which this region is famous.

Climbing again up the steep slopes on the eastern side of the valley, past junctions where branches of the railroad run out to copper mines hidden among the mountains, we come to the boundary of Bolivia. If we had time we should like to take a side trip and visit a copper mine. Some in this region had been worked for centuries before the Spaniards came to South America. Some which have been opened in recent years are among the most famous in the world. These western slopes of the Andes Mountains are very rich in copper. On the little branch lines that connect with the main line of the railroad great quantities of ore are brought down to the smelters, where the copper is separated from the rock in which it is found. Quantities also are carried down the mountains on the backs of llamas and mules.

The railroads that lead up to some of these mines are among the highest in the world. One of them reaches almost sixteen thousand feet above the level of the sea, or about half a mile higher than the top of Pikes Peak. At such a height the air is so thin that you would probably suffer from mountain sickness. During the southern winter these branch lines are often blocked with snow, and if your visit were in July—their coldest month you might be held at this great height in the drifts for several days.

Continuing our journey we see off at our left another glittering lake of borax. This lake is more than twelve miles long, and there is one a little smaller not far away.

Figure 129—Large quantities of copper are brought down the mountains on the backs of llamas.

Figure 130—A Borax Lake

Great quantities of borax are shipped from this region and from parts of Peru. Borax is found also in other rainless parts of the earth,—in California, Siberia, and sections of China,—but the lakes of South America yield the greater part of the world's supply. The laborers dig the borax out of the lake in huge lumps, which are spread around the factories to dry. It is then heated in furnaces until it forms a powdery mass of crystals. After this it is packed in bags and sent by rail down to the coast towns to be shipped to Europe and the United States.

Leaving the borax fields we continue our trip into Bolivia. What a bleak, barren country it is! Nearly all this western portion in which we are traveling is a high desert plateau inclosed by two lofty chains of the Andes Mountains. Though cold and unattractive it is one of Nature's storehouses. On the bare, rough slopes and deep in the rocky soil are hidden vast treasures of copper, tin, silver, and gold. Millions of dollars' worth of these minerals have been taken from her hoard, yet this enormous amount is very little compared with the quantity that still lies buried, waiting for money to develop the mines, to import machinery, and to build more railroads. Railroads are one of the greatest needs of Bolivia, but in her mountainous country it costs immense sums to build them, often several hundred thousand dollars a mile. In spite of this enormous cost, Bolivia is every year extending her lines to connect with those of other nations and with the oceans on either side.

Not all of Bolivia is the high, barren plateau that most people imagine the country to be. More than half

Figure 131—It costs immense sums
to build railroads in Bolivia.

301

of the republic lies to the east of the snow-capped Andes and slopes down to the tropical forests of the Amazon basin, Much of this region is uninhabited, save by South American Indians untouched by civilization, who go about unclad, use the blowguns and poisoned arrows, and live in a primitive way. In this eastern part of Bolivia we shall find jaguars, peccaries, crocodiles, brilliantly colored birds, and chattering parrots, such as we found in the forests of Brazil. There are also thousands of acres of rich pasture land, trees of valuable hard woods, besides rubber, coffee, and cacao trees. Here grows also in large numbers the cinchona tree, from the bark of which the bitter medicine quinine is made. This tree is found in both Peru and Bolivia, and at one time these countries supplied the world with quinine. Realizing the value of the product, England, years ago, set about cultivating the tree in her possessions in the East,—in Ceylon, India, Burma, and other colonies in and around Asia. Following her lead, other nations planted large numbers of the trees in several of the East Indies, until today the larger part of the world's supply comes from the East—most of it from the island of Java.

Besides the cinchona trees that grow wild in the forests of eastern Bolivia, millions have been planted on plantations. As railroads are built and transportation becomes cheaper, the quinine industry may grow to be of more importance. It is carried on at present in a very simple way. Long, narrow strips of bark are peeled off from the trunk, and the tree is left for the wound to heal over. The bark is dried, and is then carried on the backs of men and donkeys down through the tropical forests to some branch of the Amazon or up over the steep mountain trails to La Paz, where it is shipped to Europe and the United States.

There are gold mines also on these eastern slopes of Bolivia. For hundreds of years great quantities of gold have been obtained by the Indians by washing the yellow metal from the sands of the streams. When the Spaniards first came to South America they found in both Peru and Bolivia wonderful temples with ornaments of gold and rooms whose walls were covered with it. The Indians did not care for the gold for themselves but kept it for their rulers and their temples. It is probable that much of the vast quantity which the Spaniards found came from the eastern slopes of the Bolivian mountains. It is probable also that great quantities will be mined here in the future. White men of different nations have begun to develop these riches, and in this wilderness, hundreds of miles from cities and towns, one will find today mines equipped with modern machinery for getting out the gold and crushing the ore. Long, hard journeys, which took days, and in some cases weeks, were necessary for the trains of mules and donkeys to carry the material for the mines over the mountains, along deep gorges, beside steep cliffs, and through tangled forests.

The southeastern part of Bolivia, which slopes down to the plains of Argentina, is of less value than the portions farther north. Part of this area will make fine pastures and farms, while other portions are too dry for agriculture or even for grazing. On account of the difficulty of getting in and out of the country little has as yet been done to develop the eastern portions of Bolivia. A railroad is now planned which will start from Uyuni and run southeast, to connect with the Argentine lines and thus afford a way to the Atlantic Ocean and its ports.

Today a plan is on foot in both North America and South America to build railroads and to connect those already constructed until a continuous line known as the Pan-American Railroad shall stretch from Alaska to Buenos Aires. Much of this road is already in use, and the building of some hundreds of miles by each country through which the route passes will make it possible for one to ride in comfortable cars the entire length of North America, along the Isthmus of Panama, and over the high plateaus and grassy plains of South America to Buenos Aires.

The road from Bolivia to the coast of Argentina will form a part of this Pan-American Railroad. This part of the line will follow the old trade route, which for hundreds of years led from the Atlantic Ocean through Argentina to the riches of Bolivia, and thence northward to the city of Lima, Peru—an old center of civilization. It will not be long before people can ride in a modern railroad train over the route where for hundreds of years mules and llamas and Indians have trudged on their weary journeys.

In a trip over this trail down toward Argentina we see men and boys working in the fields with their curious wooden plows, or cultivating their crops with hoes and spades the handles of which are so short

*Figure 132—We see men working in the fields
with their curious wooden plows.*

that the laborers bend low over the ground. Flocks of
sheep and goats and many cattle graze in the pastures.
Near a little village of mud huts some South American
Indian women are doing the family washing in a way-
side stream. Coming down the slopes are caravans
of mules and llamas loaded with bags of ore, while
those that are slowly toiling upward toward the high
plateaus are carrying heavy packing-cases filled with
manufactured articles which these people do not as
yet make for themselves. The Indian drivers have risen
long before daylight, prepared their simple breakfast,
saddled and loaded their animals, and started out on
their long eight-hour march. At night they stop, turn
the beasts out to forage for themselves, eat their supper,
and, wrapping themselves up in their ponchos, sleep on
the cold, hard ground under the stars. On cold, frosty

nights they creep close to the llamas in order to sleep warmer. The next day the same routine is repeated, and the next, and so on for weeks. The driver is never in a hurry. Why should he be? The days are all alike to him, and it makes no difference whether the trip takes two days or twenty. Often he has no home, and if he has, it may not be any more comfortable than his sleeping-place on the ground. The life of the Indian in South America is a hard one. Let us hope that as the country develops, the future may have something brighter in store for him.

Other railroads besides this one over the old Spanish trade route have been planned to connect Bolivian cities on the plateau with the waterways that flow down the eastern slopes of the mountains into the Atlantic Ocean. There are many streams in eastern Bolivia which flow into the Madeira River and thence into the Amazon. These rivers would furnish means of transportation to the Atlantic were it not for the falls of the Madeira, which prevent ships from passing. You read in Chapter VI of the railroad which Brazil has built around the falls and which is proving of great help in opening up the riches of eastern Bolivia.

It will be many years, however, before travelers can visit the industries in the eastern part of the country as easily as those on the plateau between the mountains. It is western Bolivia and its mineral wealth which is today attracting attention. So, although the thin air of the high plateau makes breathing difficult and the cold makes traveling uncomfortable, we will continue our journey through this part of the country and learn all that we can about the great riches which are stored in such an inhospitable place.

At Uyuni we learn more about the railroad which is to run down toward the Argentine boundary and to Buenos Aires, thus connecting the Atlantic and Pacific oceans. Here also we take a side trip to the famous silver mines at Huanchaca. The town itself is interesting, though it would not prove a pleasant place for a long visit. The houses, like those in most of the towns and villages of Bolivia, are built of mud bricks with roofs thatched with straw. The buildings are so low that a person standing on the ground can easily reach the roof. The door cut in the side is an opening so small that we have to stoop to get in and out. The mules and llamas

Figure 133—The houses are low, and the doorways are so small that one has to stoop to enter.

and the plows and other farming tools fill most of the space inside, so that there seems to be little room left for the people. There is nothing in the hut that looks like a bed, and we are told that the family do not lie down on the earth floor to sleep at night but sit up and lean against the wall. We see no furniture, not even a stove. As no trees grow on the greater part of the plateau and as coal costs from thirty to fifty dollars a ton, the question of fuel is a serious one, and none can be spared for heating the houses. At this height the air is so thin that the sun's rays are hot, and if we stay in the sunshine we shall keep fairly warm during the daytime, perhaps sometimes uncomfortably so. But on cloudy days, and especially at night, the air is cold and disagreeable. Indeed there are few nights on the plateau when ice does not form. With no stoves to heat the houses and with the air so thin and rare that violent exercise is impossible, the only way to get warm is to go to bed.

The cooking is usually done out of doors. A hole is made in the ground about a foot and a half deep and covered with a roof of clay. The covering contains holes of various sizes on which the cooking vessels are placed. The only material which can be obtained for fuel is the manure of the llama. This is collected and dried and then piled beside the huts in much the same way as is the dried manure of the yak on the highland of Tibet in Asia.

A legend concerning the Huanchaca silver mines tells us that they were shown to a poor prospector, who had hunted all his life for riches, by a South American

Indian woman whom he had befriended. It is wonderful to find here in this dreary desert land, two and a half miles above the level of the sea, mines equipped with the best modern machinery, with thousands of laborers, with more miles of tunnels than any other silver mines in the world, and with an output of millions of dollars' worth of silver a year.

Interesting as these mines are, they are not so wonderful as those at Potosi, a considerable distance off to the east. It is only very recently that a branch has connected Potosi with the main line of the railroad on which we are traveling. Before the building of this branch all the product of the many mines around Potosi and all the machinery and supplies needed in them were carried on the backs of llamas and mules.

As we approach the town we notice the ruins of buildings, the abandoned openings of mines, the large smelters, and the piles of rock waste, all testifying to the fact that Potosi was and is an important mining center. At one time it was the largest city in the Western Hemisphere and was a flourishing center, ten times its present size, when the early settlements in the United States were only small villages and towns.

Did you ever hear of a mountain of silver? That is what Mount Potosi is often called, for not even the treasures found by Aladdin in his wonderful cave equal the riches hidden within its rocky slopes. Millions and even billions of dollars' worth of silver have been taken from it, until the mountain has been turned almost inside out. It is said that there are more than six thousand abandoned mines on its slopes besides those that are being worked today. Now that a railroad connects Potosi with the seacoast, thus lessening the cost of shipping the metal, it is probable that some of these abandoned mines will be reopened and the mineral output greatly increased.

Silver and tin are the two minerals which are found most largely in the mountain. In early days the miners, not knowing the value of the tin, worked the mines for the silver only. As the workings become deeper it has been discovered that the amount of tin is greater than that of silver. The latter is still obtained in quantities large enough to pay the expenses of mining, so that the profits of the mining companies come from the tin which is obtained.

Let us go up on the mountain and see how the mining is carried on. We may visit if we choose an up-to-date mine with elevators, cars, electric lights, and modern smelters for crushing the ore and separating the metal. If we prefer, we may see one where the Indians are working just as they did three or four hundred years ago, crawling in through the small opening on their hands and knees, digging up the rock with pickaxes, bringing it out of the mine in sacks on their backs, and pounding it by hand to break up the ore. The miners wear thick knitted caps to protect their heads from falling stones, and leather pads over their knees. Those that carry the ore out of the mine wear a heavy leather apron on their backs.

Deposits of tin occur in but few places in the world.

The Malay Peninsula, a small area in India and Australia, Banka and Java in the East Indies, southwestern England, and the country of Bolivia are the principal places where it is found in quantities large enough to pay to work. Tin is found in several of our states, and it is expected that in the future large quantities will be mined on Seward Peninsula in western Alaska. Bolivia, however, has the richest deposits in the Western Hemisphere, and this one country of South America produces about a fifth of the world's supply.

In former years all the tin exported from Bolivia was sent to Europe to be smelted. Tin from Bolivia is now imported into the United States, and large establishments have been erected in New Jersey to smelt it. As the years go on and South America develops more and more, tin will be smelted near the mines in Bolivia, as a little of it is today. Large quantities of refined tin will then be shipped to the United States, for we use more tin, especially in canning, than all other countries put together.

Returning from the mines we will stop for a little while in the town of Potosi and see the old mint which was built three hundred years ago to receive the plunder that the Spanish conquerors forced the Indians to dig out of the hill. Its windows are covered with heavy bars, and its roof with red tiles. One can still see the old dies, the little cars built to carry the silver bars to the stamping machines, and the records made centuries ago. The carved stone head on the front of the building, which smiled down on the glittering treasures of the Spaniards, still looks down on the Indians and their droves of llamas which gather around the fountain beneath it.

Potosi is situated in the torrid zone, yet the warmest day ever known in the city was below sixty degrees, while during the winter the mercury sinks to between twenty and thirty degrees. Every afternoon the wind sweeps across the bleak height, chilling one to the bone. It is no wonder that years ago the people of Potosi looked about for a pleasanter place in which to live. Such a place was found in a fertile valley a few days' journey to the east, where there was an abundant water supply. Here the city of Sucre, the capital of the inland country of Bolivia, was built. In this old city, shut off from the rest of the world by many miles of lofty mountains, dreary deserts, and deep forests, live many of the wealthy families of Bolivia, who can trace their descent back to the Spanish conquerors.

On account of the location of Sucre and the long journey necessary to reach it, much of the government business has for years been carried on at La Paz. The railroad that connects Potosi with the main line to the coast will soon be extended to Sucre, but for many years to come the old Spanish city with its low houses, its quaint market scenes, its old churches, and ancient customs will remain much as it has been in the past.

From Uyuni the railroad runs north to Oruro, three hundred miles away. From the car windows we catch sight of Bolivians at work in the fields. More than half of the people of the country are South American Indians. They work in the mines, drive the llama trains, and raise

Figure 134—Alpacas Feeding on the Plateau
Eighteen Thousand Feet High

the stunted grains and vegetables that will grow on the bleak plateau. Few of the people own the little farms that they till. Most of the land of Bolivia, like that of Chile and other South American countries, is divided into large estates. These are dotted here and there with little stone or mud huts occupied by the Indians who live on the estate and work for the owner. They cultivate the ground and tend the animals—the cattle, sheep, goats, alpacas, and llamas. In return for their work the landowner supplies his laborers with wool for clothing, and with salt, sugar, and other articles of food which they cannot produce for themselves. Each Indian has also a small piece of ground to cultivate for himself. Here he raises a little stunted wheat, barley, potatoes, and quinoa. Quinoa looks like a weed, but it is a very useful food plant to the Indians of the high Andean plateau. They boil its leaves for greens and cook the seeds into a kind of mush.

Many of the Indians of both Bolivia and Peru are llama drivers and spend their time on the trails. Much of the ore and other freight has to be carried long distances over steep rocky paths. These trips take days and weeks and even months. Some of the freight is carried by donkeys and mules, and on the higher elevations by llamas. The llama is a graceful animal with long neck and slender legs, its little head carried high in the air, its soft brown eyes and its sharp-pointed ears always alert like those of a high-bred dog. What the reindeer is to the Eskimos in the Far North, the camel to the inhabitants of the great deserts, and the yak to the people on the high plateau of Tibet, the llama is to the Indians of Bolivia. They make cloth from its coat, eat its flesh, and load it with their burdens.

Like the camel, the llama can go for days without food. When turned out to forage for itself, it satisfies its hunger by nibbling the tough grass or the low, prickly shrubs that grow on the high table-land. On long trips, when a place is reached where there is good food for the animals the driver always halts and lets them feed. It makes no difference whether he stops for a few hours or a few days, for time is of little value to a Bolivian Indian.

The llama is an intelligent animal. It knows better than anyone else just how heavy a load it can carry over the rough mountain paths, and it will carry no more. If the driver fastens onto its back a load heavier than the llama knows it can carry, it will lie down, and no amount of coaxing or whipping will make it get up until the load is made smaller.

Off to the right we can see a train of llamas making their way across the wind-swept plateau. There must be forty or fifty of them, and they are accompanied by an Indian driver and his wife, who walk beside the animals and who can make as long a day's march as their four-footed companions. What an odd-looking couple they are! The man wears a close-fitting cap with long ear lappets hanging down on either side. He wears a poncho which was once very brilliant, but the dirt on it has softened and toned down its bright colors. His feet are bare, though the morning was so cold that ice formed on the water in our car.

His wife is as odd-looking as he is. She wears a small felt hat from under which her hair hangs in two long braids down her back. She has on so many short, heavy skirts, all very full around the waist, that it seems as if

*Figure 135—The llama knows
just how heavy a load it can carry.*

315

it must be tiresome for her to walk and carry such a weight. All the skirts are very bright-colored, and each one is of a different hue. If the weather grows warm, or if the sun is too hot, she may remove the outside red one and show a purple one beneath. Under this there may be one of bright green, and the next may prove to be a vivid blue. The women are very proud of these skirts and are as fond of showing their number and their bright colors as some women in our country are of showing their fine dresses.

Figure 136—Even when climbing the hardest trails the fingers of the Indian women are always busy twirling the spools and winding the wool.

As the llamas and their drivers come nearer we see that the woman is spinning as she walks. It is seldom that one sees an Indian woman with empty hands. In their hard life they have but few minutes in which to sit down and spin the llama wool, so nearly all of them carry with them on their trips their bundle of carded wool and the large spools on which they wind their thread. Even when climbing the hardest trails their fingers are always busy twirling the spools and winding the wool into yarn. Later, in her little hut somewhere on the high plateau, she will dye the yarn with the juice of some plant and knit a cap like the one which the man beside her is wearing. Or she may weave a poncho so close and firm that it will shed water as well as the best raincoat made in the United States. Her loom is simply two logs laid on the ground, between which the long warp threads will be stretched. Her shuttle, with which she weaves her thread over and under, over and under, is made from the bone of a sheep. In this simple way are made the ponchos which most of the Indians wear.

Figure 137—Women Weaving Ponchos in Bolivia

It is interesting to see the driver guide his llamas. He carries with him a sling shot and a little bag made of llama wool filled with small stones. With these he urges the slow animals forward and checks those which would stray from the trail.

Both the llama driver and his wife are chewing, not gum, as one might think, but the leaves of the coca plant. Do not get this plant confused with the cacao tree from the beans of which our cocoa and chocolate are made. The coca plant is a shrub from four to six feet high which grows on the eastern slopes of the Andes Mountains over toward Brazil. The Indians pick the leaves and pack them in skin bags, which are carried by mules and llamas up over the mountains to the cities and towns on the plateau. The cultivation of the coca plant is an important industry in parts of eastern Bolivia. Some of the leaves are shipped abroad to Europe and the United States to be used in the manufacture of cocaine. When you have had a tooth pulled, perhaps the dentist put some cocaine on your gum to deaden the pain.

The Indians of Peru and Bolivia think that they cannot work unless they have coca leaves to chew. In whatever occupation he may be engaged, a workman is given, besides his regular wages, a quantity of these leaves. Without his coca he might not be able to endure his hard life but it may be that the constant chewing of these leaves is one of the causes which has helped to dull the ambitions of the Indian of the Andes Highland.

The food of the Indians is not very plentiful or very nourishing, and we do not wonder that they need something more to enable them to do the hard work in the mines and on the farms, and to take their long journeys over the rough mountain trails. One of their favorite dishes is *chupe*. This is a kind of stew made of scraps of llama meat, frozen potatoes, and other vegetables, and is very highly seasoned with red pepper. In any village into which we might go we should be sure to find a kettle of *chupe* cooking over the little clay stove.

As we go northward we see many llamas feeding on the plateau. We see also herds of alpacas, which at a distance we mistake for llamas, and we catch glimpses now and then of herds of vicuñas. No great quantity of vicuña wool is produced, and the most of this is used in South America for making beautiful ponchos, warm rugs, fine blankets, shawls, caps, and mittens.

Continuing northward past a large lake—the outlet of Lake Titicaca, on which we are to sail later into Peru we come to the town of Oruro, at the end of the Antofagasta and Bolivia Railroad. We should know that Oruro was an important mining center from the piles of rock waste, the chimneys of the smelters, and the gaping mouths of the mines which we see as we approach. If we had time to make some trips off into the hills we should find copper, tin, and silver mines—some with modern machinery, shafts, elevators, cars, smelters, and stamp mills, and others where the Indian laborers work with pickaxes and shovels and climb in and out of the mines through small holes, not much too large to accommodate a good-sized dog, just as they did in the days of the Spanish explorers. Some of the mines are connected with the railroad by little branch lines, while others still send the ore to the railroad in bags of fifty pounds each on the backs of llamas.

Oruro does not impress us as a very pleasant place for a visit. The narrow streets are lined with low, one-story houses of sun-dried brick, some of which are painted in bright colors. Those in which the Indians live have no windows, furniture, or stoves. There are llama trains in the streets, Indian women with full, bright-colored skirts in the market place, and smelters with tall chimneys outside the town. There are several mining companies which have offices here in Oruro, and we shall meet many foreigners—English, Germans, Chileans, and men from the United States. Few of the mines belong to the Bolivians. Nearly all of them are in the hands of people from other nations, and much of the development of the country is due to their efforts. There is, of course, a plaza in Oruro such as all Spanish towns have, on the sides of which are a few good shops, a cathedral, and the government buildings. On either side of the town rise the brown hills and beyond them the mountains to whose mineral treasures Oruro, with its twenty thousand people, owes its existence.

From Oruro we will continue our journey northward over a Bolivian railroad which extends to La Paz. On either side the mountain view is wonderfully fine. Along the eastern horizon rises a great wall of snow-capped mountains, whose heads touch the sky. On the west, also, rise high peaks, while toward the north, ahead of us, stretches the vast plain. We pass some little groups of mud huts, near which some Indians are working in the fields. Their plow is a crooked stick with one handle and a flat piece of iron fastened to the point by a string of rawhide, which makes a furrow only five or six inches deep. Instead of a yoke the bullocks which draw the plow wear a crosspiece of wood lashed behind the horns. A woman and child follow in the furrow to break up the heavy clods of earth. Few crops can be raised on the cold, dry plateau of Bolivia except barley, wheat, corn, potatoes, and quinoa.

What large numbers of llamas there must be on these high plateaus! We meet many long trains of them with their Indian drivers, and we see large herds of donkeys and llamas feeding on the tough brown grass.

On the bleak, level table-land, thirteen thousand feet high and stretching for miles to the distant mountains, we stop at the station of Viacha. This is the point where the railroad branches, one line going to La Paz, another swinging westward to the southern end of Lake Titicaca, while a third winds its way through the western mountains down to Arica, on the Chilean coast. We continue toward La Paz, and soon the conductor tells us that we are approaching it. We look eagerly about us for our first view of the city. We see Indians, little groups of mud huts, and trains of llamas on the broad, level table-land, but we catch no glimpse of houses, streets, churches, and shops such as a large city like La Paz would be likely to contain. The train stops and we alight, but still no city comes into view. Wondering what it can mean, we walk from the car a few steps around the station. Suddenly we stop in amazement. Before us, over the edge of a steep cliff, fourteen hundred feet below the level on which we are standing, lies La Paz, a mass of red roofs, tall spires, white and bright-colored houses, and tree-lined streets.

Through the center of the deep gorge in which the city lies rushes a little river. When the Spanish explorers first entered Bolivia they found that the Indians of this region washed gold from the sands of this stream. The Spaniards started a little settlement on its banks, and forced the Indians to continue the washing of gold for them. The mining has long since been abandoned, but the sheltered position, the abundant water supply, and the opening at one end of the gorge where a ravine made possible a trail down to the forested country on the eastern slope of the Andes caused the settlement to grow and prosper, until today La Paz is the largest city of Bolivia. In spite of the fact that it is in a gorge fourteen hundred feet deep, it is one of the highest cities in the world, being nearly two and a half miles above the level of the ocean.

But let us descend from the bluff and see what a nearer view will tell us about this ancient Spanish city. Until recently a narrow roadway carved out of the side of the cliff led from the plateau down to the bottom of the gorge, and a stage drawn by mules carried the passengers down the winding path. The driver, liking to show his skill, was not always careful to slow up around the sharp corners or on the steepest places. We are glad that instead of the old coach and its reckless driver we can zigzag down the cliff in an electric car fitted with powerful brakes.

La Paz is one of the quaintest cities in the world.

*Figure 138—La Paz lies fourteen hundred feet
below the level of the cliffs which surround it.*

The houses are painted in gay colors, and the land is so hilly that but few of them stand on level ground. Some of the buildings are one story high on one side and three stories on the other. How steep the hills are! It is no wonder that there are few wagons in the city, as no animal could pull a load up such steep grades. Most of the freight is carried on the backs of mules, donkeys, llamas, or Indians, and in some places the narrow streets are crowded with these burden-bearers. Here come some llamas carrying bags of coca leaves. Behind these come others loaded with the bark of the cinchona tree, from which quinine is to be made. Some of the animals are bringing into the city balls of rubber and bags of fruit from the tropical lowlands to the east, while some are climbing down the steep trail from the plateau above with goods which have been brought by rail and water from other countries, cloth, boots and shoes, machinery, sugar, rice, and dozens of other articles, large and small, which the people of a civilized city need.

The people interest us more than anything else. There are so many Indians on the street dressed in such bright colors that they make the city seem very gay. The long ponchos of the men and the full skirts of the women are as brilliant as the plumage of the parrots in the Brazilian jungle. The ladies whom we meet on the street just coming from the cathedral are dressed in black, and the colors that the Indians wear are so very bright that they make the black costumes all the more noticeable.

Besides the Indians and the Spanish there are also in La Paz many *cholos*, or mestizos. The men dress much as the men in our country do, but the women still cling to the gay shawl and the many full, bright skirts. Some of them wear shoes with stockings as bright as their skirts, while others wear no stockings at all.

Many of the *cholos* are the business men and keep the stores in the older part of the city. Some of these shops are small, dark rooms with no windows. Through the open doors we can see the proprietor and his assistants at work, for in many cases the merchant makes the articles which he sells. The little shops are so small that the men sometimes do their work in the narrow streets, thus making them seem even narrower.

*Figure 139—The women wear the gay shawl
and the many full, bright skirts.*

Formerly all the shops of La Paz were like these—small, dark, and shabby. Now, in the wealthier part of the city, we find large, well-lighted stores and an attractive supply of goods.

Many of the people, especially the Indians, do not trade much in the stores but buy what they need at the market. Sunday is the best time for us to visit the market, for the crowds are much greater on that day than on any other, and the amount of goods displayed is much larger. Not only in the market buildings but in the streets and squares around there are many buyers and sellers. The narrow alleys are crowded with loaded llamas and donkeys, Indian women with bundles of produce or babies wrapped in bright-colored shawls on their backs, and Indian men in bright ponchos, with a lump of coca leaves in their mouths.

The sides of the streets are lined with piles of goods, with the owners squatting on the ground behind them. There are no scales for weighing, as one buys by the pile instead of by the pound. Here are mounds of wheat, barley, and quinoa, and attractive-looking fruit. On the other side of the street there are piles of parched corn, dried peas, beans, onions, and other vegetables, and close beside them some small, hard, white balls. These are frozen potatoes, one of the most common articles of food of the Bolivians. They were frozen and dried, after which the skins were rubbed off. They were then wet, frozen, and dried again. In this state they keep for years, or until they are needed in the stew which is

Figure 140—A Sunday Market Scene in La Paz

eaten almost daily by the Indians. Let us stop at these stalls where some Indian women have displayed some bright blankets, gay striped ponchos, and the heavy woolen cloth of which their skirts are made. There are stalls also where one can buy native jewelry,—chains, earrings, bracelets, and the long pins with which the women fasten their shawls.

Figure 141—The splendid white peak of Illimani overlooks the city of La Paz.

Our visit to La Paz has been most interesting. We have enjoyed seeing the deep gorge in which the city lies, the rushing river that flows through it, the beautiful colors of the cliffs, and above all the splendid white peak of Mount Illimani, one of the highest mountains of the Andes, which looks down over the city. We should not like to live here all the time. Though the mercury in the thermometer touches eighty in the daytime, it may sink at night to several degrees below freezing. There are very few stoves for heating in La Paz, and our evenings would be most uncomfortable. On account of the height and the thin air we should not be able to walk fast enough to keep warm even on level ground, and we might feel dizzy and sick if we attempted to climb any of the steep hills. We shall not be sorry to take the electric cars up to the plateau and start again in the train on our journey northward. We will sail across the highest large lake in the world, and in Peru we will gradually descend to the lower levels, where we shall find the climate warmer and the air easier to breathe.

TOPICS FOR STUDY

I

1. The Antofagasta and Bolivia Railroad.

2. Copper mines of Bolivia.

3. Lakes of borax.

4. Eastern Bolivia.

5. The cinchona tree and quinine.

6. The Pan-American Railroad.

7. Indians of Bolivia.

8. Huanchaca silver mines.

9. Potosi and its tin mines.

10. Sucre, the capital of Bolivia.

11. Llamas, alpacas, and vicuñas.

12. Coca leaves and cocaine.

13. The mining town of Oruro.

14. The quaint city of La Paz.

II

1. Sketch a map of South America. Show the country of Bolivia and the routes into it from the east and west. Write the names of the cities on these routes.

2. Locate the places mentioned in the chapter where tin is found. From what port on the Malay Peninsula would it be shipped? From what port on the island of Java? On what waters would a vessel sail in going from the Malay Peninsula to an English port?

3. For what is borax used?

4. What advantages in the production of quinine has southern Asia over eastern Bolivia?

5. Write a list of all the animals of the world whose coat is used in the making of cloth.

6. Make a list of the places mentioned in Topic III which you think are so important that you should always remember them.

III

Be able to spell and pronounce the following names. Locate each place and tell what was said of it in this and in any previous chapter. Add other facts if possible.

Peru	Pan-American Railroad
Argentine Republic	Lake Titicaca
Brazil	Paraguay River
California	Amazon River
Alaska	Loa River
England	Madeira River
Australia	Andes Mountains
India	Mount Potosi
Siberia	Pikes Peak
China	Antofagasta
Tibet	La Paz
Ceylon	Buenos Aires
Burma	Lima
Java	Potosi
Banka	Sucre
East Indies	Oruro
Seward Peninsula	Uyuni
Malay Peninsula	Huanchaca
Isthmus of Panama	Viacha

CHAPTER XVII

A SAIL ABOVE THE CLOUDS INTO PERU

TODAY we will continue our trip northward into Peru. On the way from La Paz to Lake Titicaca we see on our right the mountain wall of the Sorata Range, one of the greatest continuous snow ranges in the world. On the left are the lower hills of the coast range, and in front of us stretches the seemingly endless plain on which we have been riding for some days. This plain is a part of the bed of an ancient lake, of which Titicaca is only a small remnant. The old lake bed is now covered with sand and gravel and dotted with South American Indian villages of mud huts and little patches of barley, potatoes, and quinoa.

At Guaqui we take a boat for our sail across Lake Titicaca into Peru. As we step aboard the fine, large steamer at the wharf we can hardly realize that we are two and a half miles high in the heart of the Andes Mountains. The only way to get the boats into this region was to bring them in parts up the steep slopes of the mountains and put them together on the shore of the lake.

331

Our steamer is much like those on the lakes and rivers in the United States, but the small boats around us are different from anything we have ever seen. They are made of reeds more than twice as tall as you are and not much larger around than your thumb. These are bound together with strings of grass into large bundles, which are sewed together in the form of a boat. The reeds are very light, but soon become water soaked. The boats are then of no further use and are torn apart, and the reeds are used for the roofs of huts and other purposes. The loss of their boats troubles those people but little, for the reeds grow plentifully along the shore, and time is of little value to these South American Indians.

The frail little balsas, as they are called, carry animals, people, and freight. Some of them have sails made of reeds; some, used near the shore, are pushed along with poles; and in others paddles are used.

Lake Titicaca is the highest large lake in the world. As we sit on the deck of the comfortable steamer we are more than twelve thousand feet above the level of the sea. The little blue spot on our maps that shows the location of the lake is so small that we had not realized that it represented a body of water about a hundred miles long and three times as large as the state of Rhode Island. It was once much larger than it is today and stretched nearly to the border of Argentina. In our trip through Bolivia we traveled most of the time over its ancient bed of sand and gravel, and the lake that we passed on our way to La Paz is another remnant, not yet evaporated, of this ancient body of water.

Figure 142—The native boats,
called balsas, are made of reeds.

Lake Titicaca is fed by mountain streams that bring down the waters of the Andes glaciers. Put your hand into the water and you will find it icy cold. Few of the people who live near the lake have ever learned to swim, and it is said that anyone falling into the water would perish quickly from the cold.

Lake Titicaca has no known outlet to the ocean. Yet in the waters along the shores of northern Chile there are found at times reeds, grains, and bits of plants that grow only around this high mountain lake, and it is thought that these materials find their way to the Pacific through underground streams.

The color of the water of the lake is a cold, steely blue, not at all like the soft, deep blue of lakes on which the rays of the tropical sun beat down. It is so cold here on the plateau that ice forms around the shores nearly every night in the year, though the body of the lake never freezes.

There are several islands in Lake Titicaca, some of which are occupied by Indians. Two of the islands, the Island of the Sun and the Island of the Moon, are held in great reverence by the natives. One of their legends relates that from the Island of the Sun came the first Inca, or ruler, and that from the Island of the Moon came his wife. From this couple were descended a long line of Incas, who, when the Spaniards first came to South America, ruled over the largest Indian empire in the world. It stretched for two or three thousand miles through the Andean region, from Ecuador in the north through Peru and Bolivia and more than halfway along the narrow strip of Chile.

Stories of this kingdom sound like fairy tales. According to the old legend of the Indians, the Creator gave the first Inca who came from the Island of the Sun a rod of gold which he was to drive into the earth wherever he stopped in his travels. When he reached a place where the rod went into the ground without pressure, there he was to build a city which should be the capital of his empire. This happened at Cuzco, Peru, a quaint old city which we shall visit later. Here the capital was built, and here began the reign of the Incas.

The rulers divided their vast empire into provinces, and appointed governors who ruled over their millions of Indian subjects. These Indians were hard-working people—farmers, shepherds, and mechanics. They built terraced gardens on the slopes of the mountains, dug canals, and irrigated millions of acres of land; they tended large flocks of llamas and alpacas and hunted the timid vicuñas in the mountains. The women spun and wove the soft, silky wool of the vicuña and the coarser wool of the alpacas and llamas into cloth, which they dyed in brilliant colors with the juice of plants. The men made beautiful ornaments and decorations for their temples with the gold which they washed from the sands of the streams on the eastern slopes of the Andes. They used copper and silver also, which they dug from the rich veins in the rocks of the plateau.

The Incas had roads built in different parts of their empire and established rest houses for travelers. They had a regular system of runners, so that news was carried very quickly for great distances. By means of these runners fruits from the low, tropical regions near the ocean and even the fish from its waters were enjoyed by the rulers on the high, inland plateau.

Most of the roads and many of the irrigation systems and canals have been destroyed, but the little mountain farms with their terraced walls remain, an example of Indian industry. Many of these farms, once green with grain and vegetables, are now brown and bare, for the Indians of today use but a small part of the area which was cultivated in the time of the Incas. They carry on farming in just the same way that their ancestors did hundreds of years ago. They stir the ground with a little wooden plow which turns up the soil only a few inches, and they thresh their barley by driving their oxen over and over the grain, as you see in Figure 143.

Figure 143—They thresh their barley
by driving oxen over and over the grain.

Many conflicts took place between the Spaniards and the Indians of Peru and Bolivia. The Spaniards were greedy to obtain the gold with which the temples of the Incas were decorated and which the Indians could also obtain for them from the rich deposits in the countries. In many places the rulers were killed, the temples robbed of their golden treasures, and the Indians became the slaves of their conquerors. In many cases, rather than see their sacred vessels and ornaments fall into the hands of the Spanish, the Indians fled carrying great quantities of treasure with them. Some they buried in the ground, some they threw into lakes and caves, so that in many parts of Peru today one hears stories of the vast riches which are hidden in the earth or water.

Perhaps the most treacherous of all the acts of the Spaniards was the capture and killing of Atahualpa, an

Inca emperor. This ruler went in friendship to visit the Spanish conqueror, Pizarro, who imprisoned him in a room fourteen or fifteen feet square. In return for his freedom Atahualpa promised Pizarro to fill the room with gold as high as he could reach. To secure this great treasure, Pizarro promised to free him, and the order went forth to all parts of the empire to bring in the gold. It was brought on the backs of Indians and llamas,— statues, vases, plates, and chains of solid gold,—until the room was full to a height which Pizarro was willing to accept. The treacherous Spaniard, however, instead of giving Atahualpa his freedom as he had promised to do, kept him a prisoner and later put him to death.

At the Peruvian side of the lake we will leave the boat and continue our trip by train through the land of the

*Figure 144—Two Cuzconian belles and their llama
start off on a long trip over the mountains.*

Incas and to its ancient capital, Cuzco. Peru is in many ways a land of "big things." The country itself is nearly as large as Texas, Arizona, New Mexico, California, and Oklahoma. It contains some of the highest mountains on earth, it is the birthplace of one of the greatest river systems of the world, and under its bare, rocky surface are buried some of the richest mineral deposits to be found in any country. On its plateaus and mountainsides are some of the highest cities and towns in the world, and important industries are carried on in Peru nearer the sky than in any other place on earth.

On our way northward we pass a lake about which the Indians tell an interesting legend. Many of them think that in this deep lake there lies a great golden chain, a quarter of a mile long and made of links a foot or more in length, which once inclosed the square in front of the Temple of the Sun at Cuzco. To save it from falling into the hands of the Spaniards, so the legend runs, the Indians tried to take the chain with them in their flight from the city, but its weight hampered them so much that they threw it into this lake. Companies have been formed and individuals have tried in various ways to recover the treasure, but if it were really buried here it still lies in the cold waters.

Now the train begins to descend the valley of a little river toward Cuzco. From the view out of the car windows we begin to understand how it was possible that these high plateaus could support in comfort the millions of people whom the Spaniards found here. We can see large herds of sheep, llamas, and alpacas feeding on the coarse grass, while the land around is dotted with

*Figure 145—The people whom the Spaniards found
in the Andes cultivated these high plateaus.*

the stone and mud huts of the Indians like a meadow
with haystacks. Everywhere we see fields of wheat and
barley and patches of qninoa and vegetables. The steep
sides of the valley are lined with little gardens terraced
up with stone walls to prevent the soil from washing
down the slopes. Some of the farms in the lower part of
the valley where irrigation is carried on are surrounded
with low mud walls to hold in the water. The land here,
as in many parts of South America, is divided into large
estates owned by wealthy white men or mestizos, and
their Indian laborers live in the little huts which we have
seen scattered over the high plateau country.

Situated on the great plateau, at the head of the little
valley through which we are riding, is Cuzco. From
what we see of the city as we go from the train to the
hotel we should never dream that it was once the capital
of a great empire. The streets are narrow and dirty, and

the low stone houses with their red-tiled roofs and their gayly painted fronts set close to the narrow sidewalks.

Figure 146—A Water Carrier in Cuzco

Cuzco today is only a tenth as large as it was in the time of the Incas, and it is more famous for what it has been than for what it is. The ruins which lie in and around the city tell us something of its former size and importance. The walls of these ancient buildings are made of blocks of stone each of which must weigh several tons. These were brought from long distances and were fitted together without mortar or cement so closely that it is impossible to put the blade of a knife into the cracks. The houses of Cuzco present a peculiar appearance, for the lower story of many of them is formed by the thick walls of the ancient buildings. One of the largest churches in the city is built on the walls of the old temple of the Incas.

To judge from the descriptions of the Spaniards who first visited Peru, this old Temple of the Sun must have been a wonderful building. Covering the roof were great plates of gold, like the lids of chests, which gleamed and glittered in the sunlight. On the inside, the walls and ceiling were covered with sheets of gold. On the eastern wall an immense oval golden plate, sixty feet in diameter, represented the Sun, the god before whom these ancient people worshiped. In this part of the temple were golden thrones and shrines, and a sacred fire was always kept burning, tended by the virgins of the Sun, beautiful maidens who lived in a large building near at hand. The vessels used in the temple worship and all the images and decorations were of gold. In the large garden or park connected with the temple were statues of men, birds, animals, and reptiles, all of gold. The Spaniards took millions of dollars' worth of the precious metal from this one temple, besides much from other places, and the Indians carried away and hid millions of dollars' worth more.

There were temples sacred to the sun in several cities of Peru and many other temples and palaces in Cuzco. If half of what the Spanish explorers told of the riches and glories of these old buildings is true, they must have been wonderful almost beyond belief.

On a hill behind Cuzco, overlooking the city and the beautiful valley in which it lies, are ruins of temples, palaces, and forts which are more remarkable than anything in the city itself. The walls of an old fortress which crowns one of the summits are made of enormous blocks of stone, some of them from ten to fifteen feet high and nearly as wide. How these ancient people with no knowledge of machinery managed to draw the heavy blocks from the quarry several miles away, lift them to the top of this hill a thousand feet above the plain, and fit them together is a mystery which has never been solved.

*Figure 147—The walls of the old fortress
are made of enormous blocks of stone.*

We should like to remain on the plateau of Peru, the center of its wealth and population, and continue our trip toward the equator without going down to the coast. We should find such a route very difficult. No trains run northward from Cuzco, and we should be obliged to go by muleback on a long, uncomfortable journey of about four hundred miles in order to reach Cerro de Pasco, which is the nearest point in the North where we should find a railroad. Some day, when the long Pan-American Railroad from Alaska to Buenos Aires is completed, one will be able to ride among the mountains of Peru from the border of Ecuador to the boundary of Bolivia. Some day also the short railroads stretching up from the Pacific Ocean will be continued by lines which will run down through the tropical lands east of the Andes to branches of the Amazon River. Then goods from eastern Peru will be sent to both the Atlantic and Pacific oceans, and imports into the country will be brought by the same routes. Today, however, in order to visit the parts of Peru farther north we must take the train at Cuzco for Mollendo, on the coast. Then we will sail along the shore to Callao, where we shall find another railroad that will take us up into the mountains again. Trace this route on your maps so that you will know just where we are going to travel.

Most of the interior towns of Peru have at present no connection with one another or with other countries. Not only are there no railroads in these regions but

Figure 148—Plaza at Cuzco—Cuzco is set on a great plateau between two rows of mountains.

*Figure 149—Goods are carried for long distances
on the backs of llamas.*

there are also no roads, and goods must be carried over rough, stony trails on the backs of llamas and mules. Nowhere in the country except in the few principal cities shall we see wagons drawn by horses. In a trip far away from the railroads and in some places near them we shall meet pack mules and llamas, each with its load of ore or provisions. They climb rough, stony paths on narrow trails where in places a single false step might hurl them to death on the sharp stones hundreds of feet below. Behind the animals trudges the Indian driver wrapped in his poncho. Often he is accompanied by his wife, as unkempt as he is but more industrious, for as she walks she twirls the spools on which she is spinning the llama wool. As they journey, both man and woman are chewing coca leaves, for without them they might not be able to endure the hard climb, the cold, and the scanty food.

The Southern Railroad of Peru, on which we are riding, is an important railroad in the country. It is the main route from the ocean not only into southern Peru but also to Lake Titicaca and Bolivia. The road winds through the pleasant valley of Cuzco and out again into the wide plain, once a part of the ancient bed of Lake Titicaca. We are more than two miles above the level of the Pacific Ocean, toward which we are bound, but we shall wind half a mile higher before we reach the large cross which marks the top of the bleak, wind-swept mountain pass that separates the high central plateau of Peru from the Pacific slopes. Even here on this dreary height we see a few huts of some Indian shepherds.

The air is thin and hard to breathe, and the cold chills us to the very bones. As we descend to lower levels we begin to see patches of green grass between the piles of rock and beds of lava stone. We pass large flocks of llamas and sheep and herds of cattle feeding on the tough, wiry growth, and here and there we glide by little Indian huts surrounded by patches of grain and vegetables.

Figure 150—An Indian Mother and Child at the Door of their Hut

345

What comfortless lives these poor people live! The hut is no better than a hencoop—not so good in fact as many which may be seen on prosperous farms in the United States. The door is a hole cut in the side, through which we must stoop to enter. The inside is dark and ill-smelling. We see no furniture, not even tables and chairs. There are no beds, and the people huddle together at night on the cold stone floor or lean up against the hard wall, wrapping their ponchos around their heads and shoulders and leaving their feet bare to the frosty air. In one corner is a little fire of llama manure, the only fuel which can be found on the high plateaus. On the hot stones surrounding the coals is a dish in which is cooking a stew made of goat's meat and frozen potatoes. These people desire nothing better because they know nothing better. For a few cents a day they work on the hard trails, in the mines, or on the

Figure 151—What comfortless lives these poor people lead.

farms, asking for nothing except plenty of coca leaves, which take away the feeling of cold, fatigue, and hunger.

Farther down the slope, about a hundred miles from the Pacific Ocean, guarded by towering peaks, some of which are four miles high, and washed by the waters of a mountain river, we come to Arequipa, the second city in Peru and the most important place in the southern part of the country. The stream on whose banks Arequipa stands is only a mountain torrent rushing down from the snows above, but it furnished the only water in the desert around and so decided the location of the city. Arequipa has electric cars, electric lights, and telephones. The little mountain river not only makes green this oasis in the desert and covers it with vegetables, fruits, and grains like those raised in the United States, but it also furnishes power for the making of electricity.

Here at Arequipa we are higher than the top of Mount Washington. The air is clear and pleasant. The sun is hot in the middle of the day, but the nights are nearly always cool. The river gives plenty of water for the gardens and fields, and if the city were not separated from the rest of the world by miles of desert it would be a pleasant place to live in. Like other Peruvian cities Arequipa has its low, one-story houses set close to the streets and painted in all the colors of the rainbow. There is, of course, a large plaza in the center of the city, one side of which is completely filled by a great cathedral. Service is just over, and the crowds of black-draped ladies and Indians in bright-colored clothes are pouring out into the narrow street.

Arequipa is a busier place than some of the cities which we have seen. There are factories for making cloth from the wool of the sheep, llamas, and alpacas which feed by thousands in the high pastures. There are car shops where the employees of the Southern Railroad of Peru, on which we are riding, make and repair cars. There are cotton mills, a flour mill, a chocolate factory, and other industries which tell us that the people are developing more and more their opportunities for manufacturing and commerce.

There are few places in the world that have more clear days and starlit nights than Arequipa. Therefore, when a wealthy man left some money to Harvard University to be spent in building and equipping an observatory for the study of the stars, it was decided to locate the building here at Arequipa. The observatory has been erected on the slopes of Mount Misti, a beautiful volcano more than three and a half miles

Figure 152—The Beautiful Plaza at Arequipa

high, which rises near the city. Here the stars of the southern sky are watched through great telescopes, one of which has a lens two feet in diameter. We should enjoy a trip to the station and a peep at the sky through the great glass on some bright, starlight night. On the summit of Mount Misti another station has been built. This is furnished with wonderful instruments which record facts about the wind, the pressure of the air, and the temperature which are useful to scientists. Every few weeks a long, hard trip is made to the top of the mountain to get the records, to see that the instruments are working properly, and to adjust them. The trip is too difficult to be very enjoyable, so we will content ourselves in looking about a little more in Arequipa before we start again on our downward trip to the coast.

What are those bells ringing for so much of the time? If they are fire bells there must surely be a great fire somewhere in the city. They are not fire bells but church bells. Arequipa has many churches, and the bells clang all day long. In some of the churches the bells are not rung but are struck with a hammer. This produces a clanging very different from the ringing to which we are accustomed.

The people of Arequipa do not dread fire as much as they do earthquake shocks and volcanic eruptions. Mount Misti gives to the city much of its beauty, but it gives also to the people a fear of what it may sometime do. Arequipa was once almost entirely destroyed by an earthquake, and thousands of people were killed. On the seal of the city there is a representation of the mountain with smoke rising from the top of the peak.

Figure 153—Mount Misti, a beautiful volcano more than three and a half miles high, rises near the city.

All along the western coast of South America we are in earthquake land, and in all the cities great care is taken to make the houses "earthquake proof." Here at Arequipa most of the buildings are only one story high, and the walls are made of stone from five to nine feet thick. These are plastered over and painted in gay colors, so that in passing along the street one does not realize their thickness. Most of the buildings which we see have courtyards, around which the houses are built. To us the rooms seem dark and gloomy and we shiver in going into them, for in none except a few of the most modern ones are there any stoves for heating. You would scarcely wish even in the summer to stay in a place as high as the top of Mount Washington without a fire at least a part of the time, and at Arequipa it is often much colder than any summer temperature on Mount Washington.

Leaving Arequipa we zigzag downward again toward Mollendo on the Pacific coast. This part of our ride takes us through one of the dreariest deserts to be found anywhere on earth. It is a continuation of the great desert strip which we found along the coast of Chile and which stretches northward through Peru as far as the boundary of Ecuador.

Figure 154—The railroad zigzags down the mountains.

The trade winds from the Atlantic Ocean prevail here. They have lost their moisture on the eastern side of the mountains and have none to give to the land on the Pacific slope. The cold Antarctic current which sweeps up the western coast chills the air and causes clouds and fogs to hang over the shore for weeks at a time; and these increase the gloomy appearance of the desert.

The land here is warmer than the ocean, and the

clouds are not condensed into rain or snow till near the summits of the mountains. This is the reason that on the high slopes and the high plateau between the ranges some grass grows and vegetables and grain can be raised. Near the shore not a blade of grass or a green shrub can be seen, except in the valley of some mountain stream. Wherever we find a town or a city on the coast of Peru we are sure to find also a river rushing down to the sea.

These coast towns are all more or less alike. They consist chiefly of low houses of sun-baked mud, a few stores and offices, and the railroad station. A short line usually runs up into the mountains to some mineral deposit, and the ore which is sent down to be shipped away forms the principal article of freight.

Peru is divided into three sections. First, there is the desert coast strip, fourteen hundred miles long and from fifty to a hundred miles wide, brown and bare everywhere except where some little river makes its way down from the snows above to the ocean. In this region it is often cloudy, but rain seldom if ever falls. There is no life except in the river valleys, and no wealth except in mineral deposits. Save in the few places where railroads can be found, if one wishes to get to the interior of the country he must go on a long journey on muleback up some stony trail or dry river bed.

Nearly two thirds of Peru is included in the second division. This is the eastern section of the country, which slopes eastward from the mountains down toward the Amazon basin. Here are rich timberlands and streams whose sands have yielded millions of dollars' worth of gold. Farther down these slopes are great grassy pastures, and still lower are the dense tropical forests, where thousands of rubber trees grow. In this section of Peru, besides the quinine and rubber trees, tropical fruits, and gold deposits, there are vast areas of fertile soil where cocoa and sugar might be raised and rich pastures where thousands of cattle might feed. At present the cost of taking goods from this region to the coast is so great as to prevent settlers from developing the land, and there are few people except Indians unreached by civilization living here today. When the northern railroad of Peru which starts inland at Paita is continued over the mountains to Iquitos on the upper Amazon River, known as the Marañon, it will help greatly in developing this rich eastern region. Iquitos is twenty-five hundred miles up the Amazon, a distance as great as from our capital city of Washington to the Pacific coast, yet ocean steamers from European countries come up the great river to the wharves of the town. With the railroad connecting the western ports and the river opening the way to the east, Iquitos will some day be a large city, the center of a rich agricultural region.

The third division of Peru, and the most important one today, is the central part, the great plateau from fifty to one hundred miles wide, which is inclosed by the high Andes on the east and the west. This plateau averages more than two miles above sea level, and the pastures on the slopes of the mountains, where llamas, alpacas, and sheep feed, are even higher. There is no pass from the coast lands into the plateau lower than fourteen hundred feet, yet it was in this central table-land that the empire of the Incas developed, and it is in this part of the country that most of the people live today.

The plateau is a great treeless waste, containing vast swamps and lakes. Some of the river valleys are fertile, but most of the region is covered with a coarse grass, on which Indian shepherds tend their flocks.

Figure 155—The plateau is a great treeless waste.

As we descend nearer the coast the country becomes more and more barren. Dark, furrowed mountains, black volcanic peaks, and stretches of sand, pebbles, and jagged rocks are all that we can see. Near the railroad there are some curious-looking hills of sand shaped exactly like crescent moons. The conductor tells us that they are always of this shape and that the wind, which blows here strongly and steadily from the south sweeps them slowly along. Sometimes they block the railroad track, and in places there are large stones piled up to break the force of the wind, and so prevent these curiously shaped sand dunes from interfering with the passage of the trains.

Mollendo is the port on the Pacific Ocean at the end of the Southern Railroad of Peru. It lies close to the shore, hemmed in by bare, brown hills. There is little that is attractive in the town. Even the water to drink has to be brought in pipes from a river miles away. For most of the year the gray clouds make the place appear even more gloomy than it otherwise would be, but the cloudy weather is probably much more comfortable than if the tropical sun were blazing down on the bare, dry earth.

Figure 156—Near the railroad are some curious-looking hills of sand shaped exactly like crescent moons.

In spite of its unattractive appearance and its poor harbor, Mollendo is an important port, opening up southern Peru to trade. Great quantities of goods from foreign countries are received here to be sent to Bolivia, and many exports from the plateau region are sent away from this Peruvian port.

We are surprised that so much commerce is carried on from the port of Mollendo. The harbor is a poor one. Ocean-going vessels cannot come up to the wharves but have to anchor some distance out from the shore and discharge their passengers and freight into small boats, which take them to land. This method of unloading is common at most of the west-coast ports of South America. If the continent had more good harbors its commerce would have grown much more rapidly than it has.

It is a two days' sail from Mollendo to Callao. It seems impossible to believe that we are in the torrid zone, for the sea looks cold and gray and the air is chilly. Clouds hang over the shore and hide the mountains behind. Even if the sun were shining there would be little to see on land except the bare, brown desert coast; and it is more interesting to watch the sea lions leap and play in the water and the long-billed pelicans dart down for fish.

Callao is the most important port of Peru, and all the commerce of Lima, the capital, and of central Peru passes through its doors. The city has been destroyed by earthquakes and tidal waves and showered with bullets. It has been said that in Peru, as in some other countries of South America, the chief product is revolutions, and Callao has had her share in these.

We will take the electric car from Callao to Lima, seven miles away. Vineyards loaded with grapes line the road for a part of the way, and we pass by great fields of sugar cane and long rows of Indian corn taller than any that we have ever seen in the United States.

Lima is a city about as large as Atlanta, Georgia. It is the most attractive Peruvian city that we have yet visited, though it is not so pleasant, it seems to us, as the cities in our own country. It is always cool enough in Lima to make one wish for a fire, but it is never quite cold enough to have one. For nearly half the year the weather is cloudy. During these cloudy months it never rains, yet it is never quite dry. For the rest of the year it is clear and pleasant, and one's impression of Lima depends very largely on which part of the year he visits it.

On Sunday the narrow streets are full of people. Most of the women are dressed in the black gown and head-dress which they wear to church. Many of them have just come from worship in the great cathedral which occupies one whole side of the central plaza. Most people who stop at Lima visit the cathedral to see the bones of Pizarro, which are displayed there in a glass coffin. Pizarro was doubtless a great conqueror, but he was also so cruel a man that his bones interest us but little, and we hurry out onto the streets again to see the sights there.

The word *Lima* comes from *Rimac*, the name of a little river which rushes down from the mountains

Figure 157—The Rimac River rushes down from the mountains and furnishes water, light, and power for Lima.

and which by its waters makes possible the city, the fields of grain and vegetables, and the vineyards and orchards around. The electricity which lights the city and which runs the cars to Callao and seaside resorts is also due to the water power of the little river.

We are glad that we decided to remain a day or two in the city, for we wish to visit some of its stores and see something of its everyday life. How different the buildings seem compared with ours at home! We do not like the narrow streets, with the walls of the houses close to the sidewalks, as well as we do our broader roads, wider sidewalks, and smooth green lawns. We know that behind these walls are courtyards with flowers and trees and fountains which the owners enjoy, but it would make the city seem pleasanter if other people could enjoy them too.

Most of the stores are small and dark. Families usually occupy the second floor, and odd-looking balconies are built out over the sidewalks so that the women can see what is going on in the streets. The houses look much more solid than they really are. The plaster with which they are coated gives the appearance of stone, but they are really built of sun-baked mud laid over a framework of bamboo. The walls of the low, one-story houses and those of the first floor of the higher ones are often several feet in thickness. The flat roofs are made of light poles covered with earth. We cannot help wondering what would be left of such buildings if a long, heavy rain should come. It never does come, however, and the people do not care to have their houses rain-proof as much as they do to have them earthquake-proof. Many earthquake shocks occur, but unless they are severe ones the mud-covered bamboo houses shake but do not fall.

Let us go up in this high church tower and take a view of the city. There are no chimneys rising from the flat roofs, but instead we see some little structures on the tops of the houses which look like chicken coops. A person who has lived for a long time in Lima tells us that thousands of hens are raised on the roofs and never set foot on the ground. The inner rooms of the houses get their light from the courtyards around which the buildings are placed. If there is a double row of rooms, the outer ones are lighted by little dormer windows in the roofs, which look so much like the chicken coops that it is hard from a distance to tell one from the other. Many of the better houses in Lima are large

Figure 158—View of Lima, Peru—The great cathedral occupies one whole side of the plaza.

and comfortable, with pretty courts and airy rooms. The poor people herd together in very close quarters, a whole family occupying one of the rooms opening onto a courtyard which all share in common.

In the afternoons the shopping streets of Lima are crowded. Everyone seems to be out for a good time instead of for business. No one seems in a hurry. The ladies linger to laugh and chat, and the men saunter along in a leisurely way. It all seems very different from the hurrying crowds and the bustling people who throng the sidewalks of our large cities.

Now let us start on our last visit up into the mountains and high plateau regions of Peru. The Central Railroad, which we shall take from Lima, was built under the supervision of a man from the United

States. It is said to be the most wonderful road, as well as the highest, to be found anywhere in the world. Before we have gone a hundred miles from the Pacific Ocean we have climbed three miles toward the clouds or perhaps have risen above them. The road clings to the sides of the hills, creeps along the edges of cliffs hundreds of feet high, winds through dark tunnels, and goes over cobwebby bridges where far below us we can see dashing torrents rushing down to the ocean. There is a tunnel and a bridge for every two miles of track. In building the road there were places where the workmen had to be let down over the cliffs by ropes from above, and in some cases they had to cut ledges in the rock on which to stand while they worked.

For the most of the way we follow the Rimac River, which flows through Lima. It rushes down from the

Figure 159—The railroad goes over cobwebby bridges.

*Figure 160—We glide down steep grades
beside swift mountain rivers rushing toward the sea.*

glaciers on the mountains, falling in sheets over tall cliffs, foaming through deep gorges, here losing some of its waters to irrigate a field of cotton, there flowing in ditches between rows of tall sugar cane, and again making green some terraced fields of alfalfa. These terraced farms extend high up on the mountain-sides, and far above those which are cultivated today we can see the old wall-inclosed fields which bore flourishing crops in those early days when the Incas ruled all this Andean land.

Nowhere on the lower slopes except in these irrigated patches is there any vegetation, and it is not until we are nearly two miles high, where it is cold enough to chill the air and make it drop the moisture which it contains, that the bare brown desert changes to green.

362

Here and there we pass little groups of Indian huts clinging to the rocks. See the train of llamas and their Indian driver coming up out of that steep, rocky trail at our left. The man is dressed in his poncho and close cap with tabs hanging down over his ears. His wife in many bright-colored skirts trudges beside him, spinning as she walks. Still higher up we see some Indian women spinning as they stand watching the flocks. On the little terraced fields some men are bending over their work, hoeing what looks to be small patches of potatoes. If they are not careful, a backward step or two will send them rolling down the steep slopes.

Now we have climbed another mile higher. We are nearer the sky than we should be if we were on the tiptop of the highest mountain in the United States. When we are nearly sixteen thousand feet high we go through a tunnel under the lofty mountain pass overhead, and descending a little we find ourselves for the second time in the central plateau of Peru—the part, as we have said, which was the most developed region of the Inca empire and the place where most of the Peruvians live today. Here, as farther south, the plateau is covered with thin grass and moss. Vegetation is scanty, but it is sufficient for immense flocks of sheep, llamas, and alpacas. Most of the land is divided into large farms cared for by the Indians who belong to the estates. A few mestizos and Indians have small flocks of their own, but by far the larger number work on the big haciendas. The owners of some of these large estates own thousands of animals, which produce great quantities of wool every year.

How would you like to live on one of these great estates twelve thousand feet or more in the air? In their winter, from May to September or October, the sun shines all day from a clear sky. The days are warm and the nights crisp and cool. In their summer, from October to May, the rainy season prevails. During these months it rains or snows nearly every afternoon. It is chilly and disagreeable at this time, but you could enjoy no bright fires or well-warmed, comfortable houses, for here, as in other parts of South America, the people have no such conveniences.

We did not come up into the mountains to see the Indians, the animals, or the farms, for these are very much like those that we saw in the southern part of the plateau, near Cuzco. On this trip we are going to visit instead some of the famous mining towns of Peru. The minerals of Peru are worth more than all her other products put together. It was the desire to obtain these mineral treasures, especially the gold, which made Pizarro and his followers treat the Indians so cruelly. Most of the gold is found on the eastern slopes of the mountains near the streams which flow into the Amazon River. It was in this region that the Indians, by washing the gold from the sands of the rivers, obtained most of the material which decorated their temples, and today we might see hundreds of natives here obtaining the gold in the same simple way.

Billions of dollars' worth of silver have been taken out of the mines on the central plateau, and they still yield silver today but in much smaller quantities. At the present time copper is the most valuable mineral in Peru, though immense wealth in silver and gold still lies hidden in the rocks.

We are going to visit the highest mining town in the world. We shall have to begin climbing again until we are as high as the pass over which we rode when we came from Lima up onto the central plateau. You must be prepared for a cold, uncomfortable trip and perhaps for an attack of mountain sickness. Your nose may bleed, your head may ache, and you may feel dizzy and faint.

As we shiver in our heavy coats we can hardly realize that we are no farther south of the equator than tropical Panama is north of it. At night the thermometer often sinks to zero or near it, yet not one of the little mud huts of the Indians contains a stove for heating or any other means of making the room comfortable.

The name of this mining town is Cerro de Pasco. There are deep, gaping holes in dooryards and courts where the Indians carry on mining in just the same way that they did in the days of Pizarro. They dig the hard rock with their pickaxes and bring out the ore in bags made of skins.

Some wealthy Americans, knowing the value of the minerals here, have formed a company, bought large areas, and opened mines where several thousand Indians are employed. They have built a railroad seventy-five miles long to connect with the Central Railroad of Peru, so that they may ship the silver and copper more cheaply and quickly than it can be carried

*Figure 161—Before the building of this railroad
all supplies were carried to the mine by llamas and mules.*

by llama trains. They have built homes and stores for the Indian workmen and pay them higher wages than is usual in Peru.

Of course there are hundreds of other workmen in these mines besides the unschooled Indians. There are managers, overseers, engineers, doctors, and other skilled mechanics and professional men. These people come from the United States and from different countries of Europe. To make them comfortable the company has built stone houses with modern improvements, where the men and their families live. They have clubs, tennis grounds, ball grounds, and provisions for other amusements such as you might find in any large city of the United States.

The mining here is carried on in as up-to-date a fashion as in any other mines in the world. The tunnels are lighted by electricity, and the ore is carried by electric cars to the shaft, where it is taken up by elevators to the cars that carry it to the smelter. A few miles away are some coal mines that belong to the company, and at the town of Oroya, where

Figure 162—A Smelter in the Mountains

their railroad joins the Central Railroad of Peru, they have built an electric plant on a waterfall high enough to furnish more electricity than they can possibly use.

It is surely a wonderful enterprise which is carried on here in the heart of the Andes Highland. And what makes it more interesting to us is the fact that it is in the hands of people from the United States, is run by money from the United States, and is equipped with machinery from the United States.

The opening of the Panama Canal brings Peru thousands of miles nearer to the eastern ports of the United States than she was when the shortest ocean route to Callao was around Cape Horn, at the southern tip of the continent. Our trade with this South American country is already large. Now that a trip to Callao is no longer than one to England or France there is no reason why our commerce with Peru should not be greater than that of any other country. Peru needs our manufactures, and we need her minerals, wool, and other products.

Our trip down the mountains to the coast is even more exciting than the ride up to the plateau. The brakes are strong, however, and the engineer skillful, and we reach Callao without accident. We make our way to the vessel over wharves filled with bales of cotton and wool, bags of sugar, piles of hides, packages of coca leaves, and bars of silver and copper. As we think of the great riches of Peru which are as yet undeveloped we predict that in the future both the exports and imports will be much greater than they are at present and that the port of Callao will grow in importance with the growth of the country.

Leaving the harbor we steam out once again into the Pacific. How thick the birds are around us! At times they actually darken the sky as they fly overhead. For centuries great numbers of sea fowl have made their nesting places on the islands off the coast of Peru. Here they have lived and died, and here large herds of seals have come to breed. The droppings of these millions of animals and their accumulating dead bodies have decayed into a fine grayish powder hundreds of feet thick. Years ago it was discovered that this material made splendid fertilizer, one that would "make two blades of grass grow where but one grew before." This decayed animal matter is called guano. Millions of dollars' worth of it have been carried away from the islands of Peru, until today comparatively little of it remains. It is thought that not nearly so many animals and birds make their homes here as in former years, and the government has recently closed the islands to shipping during the breeding season in order that these inhabitants may not be driven away. There is still enough guano left on the islands to be a valuable product for some years to come, but the amount shipped away as the years go by will grow smaller rather than larger.

There is one other port in northern Peru at which we should like to stop. This is the town of Paita, where a railroad starts up into the mountains. This is the road of

Figure 163—Paita is a little desert city.

369

which we have spoken that will some day be continued across the plateau and over the eastern ranges down to Iquitos, in the Amazon valley.

Paita is a desert city with narrow, sandy streets and low mud houses painted all colors of the rainbow. Around, watered by the little river on which the city is built, are great fields of cotton. The plants here in Peru might well be called trees, for they grow much taller than the cotton shrub does in the United States and are kept cut back to a convenient height. The cotton fiber is longer and more like wool than that produced in our Southern states and is valuable to mix with wool in manufacturing cloth, hats, and stockings. Cotton is an important product of northern Peru. Most of it is exported, but in recent years large factories have been built in Lima in order that some of the product may be manufactured there.

Petroleum has recently been discovered in the northern part of Peru. Most of it is shipped from Paita, and as the industry develops, oil will be shipped in larger and larger quantities from this northern port.

You will probably be more interested in the Panama hats which are made in and around Paita than in petroleum or cotton trees. Perhaps you have thought, as many people do, that Panama hats are made in Panama. We shall see many of them for sale here at Paita, but we shall see many more and learn more about how they are made in Ecuador. So with a farewell look at the Peruvian coast we will steam northward for a trip into that country.

TOPICS FOR STUDY

I

1. A sail across Lake Titicaca.

2. The Incas and their great South American empire.

3. The Spanish conquest.

4. Resources of Peru.

5. The great central plateau of Peru.

6. The old city of Cuzco.

7. Railroads of Peru.

8. Arequipa and Mount Misti.

9. Peruvian coast towns.

10. The three divisions of Peru.

11. Callao, the chief seaport.

12. Lima, the capital.

13. Minerals in Peru.

14. The mines at Cerro de Pasco.

15. Guano and its use.

16. Paita, a northern seaport.

II

1. Sketch a map of South America. On it show the route we have followed from Valparaiso, Chile, to Paita, Peru. Write in the proper place the names of the places passed, the animals seen, and the products mentioned.

2. On the map show the railroads of Peru mentioned in the chapter.

3. Arrange in a column the names of all the places in Peru spoken of in the chapter. Beside each name write a word descriptive of the place.

4. Find the route that Pizarro followed in going from Spain to Peru.

5. Write a list of any other Spanish explorers of whom you have heard.

6. Write a list of some large lakes of the world. Locate each. Which one is the largest? the highest? Which ones are salt?

7. Why is an observatory which is located south of the equator of especial advantage?

8. What are trade winds? In what zone do they prevail? In what direction do they blow?

9. Make a list of the places mentioned in Topic III which you think are so important that you should always remember them.

III

Be able to spell and pronounce the following names. Locate each place and tell what was said of it in this and in any previous chapter. Add other facts if possible.

United States	Isthmus of Panama
Argentine Republic	Sorata Mountains
Bolivia	Andes Mountains
Chile	Mount Washington
Ecuador	Mount Misti
Spain	Antarctic Current
France	Cape Horn
England	Guano islands
Texas	Pan-American Railroad
Arizona	Southern Railroad of Peru
New Mexico	Central Railroad of Peru
California	La Paz
Oklahoma	Guaqui
Alaska	Cuzco
Panama	Cerro de Pasco
Lake Titicaca	Mollendo
Amazon River	Callao
Marañon River	Lima
Rimac River	Arequipa
Panama Canal	Paita

Iquitos   Washington
Oroya   Atlanta
Buenos Aires   Plymouth

CHAPTER XVIII

ECUADOR AND ITS COCOA PLANTATIONS

BEFORE we go to our staterooms for the night we take our last look at the shore of Peru. There is nothing in sight but the same bare rocky coast and brown hills that we have seen ever since we left Valparaiso. When we awake in the morning and catch our first glimpse of land we rub our eyes in astonishment and wonder if we are still dreaming. We think of stories that we have read of fairies and genii, of enchanted lands, and of marvelous journeys taken in a night to far-away countries. The bare desert shore has entirely disappeared, and in its place we see a tropical fairyland of green. Huge trees wave their blossoming branches high in the air. Their trunks are completely hidden by clinging vines which are trying to find a support for their dense masses and which in climbing upward often pull the forest giants to the ground.

The great desert which extends for more than two thousand miles along the western coast of South America ends near the boundary between Peru and Ecuador. From here through the Panama Canal we

COLOMBIA, ECUADOR,
AND PANAMA

SCALE OF MILES

0   50   100   150   200   250   300

shall see tropical vegetation, waving palms, tall grasses, masses of vines, and dense jungles of vivid green. Owing to the cool air from the Antarctic Current and the mountain winds from the high Andes, the heat of the coastal regions of Ecuador is not nearly so great as in the same latitude on the Atlantic side of the continent.

As we approach Guayaquil we hear some of the passengers telling stories of yellow fever, plague, and other diseases which have visited the city and caused the death of hundreds of people. The authorities have finally taken the matter in hand and have made great efforts to clean up the city and to rid it of mosquitoes, rats, and fleas, which people now know are the carriers of these tropical diseases.

The opening of the Panama Canal was the chief cause of the cleaning up of Guayaquil. This city is the first large port south of the Canal. It is nearer to New York than any European port, and much more commerce than at present will be carried on through the Canal between Ecuador and the United States. The officials of Guayaquil knew that the health officers of the Canal Zone would not allow vessels to pass through the great waterway if there was any danger of their spreading disease germs. The future growth of Guayaquil and the development of the riches of Ecuador depended therefore on the banishment of flies, rats, mosquitoes, dirt, and anything else that might cause epidemics in the country. Ports of Brazil, no hotter than the coast cities of Ecuador and formerly as unhealthy, had been made as free from disease as cities in the United States, and there was no reason why the same should not be true of Guayaquil. Knowing of the splendid work that had been done by the United States in Panama to make the place healthful, the city of Guayaquil invited Colonel Gorgas, the man who had had charge of the health crusade at Panama, to come to Guayaquil and make plans to improve that city. The suggestions in his report were carried out. Sewers were dug, a better water supply provided, rat-infested buildings torn down, and cleaner quarters built for the poorer classes. The people of Ecuador realize that the future growth of their country depends on the healthfulness of their front doorway, and there is little doubt that in time Guayaquil will lose its bad reputation and will be no longer shunned by the trader, the traveler, and the tourist.

Guayaquil is situated on the Guayas River, the longest stream on the western slopes of the Andes

Figure 164—A Coconut Plantation in Ecuador

Mountains. We sail up the bay and the wide mouth of the river to the city, which is situated about sixty miles from the ocean. The river water is thick and muddy with the soil that it brings from the mountains. The banks are fringed with forests of tall trees, beneath which is a tangled undergrowth of vines, reeds, and ferns. Here and there are flat, open meadows where cattle feed in grass so tall that they are half hidden in their green bed.

The harbor is a fine one, but at present the docks and wharves are entirely too small to accommodate large ocean steamers. They have to anchor out in midstream, and passengers and freight are transferred to smaller boats which can come up to the wharves. The harbor contains many vessels. Some are large steamers like the one in which we are traveling, but most of the craft are much smaller. There are many boats made of reeds or rushes. These are loaded with fruits and vegetables grown on the fertile lowlands by the river and brought by the farmers to sell in the markets of Guayaquil or to the passengers on the steamers in the harbor.

There are houseboats or houserafts crowded with men, women, and children, who raise their pigs and their poultry on board and who live contented if not clean lives. The rafts are made of a very light wood somewhat like cork. The inhabitants are equally unsinkable, for although they take frequent tumbles into the river they never seem to drown.

The river mouth narrows gradually in the shape of a triangle, at the end of which sits Guayaquil, the only large port of Ecuador. From the steamer the city appears very beautiful. Surrounded by dense foliage it slopes from the water front up the green hills behind to the still higher background of the snow-capped Andes. Nestling among the trees we see the red roofs of buildings, most of which appear to be built of stone and marble. Later, as we walk through the streets, the city loses much of its beauty and grandeur. What we thought were marble palaces and fine stone mansions are only buildings of plaster and mud spread over a foundation of bamboo cane. Such houses are cool and comfortable and, more important than all, though they sway and rock in earthquake shocks they seldom fall.

We have not yet left earthquake land. Usually earthquakes are most frequent in volcanic regions. From Guayaquil we can see high, snow-covered peaks which seem to touch the sky, and when we go farther into the country we shall discover many more. No country in the world has so many volcanic peaks in so small an area as are found in Ecuador.

Some of these are active, and smoke can always be seen ascending from their craters. Heavy earthquake shocks are not common in Ecuador, but gentle ones occur every few days. The houses therefore are low and are built of light material like those in Peru.

The tropical sun beats down on us as we land at the wharves of Guayaquil. See the bags of cocoa beans! There are thousands of them piled high one on another. They are being unloaded from small boats which have brought them down the river from plantations farther inland, and they are being loaded onto other boats to be taken out to the large ships in the harbor. These will carry many tons of cocoa beans to European countries and to the United States. The raising of cacao trees and the shipping of cocoa beans are the most important industries of Ecuador, and this little country under the equator supplies more cocoa and chocolate than any other country in the world.

Not all the freight piled on the wharves at Guayaquil is cocoa. There are hundreds of bags of nuts also, unlike any that we ever saw before. These are the tagua nuts, which grow in great quantities in the tropical forests of Ecuador. Sometimes they are called vegetable ivory nuts, for the inside is hard and white and resembles ivory. Millions of pounds are shipped away, chiefly to the United States and Germany, to be used in the manufacture of buttons. The gathering and shipping of tagua nuts is another of

Figure 165—The pods which contain the seeds grow close to the trunk.

Ecuador's most important industries. One writer humorously says that the ivory nuts of Ecuador hold up Uncle Sam's pantaloons.

See the large boxes which those blacks are carrying down to the boats. They are filled with Panama hats, many of which will be sold later in the stores of the United States. These three products—cocoa, vegetable ivory, and Panama hats—are the three most important exports of Ecuador. Besides these three articles we see on the wharves also piles of rubber, bags of coffee and sugar, and great bundles of cattle hides, with smaller quantities of alligator skins. With the development of Ecuador much larger quantities of these products, as well as many others, will be sent to other parts of the world.

As we explore the city of Guayaquil we see many blacks with heavy burdens on their backs; we meet scores of donkeys carrying bags of cocoa beans, coffee, and tagua nuts to the warehouses near the wharves; we catch glimpses of dark eyes looking out from narrow balconies at the foreigners in the street who talk in such a strange language; we pass many well-dressed people of the white race, who greet their friends very politely and who, judging from their conversation and manners, are well educated and cultured. Most of the people of Ecuador, however, are South American Indians, blacks, and mestizos, most of whom have never been in a school or handled a book.

Nothing that we see attracts our attention so much as the cocoa beans at our feet. Some of the streets are carpeted with the brown beans, which are spread out to dry in the hot sun before they are put into bags and started on their long ocean journey to northern countries. After seeing the large warehouses near the water, the piles of bags on the wharves, and the quantities of beans drying here and at the plantations, we are not surprised to learn that this little country of Ecuador, about the size of the New England States and New York, produces every year enough cocoa to give a pound to every man, woman, and child in the United States.

Chocolates are the favorite candy of most boys and girls. Now that we are in Ecuador we shall have a splendid chance to see cocoa plantations and learn more about the product from which chocolate is made. If our visit occurred during the rainy season we could make the entire trip over the plantation in a boat. Part of the time we should follow the river and part of the time we should sail across fields, through orchards, and over fences. From December to April or May the Guayas River and the smaller streams that drain the land are flooded so that the low country is like a huge lake. How peculiar it would seem to make the trip through the forest in a boat! The trees grow out of the water, and below in its clear depths, instead of sand or mud or rocks, is the green grass. Everything is very still. There are brilliant birds in the trees, but during the heat of the day they are usually silent. A few weeks before, all this great lake was dry land where people walked and cattle fed. Now the animals have been driven to the higher pastures and the people go about in boats. We meet boats loaded with cocoa beans and rafts filled with bamboo canes floating through the shadowed waters.

See the little houses on stilts. Most of the dwellings in the lowlands are raised on tall posts so that the floor may be above the water. In some houses the staircase is a notched tree trunk and the garbage pail is the water beneath the house. During the dry season the hens, pigs, and other animals live under the houses. When the floods come the animals live in the huts with the family until the ground is dry again.

These little huts are comfortless homes, but fortunately the climate is warm all the year, so that the people do not suffer from the cold. Most of the land is divided into large estates, on which the Indians and blacks work. The wages paid are small, and the unschooled workman knows little of the value of money. He buys all his supplies at the plantation store and soon falls into

Figure 166—Because of floods most of the houses in the lowlands are raised on tall posts.

debt there. According to the law of the country no laborer can leave an employer as long as he owes him money. Thus a laborer is but little better than a slave, as there is little hope of his getting out of debt. If he runs away, the expenses of the police who are employed to find him are charged to his account, so that his debt is much larger than it was before he tried to escape. It is a great pity that the children of these poor people cannot be educated. If this could be done, not only in Ecuador but in other South American countries, the condition of the laboring classes would in a short time be much better than it is today and the entire continent would profit thereby.

Here we are at the cocoa plantation and in the midst of thousands of trees. The pods which contain the seeds are shaped somewhat like a lemon, only much larger and more pointed, and they grow close to the trunk and branches. Let us walk over there where that group of workmen are cutting the pods from the trees. The stems are tough, and it takes a sharp blow from the knife at the end of the long pole to make the pods fall. What backaching work it must be to handle a heavy pole thirty feet

Figure 167—Cutting Cacao Pods

long, bending back and looking up into the trees all day long. See the piles of pods under the trees. Some workmen squatting beside them cut them open and scrape out the seeds. These are allowed to sweat or ferment for a while and are then carried to the drying floors, where they are spread out in the hot sun. These floors, often made of cement, are raised a little above the ground. The beans are spread over them to a thickness of several inches and are raked back and forth every once in a while so that all may be thoroughly dried.

Pick up a handful and examine them more closely. They are brown and hard and look something like an almond nut, only a little larger. It is from these beans that chocolate and cocoa are made. You will be astonished to learn that several hundred thousand tons of such nuts are produced every year in the tropical countries of the world. The use of cocoa has increased very rapidly in recent years, and the farmers in tropical lands have enlarged their plantations to keep pace with the demand. Some of the plantations in Ecuador contain more than two million trees, from which nearly two thousand tons of cocoa are obtained.

It would be better for us to call the tree on which the cocoa beans grow the cacao tree. Then we shall not be so likely to confuse it with the coconut tree or with the coca plant, which yields the leaves that are chewed by the natives of South America. The cacao tree is unlike either of these, and the nuts which it bears are very different from the product of the coconut palm or the coca plant.

Europeans knew nothing about cocoa or chocolate until the Spanish explorers who had visited Mexico and South America carried the product back to Europe and showed their friends how the natives prepared it. They used to grind the beans to a powder, which they mixed with water. Then they beat this mixture in a sort of churn until it was light and foamy and much thicker than the chocolate that we drink. *Latl* was their word for water and *choco* seems to have been suggested by the noise made by the dasher as it beat the frothy mixture

*Figure 168—Raking over Fourteen Tons
of Cacao Beans on the Dryers*

in the churn. So we get the word *chocolatl*, or, as we call it, *chocolate*.

See the workmen down by the river loading the bags of beans into those long boats to carry them to Guayaquil, where, before they are shipped away, they will be thoroughly dried again. From Guayaquil ocean steamers will take them to different ports in the United States and to many European countries.

The beans as you see them here at the plantation and in the streets and on the wharves at Guayaquil would be of little use to you for your candy or chocolate frosting. They have to be very carefully prepared in great factories before the fine smooth cocoa powder and the rich chocolate are ready for us to use.

When we get back to the United States we will take a trip to the largest cocoa establishment in the country and see what is done to the beans there. You would know when some distance away that you were approaching the great plant by the delicious smell of chocolate in the air. There are eleven factories clustered together, and a spur of a branch railroad track brings carloads of beans to the very doors. In the long storehouses there are tons of beans worth thousands of dollars. These have come from Mexico, Central America, Brazil, Ecuador, Venezuela, and even from far-away Ceylon. Different flavors and shades of color are given to the chocolate by mixing the different varieties.

The cocoa beans are not the only product that the company buys in large quantities. To make their sweet chocolate, an enormous amount of sugar is used, from eight hundred to a thousand barrels a week. It would almost seem that with such a quantity of sugar this one company might make enough sweet chocolate to supply the whole world. But each one of Uncle Sam's children has so sweet a tooth that many other companies are working to supply the demand.

When the beans arrive at the factory they are thoroughly cleaned. Then they are roasted for three or four hours in huge ovens, each one of which is large enough to hold a ton. Thirty such roasters in one building will roast thirty tons at a time. With four roasts a day one hundred and twenty tons of beans can be roasted in one building, and there are several buildings where the same process is going on.

After the beans are cooled they are crushed into broken pieces called nibs. These are sorted by passing over sieves with meshes of different sizes, while a blast of air carries away the shells.

Next comes the grinding. The beans flow down between two huge steel cylinders three or four feet across, which revolve rapidly against each other. In a day one of these monster mills grinds more than half a ton of nuts into a thick dark liquid which looks somewhat like cold molasses. This is the unsweetened cooking chocolate. Sugar is added for sweet chocolate. One great machine, used in making sweet chocolate, is a wonderful invention. The cocoa beans and sugar are put into one part of the machine, and from another part perfectly formed cakes of chocolate are turned out at the rate of five tons a day.

Nearly half of the cocoa bean is made up of fat, usually known as cocoa butter. This large amount of fat makes chocolate too rich a drink for many people, and so some of the fat is removed, leaving a fine dry powder. This is our common cocoa. Wonderful machines pour the powdered cocoa into cans, put on the covers, roll the cans into their labels, and even nail the covers onto the wooden boxes in which the cans are packed.

Some of the fat that is removed in the making of cocoa is put into sweet chocolate to absorb the sugar. Some companies do not use the cocoa butter in this way but sell it to other firms to use in making cold cream, face lotions, and medicines.

In the refrigerating and cold-storage rooms the thermometers indicate that the temperature is below freezing. Here on either side are pans upon pans and cakes upon cakes of sweetened and unsweetened chocolate. It is astonishing that so much chocolate is used in the world and that one factory can manufacture so much. The next time that we drink a cup of cocoa or eat a piece of chocolate cake we will think of the great plantations on the low, hot plains of tropical countries and of the large factories in the United States and Europe where people are preparing for us this delicious food.

Let us go back to Guayaquil and take the train for Quito, the capital of Ecuador. We are glad to leave the low, hot coast plains and climb a little higher toward the mountains, where it is cooler and pleasanter. For the first few miles the ride takes us through tropical lands, where on either side we see banana and orange groves, orchards of cacao and coffee trees, rice fields, pineapple

*Figure 169—In the tropical lands near the coast
we see large sugar plantations.*

gardens, and sugar plantations. Now and then we glide by grassy meadows where cattle are feeding in the tall grass. Here and there are little scattered villages of thatched huts raised on poles to avoid the floods. Now we pass large forests where the tagua nuts grow, and on a little river we see some Indians paddling large rafts piled with nuts down to Guayaquil.

The tree on which these nuts grow looks like a stunted palm from ten to twenty feet high. It has a large trunk and a bunch of long, feathery leaves at the top. The cases, or pods, which hold the nuts are as big as your heads and are covered with a sort of burr like a chestnut burr, only very much thicker. When ripe, the shell bursts open and the nuts, usually from ten to thirty in each burr, fall to the ground. When these nuts are green they are filled with a sweet, clear liquid not unlike the milk of a coconut. This gradually thickens and hardens until, when the ripened nuts fall from the tree, the liquid which filled them has changed to a solid substance hard and white like ivory.

The gatherers collect the nuts and take them on rafts or on mules to Guayaquil, where they are shipped to Germany and the United States to be used in the button factories. The United States buys so many of these nuts that if they were carried in teams from the forests to Guayaquil it would take ten thousand horses to draw them to the port. Some tagua nuts are collected in other South American countries, in Colombia, Brazil, and the hot regions of Peru, but by far the greater quantity comes from Ecuador.

In a button factory the nuts are first dried until they shrink enough to rattle in the shells. Then they are passed through great cylinders fitted with special contrivances for cracking and removing the shells. Then with circular saws the nuts are cut into slices of the required thickness from which the round buttons are turned out. All this work requires many skilled laborers and fine tools in order that the ivory may be used to the best advantage.

See those Indians cutting the big leaves from those pretty, drooping shrubs which look like dwarf palms. These are the toquilla plants, from the straw of which the well-known Panama hats are made. The toquilla and similar plants grow in most of the tropical countries of Central and South America, but none thrive so well or yield such fine straw as those from the damp forests of Ecuador.

How would you like a hat so fine and soft that you could fold it into a package no larger than your father's watch? A hat which was sent from Ecuador some years ago as a gift to the Prince of Wales made a package no larger than that. Wealthy planters of South America sometimes pay seventy-five to a hundred dollars for a hat so soft that it can be folded up and carried in the pocket. We seldom see such fine hats for sale here in the United States, but some of the best ones which we import are well woven and will wear for years.

To make the best hats the straw has to be very carefully prepared. The leaves must be cut before they are fully open, stripped of the outer fibers, and then plunged into boiling water, drawn quickly out, and

Figure 170—This is the toquilla plant from the straw of which Panama hats are made.

plunged in again. They are shaken thoroughly, dried in the shade, and then spread in the sun for further drying and bleaching.

Let us stop for a moment at this little thatched hut and watch the Indian woman at work. She takes the bleached straw and divides it with her thumb nail into the width she desires. Beside her she has a large pile of such straw tied up in a bunch. Look at the hat which she is holding up for us to examine. What a fine straw it is and how beautifully woven! It is only partly finished, but she will not do any weaving on it now while the sun is so high. All the better grades of Panama hats are made between midnight and six or seven o'clock in the morning, while the air is damp. If the straw is worked in the daytime it becomes brittle and is likely

*Figure 171—In this little thatched hut
a woman is weaving a hat.*

to break. When a strand breaks, the weaver fastens on the new piece so carefully that you could not find the place where it is spliced. The length of time that a hat will last depends largely on the skill with which the strands are lengthened.

The Indian weaver has been at work for three months on the hat which she is showing us, and it will take her several weeks yet to finish it. When it is done it will be a very fine hat, that will sell perhaps for more than a hundred dollars. Besides this one she shows us also some cheaper ones which her little girls have made in a day or two from some coarser straw.

Figure 172—Packing Panama Hats for Shipping

A good deal of toquilla straw is sold into Peru, and Panama hats are shipped from Paita, the northern port of that country. The straw grows also in Colombia, and some hats are shipped from there also. A president of

Panama thought that a product named for his country ought to be made there, so he introduced the toquilla plant, employed teachers from Ecuador, and established weaving schools. The industry flourished, and today many Panama hats are really made in Panama. The occupation has spread into other Central American states, but the great bulk of the hats still comes from Ecuador, where thousands of men, women, and children are engaged in preparing the straw and in weaving.

As we approach Quito we find ourselves in a region more like the United States. Here are apple and pear trees, strawberry beds, and fields of grain. These and other crops can be raised here in this temperate climate during any part of the year. It is said that every product known to any climate of the world can be raised somewhere in Ecuador. On the low, fertile coast lands tropical products flourish. Between these hot plains and the snow-covered peaks of the lofty mountains there is found every degree of temperature and moisture. A third division of Ecuador, east of the Andes, is as little known and developed as the Amazon slopes of Peru and Bolivia. The limits of the deep forests of this region are unknown, the rubber product unworked, and the rich pastures empty of cattle. The chief means of travel are mule paths, and the few inhabitants are unkempt and unschooled. In parts of this region live Indians untouched by civilization who use blowguns and poisoned arrows.

We can scarcely believe that Quito, the capital, lies almost under the equator, for as we approach the city the air grows cooler, just as it would in a journey from the equator toward the poles. In Ecuador, as in other countries of western South America, the two main ranges of the Andes, from forty to sixty miles apart, inclose a high plateau. Here, from six to eleven thousand feet above the ocean, most of the people live and work. Quito is situated about nine thousand feet high on the plateau. It is nearer the equator than any other capital in the world and, with the exception of one or two other capital cities, is higher above sea level.

Figure 173—An Old Street in Quito, Ecuador

Not many years ago all the freight that entered Quito was carried on muleback from Guayaquil on a ten or twelve days' journey up the steep trail to the capital city. Today our trip by rail will occupy less than two days. In that time we shall see a greater variety of products than if we had journeyed from New Orleans to Minneapolis. Around Quito there are orchards of apple and pear trees and fields of wheat, barley, corn, and potatoes. The Indians here live in stone and mud huts similar to those which we saw on the high plateaus of Peru and Bolivia, drive their llama and mule trains over the mountain passes, and till the soil in the same old-fashioned way.

Some day in the future, when the people of Ecuador have a clean, healthful doorway, Quito will be visited by thousands of American tourists, just as lovely cities in Switzerland and Norway are. No views could be lovelier, no mountains in any part of the world grander, and no valleys greener than those around this South American capital.

Surely this is volcano land. At Quito we can count twenty peaks covered with everlasting snows. Mt. Cotopaxi and Mt. Chimborazo are two of the most famous peaks in Ecuador. Mt. Cotopaxi is said to be the highest active volcano in the world. It has been sleeping now for more than fifty years, but the constant grumbling that can be heard and the thin cloud of smoke that can be seen above its head show

Figure 174—Mount Chimborazo, Ecuador

that it is only slumbering and not dead. Its last eruption, followed by a severe earthquake, destroyed towns and villages and thousands of lives.

A few years later another volcano near by discharged immense quantities of lava and ashes, an earthquake caused heavy damage, and a high tidal wave from the ocean overflowed Guayaquil. The flood was so deep and came with such a rush that it lifted a vessel in the harbor from the place in the ocean where it was anchored, carried it past the houses, and deposited it in the city.

The earliest record of an eruption of Cotopaxi was at the time of the arrival of the Spaniards in South America. Quito was then a large city, and Ecuador an important part of the great Inca empire. The South American Indians and their rulers had made all their preparations to fight the Spaniards. Like other unschooled peoples, the Indians were very superstitious and saw signs and omens in things which they did not understand. They thought that the eruption of Cotopaxi was a sure sign of ill fortune for them in the coming struggle. They therefore gave up all resistance, and the country was easily conquered.

In the eruptions of some of these volcanoes the ashes have been carried so far out to sea that vessels in the Pacific Ocean have received a coating of gray dust. During an eruption a mountain may change from white to black in a single night. The hot ashes and lava in the crater melt the deep snow on the slopes, and great avalanches of mud and water flood villages and towns.

These dangerous sentinels add to the beauty of

Quito, and a view of the city from one of them is a lovely sight. The capital lies in a beautiful valley, with the peaks of eternal winter above and the tropical land of eternal summer below. The white buildings with their red roofs gleam among the trees, and beyond the city stretches a green, fertile plain. The low houses with their little balconies and projecting roofs, the narrow streets, the open markets with Indian women sitting behind their piles of produce, all make us think that we are, in some mysterious way, carried back to the seventeenth century. On the other hand, the electric lights, the cars, and the railroad tracks and station make us realize that the twentieth century has come to Quito as to other South American cities, and that years of growth, of increased trade, of higher education, and of closer relationship with the rest of the world will surely follow.

TOPICS FOR STUDY

I

1. The port of Guayaquil.

2. The cocoa industry.

3. Tagua nuts and the button industry.

4. Panama hats.

5. Quito, the capital of Ecuador.

6. Volcanoes and earthquakes.

II

1. Ship a cargo of cocoa beans from Ecuador to some eastern port of the United States. Name the waters sailed on and the shipping and receiving ports. Compare the length of the voyage with one between the two cities by way of the Strait of Magellan.

2. Write a list of the countries in which cocoa beans are an important export. From what port in each country may they be shipped?

3. Write a list of the volcanoes which you know. Write beside each one the name of the country and the mountain system in which it is located.

4. Ship a cargo of vegetable ivory nuts from Ecuador to Germany. Name the waters on which the vessel would sail. What articles would probably be sent from Germany as a return cargo? From what important seaport might they come?

5. Name as many cities of the world as you can which are situated at a considerable height above sea level. In what country is each one? In what highland?

6. Make a list of the places mentioned in Topic III which you think are so important that you should always remember them.

III

Be able to spell and pronounce the following names. Locate each place and tell what was said about it in this and in any previous chapter. Add other facts if possible.

Peru	New England States
Bolivia	Panama Canal
Brazil	Antarctic Current
Colombia	Cotopaxi
Venezuela	Chimborazo
Germany	Andes Mountains
Spain	Guayas River
Switzerland	Valparaiso
Norway	Quito
Ceylon	Guayaquil
Central America	Paita
Panama	New Orleans
Mexico	New York
United States	Minneapolis

CHAPTER XIX

HOMEWARD THROUGH THE PANAMA CANAL

IF our visit to South America had taken place before 1914 we should have been obliged to take a different route homeward from the one which we shall follow today. We might then perhaps have found a steamer that sailed from Guayaquil to San Francisco, or we might have sailed northward to Panama and there taken the Panama Railroad across the Isthmus to the Atlantic side, where we would again have changed to a steamer bound for some port in the United States. Instead of going by either of these routes we might have journeyed southward along the western coast of South America, passed through the Strait of Magellan, and thence up the eastern coast into the north Atlantic Ocean to New York. Such a voyage would have been between eight and nine thousand miles long, but it would have been the only water route between western South America and the eastern ports of the United States. Instead of taking any of these three routes we will sail northward from Guayaquil, through the Panama Canal, and thence to New York. By this route the distance is only about three thousand miles.

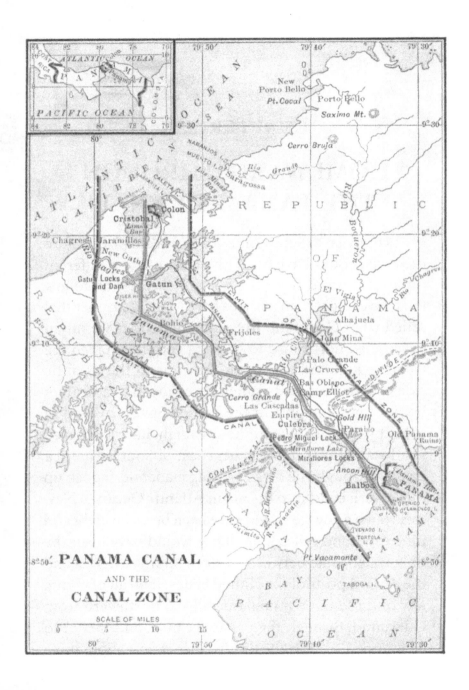

PANAMA CANAL

AND THE

CANAL ZONE

SCALE OF MILES

404

Perhaps your knowledge of isthmuses and straits is not very great, and you may have learned little about them except their definitions and their locations on maps. These little divisions of land and water are very important. Nearly every one which you can name has been claimed by some nation who saw its value as a highway for armies or a waterway for war fleets and merchant vessels.

The making of a canal across the Isthmus of Panama will probably have a greater effect on the commerce of the world than any other engineering project that has ever been accomplished, except perhaps the building of the Suez Canal. It will develop industries, change trade routes, increase commerce, and cheapen products.

As we approach the Canal a fellow passenger remarks that Panama on the Pacific Ocean is farther east than the city of Colon at the Atlantic end of the Canal. We do not understand how this can be until we look at a map. Then we discover that the country of Panama is shaped somewhat like the letter S lying on its side. The Canal is cut through the middle of the letter from northwest to southeast, thus making Colon at the north on the Atlantic farther west than Panama at the Pacific end.

The beautiful Bay of Panama is dotted with many green islands. Not far from shore lies Taboga famous for its luscious pineapples. On this island, at the top of a low hill and surrounded by tropical vegetation, we can see the sanatorium that was built by the United States for its workmen who make their homes on the Isthmus. Farther south and east are the Pearl Islands, low and green, with coconut groves overhanging a glistening white beach. Since early times these islands have been famous for the pearl oysters which are found off the shores. Back among the palm trees and coconut groves we can see the low, thatched huts of the natives, most of whom spend a part of their time in diving for pearls. When working for the merchants they wear diving suits and turn over to their employers all the oysters that they bring up. In their spare hours they dive naked at low tide, bringing up a few oysters at a time, hoping that they may be fortunate enough to find a pearl in one of them. In the days of the Spanish explorers we read of very beautiful pearls being found in these islands; some of them, the old stories tell us, were "as big as nuts."

As we approach nearer the mainland we see the yellow beach and, in the distance, the low green hills of the Isthmus. On a rocky point jutting out into the water is the city of Panama. The old city which was built by the Spaniards in the sixteenth century was east of the present town. The old Panama was the center of trade and travel between Spain and her possessions on the Pacific coast of South America. Through it passed much of the vast wealth of gold and silver which came from the mines of Peru and from the temples of the Inca empire. Ships loaded deep with treasure sailed from the ports on the Caribbean side of the Isthmus across the Atlantic Ocean to Spain. Pirates from other nations attacked and sank the Spanish vessels and tortured and killed the crews. Captain Kidd, of whom you have heard, was one of these bold robbers who sailed the Spanish Main. He was a Scotch captain who was sent to destroy the pirates. In a short time he turned pirate himself and attacked and tortured and killed as if he had been brought up in that kind of a life instead of being, as he really was, the son of a good Scotch minister. Henry Morgan, another greatly feared pirate, was a Welshman. He finally succeeded in sacking the city of Panama and obtained considerable booty which was stored there.

During our stay on the Isthmus we will drive out to see the ruins of the old Panama. The way leads past little shanties half hidden by the fields of tall sugar cane around and the palm trees above. The old walls of the ancient city are draped with green, the cobble-paved streets are covered with moss, and the old gray tower of the ruined cathedral is roofed and hung with tangled vines.

Figure 175—The old gray tower
of the ruined cathedral is roofed with vines.

After the destruction of the old city of Panama, the Spaniards built another city farther west, on a peninsula which could be easily defended. On the three water sides of this rocky point they built a sea wall from twenty to thirty feet high and in places sixty feet thick. This wall cost so much money that an old story relates that the king of Spain, standing at a window of his palace in Madrid and looking westward, was asked what he was looking for. He replied, "I am looking for the walls of Panama; they have cost me enough money to be seen even from here." Parts of these walls built before 1700 are still standing, and during our stay here we shall enjoy walking on them around the city.

People who were acquainted with Panama before the Americans took possession of the Isthmus hardly recognize the city today. In the old days the streets were deep with mud or dust. There were no sewers, and the garbage and filth accumulated in the narrow alleys and backyards. There was no water supply except what was caught in great barrels, which were filled at every tropical downpour. The Isthmus was one of the most unhealthy places on earth. Hundreds died every year of malaria and yellow fever, and few white people from other lands could live here. Today in Colon, Panama, and other towns along the route of the Canal there are dry, paved streets, sewers, and plenty of fresh water piped from the mountains. The cleaning up of the Isthmus has been a wonderful lesson for the tropical countries of South America, and many of the improvements made in their cities have been a result of the work done by the Canal Commission.

About the time that the United States began work on the Canal a wonderful discovery was made. It was learned and proved to the satisfaction of physicians that mosquitoes are the carriers of disease germs, especially those of yellow fever and malaria—the two diseases which have been the scourge of tropical countries. Because of this discovery the officials began to wage war on the mosquitoes of Panama. These pests breed in stagnant water, but the young cannot live unless they can get to the air at the surface. By pouring oil on the water a scum is formed in which the tiny insects are smothered. Millions of gallons of oil were used in the Isthmus to kill the mosquitoes. It was poured over the stagnant pools and marshes (the breeding places of the mosquitoes), rain barrels were screened, miles of ditches were dug to drain the land, and great tracts of jungle were cleared and burned over. Blacks with copper oil cans strapped to their backs and long tubes in their hands were familiar objects all along the route of the Canal. Thousands of gallons of oil are still being used each year, the homes of all white people are closely screened, and all cases of sickness are carefully looked after.

Colonel Gorgas, who had charge of the cleaning up, will always be remembered for the great work which he has done on the Isthmus and, through its influence, all over the world. It is said that the opening up of the tropics by the white man will date from the clearing up of the Canal Zone by Colonel Gorgas.

All this labor for the health of the workmen took many months and was kept up during the building of the Canal. During the earlier part of the work Colonel Gorgas was laughed at by many people who were ignorant of the real conditions in Panama and of the great work that he was doing there. Jokes were made about the Gorgas brigade chasing down a poor lone mosquito. People at home in the United States wondered why work did not begin on the Canal and talked of graft and dishonesty. Through all the criticism Colonel Gorgas kept patiently at his task, doing what he knew must be done so that the thousands of white people employed on the great work could make their homes in the Isthmus. The Americans found Panama a very unhealthy place. Today the death rate is as small as it is in many parts of the United States, and thousands of white people have lived there for several years with

Figure 176—Opening of the Panama Canal,
S.S. Ancon passing through, August 15, 1914

no touch of malaria and with no yellow-fever epidemics.

The city of Panama is the capital of the republic of that name. The city lies within the Canal Zone, the strip of land which we bought from Panama, but it is ruled and policed by the people of the Panama republic. On a hill near the city and overlooking the Canal is the new town of Balboa, built and owned by the United States, where many of the employees of the government live. Concrete houses with broad, well-screened porches have been built for the workmen, and an administration building has been erected. This covers two acres of ground and contains rooms where records, maps, and models are kept, and many offices where the "brains of the Canal" do their work. Down near the water a dry dock, capable of holding the largest ships, has been built, and many mills, shops, piers, and wharves needed in connection with canal traffic have been put up by the United States.

As we climb to the clean little town of Balboa and see its green lawns and screened-in houses, its electric light plant, sewage system, and clubhouses, we can scarcely realize that only a few years ago the hill was a tangle of tropical jungle. A pleasant house on the height, where the breeze tempers the heat, was for some years the home of Colonel Goethals. He was formerly an engineer in the United States army, and during the building of most of the Canal was the chairman of the Canal Commission. He has been called "The Czar of the Canal Zone," for he had all power to decide any question that might arise. He did splendid work in Panama, and much of the success in building the Canal was due to his efficiency, his wise ruling, and his far-sighted judgment.

At both ends of the Canal are great depots where fuel and oil are stored. Thousands of tons of coal will be kept always on hand, not only to furnish passing vessels but to supply our warships in time of need. Strong forts have been erected on both the Atlantic and Pacific shores. These are equipped with some of our biggest guns and furnished with garrisons of United States troops. Every precaution has been taken in order that the Canal may not at any time be damaged by attacks from an unfriendly nation.

On account of the fine view it will be worth our while to climb to the top of Ancon Hill, on and near which the government buildings stand. At the foot of the hill is Panama, a mass of low-roofed houses nestling under the shade of green trees. On the other side of the hill is the Pacific end of the Canal, with steamships lying along the wharves and cars waiting on the tracks. Look now from the hill toward the Atlantic and see how different the scene is. Stretching away toward the ocean are low, forested mountains with deep, green hollows between, all a tangle of trees, shrubs, and vines, so thick that one would need an ax to cut his way through. We can see no sign of the Canal, on which we are shortly to sail through this tropical country to the great ocean on the other side.

As you look out over the wooded hills and valleys can you picture the little band of Spaniards with Balboa at their head struggling through the jungle four hundred years ago? Can you imagine their joy when from one of the hills they first looked on the waters of the great ocean? Turn once more to this ocean whose waters roll at your feet. As you look out over its smooth surface can you imagine that those spots on the horizon are pirate vessels pursuing a Spanish caravel loaded with treasure, which is hurrying as fast as wind and sail will take it toward the harbor of Panama?

The thought of a canal which should join the Atlantic and Pacific oceans is no new idea. The American Indians told Christopher Columbus of a narrow strip between two great waters, and he sailed for some distance up the Chagres River in an attempt to get to the "big water" on the other side of the Isthmus. After him other explorers searched for a water passage across this narrow neck of land. Balboa, failing to find a passage connecting the two oceans, made the trip through the jungle and in 1513 reached the Pacific coast. Wading out into the water he claimed the ocean as a possession of Spain. The Republic of Panama honors the memory of this brave explorer. It has named its national coin the balboa, placed his portrait on the national postage stamp, and set aside the twenty-fifth of September, the day on which he first saw the Pacific, as a national holiday.

A few years after Balboa's discovery, Cortes, another Spaniard, weary of searching for a waterway which no one could find, laid plans before the Spanish king for the building of a canal. Ever since the time of Cortes, four hundred years ago, a canal across the Isthmus has been talked of, sometimes by the Spanish, again by the English, and often by the French and Americans.

Figure 177—Dipper Dredger at Work in Gaillard Cut

At last, in 1879, a company was formed in France, and two years later work on a canal which followed closely the route of the one now in use was really begun. At the head of the company was a Frenchman by the name of Ferdinand de Lesseps. A few years before, de Lesseps had made himself famous by digging the Suez Canal. This eastern canal is nearly ninety miles long, while the one at Panama was to be a little less than fifty. If he could do the one successfully, it surely seemed as if he could do the other. At least that is what he thought, and so organized his company, raised an enormous sum of money, and went to work.

But the making of a waterway across Panama was a very different thing from digging the long Suez Canal. The canal at Suez is without locks and is dug through a level country which, though hot, is not unhealthy. At Panama there were hills to dig through, locks to make, a river to control, and, above all, disease to fight. Yellow fever and malaria attacked the workmen by hundreds and by thousands. The French built fine hospitals and did all in their power to cure the sick, but they did little to prevent sickness. Indeed, at that time the cause of these tropical diseases was not known, and so little could be done to stop illness and death.

The chief reasons for the failure of the French to succeed in their enterprise were waste, extravagance, and dishonesty. Enormous salaries were paid to the officials, the finest machinery was bought at high prices, and splendid offices and buildings were erected. Money flowed like water. De Lesseps himself was probably honest, but he was an old man to put through such a tremendous undertaking. Many of the men associated with him, both on the Isthmus and in France, were dishonest and made themselves rich in a short time. More than two hundred million dollars was raised, but probably less than half that sum was spent on the Canal. Much of it was either stolen or wasted.

The work went on for nearly seven years, but the completion of the Canal was nowhere in sight. Thousands of the workmen had died, the money was all gone, it was impossible to raise more, and the company finally failed. Some of the officers killed themselves rather than face the angry Frenchmen. Some were tried and sentenced to prison. De Lesseps himself, now over eighty years old, was unable to stand the shame and disgrace. He was tried and sentenced to prison, but his mind gave way and he went instead to an insane asylum, where he soon died.

With the failure of the French company the people of the United States began to think more seriously than ever before about building a canal themselves. Many people thought that so important a waterway so near the States, and one which would so greatly affect our trade routes, should be built and controlled by our country.

There was much discussion as to the route of the Canal. Many favored a route farther north, which ran through Nicaragua, one of the Central American states. Such a canal would be much longer than one by way of Panama. The advantages of the Nicaragua route lay in the natural lakes and rivers which could be made use of and the lower hills to be dug through. On the other hand, the danger from earthquakes was said to be greater in Nicaragua than it was farther south. The railroad which already crossed the Isthmus of Panama would be a help in building the Canal at that point, and Colon and Panama, at either end of this route, had good harbors. Congress spent much time in discussing these and other routes, newspapers filled columns with arguments on either side, and in the end the Panama route was decided on.

The country of Panama is about the size of the state of Maine and contains half as many people. It formerly was a part of Colombia, the first country of South America which we visited. For the sum of ten million dollars we bought from the Republic of Panama the strip of land now known as the Canal Zone. It is ten miles wide and fifty miles long, and through the middle of it stretches the waterway. For forty million dollars more we purchased from the French their property and other effects and their rights to the Canal. When the people of the United States started work in Panama, they found many evidences of the work of the French. A good deal of digging had been done, which saved us time and money. Cars, wagons, dredgers, railroad tracks, and locomotives lay rusting in the jungle, but little of it was of any value. The hospital built by the French was repaired and used for the sick. Nature had done her best to hide the signs of the French failure. Moss covered the boards, and the jungle had crept up around the rusting machinery.

The Canal was finally begun by the United States in 1904, and in 1914 it was completed so that vessels could pass through. It cost about four hundred million dollars, including the sums given to the French and the Panamanians. It takes from eight to ten hours to sail through the Canal from ocean to ocean, and during the trip we shall have plenty of time to learn something about the different parts.

It was thought at one time that the best plan would be to build a sea-level canal. This was finally given up for several reasons. It would cost too much; it would take too long; it would be too difficult of navigation. The plan of the present Canal was finally decided on. Vessels entering from either side have to go upstairs until they are eighty-five feet higher than the oceans. The vessels are lifted by means of the locks, and we shall understand better how they work when we go through one of them.

*Figure 178—A lock is a huge concrete box
with gates at either end which control the flow of the water.*

Entering from the Pacific side, we sail about eight miles through the Canal, when we come to two locks, which will lift us fifty-five feet to Miraflores Lake. Here we can put on steam for a mile or two until we come to another lock, which will raise us a little more than thirty feet. Leaving these locks behind, we enter the famous Culebra Cut, now named the Gaillard Cut in honor of the late Colonel Gaillard, who had charge of this part of the work. The Gaillard Cut is nine miles long, the hardest, deepest digging that had to be done anywhere along the route. The Gaillard Cut is, in fact, the largest, deepest cutting to be found anywhere in the world.

Passing out of the Cut we can again put on full steam, for now we are in Gatun Lake, an artificial body of water covering an area of a hundred and sixty-four square miles, made by damming the Chagres River. We run for twenty-four miles through the lake, between buoys on either side which show us the channel. At the farther end of the lake is the great Gatun Dam and the Gatun Locks. There are three of these locks, which lower

*Figure 179—Gatun Lake is an artificial body of water
covering an area of a hundred and sixty-four square miles.*

our vessel the eighty-five feet which it was raised by the locks on the Pacific side. We then steam slowly for seven miles through the Canal, past the city of Colon, and at last, eight hours or more from the time that we left the Pacific Ocean, we find ourselves in the Caribbean Sea.

If you have never been through locks in a canal you will be much interested when going through the first two in watching the vessel slowly rise from the level of the Pacific Ocean to that of Miraflores Lake, fifty-five feet higher. The lock is a huge, concrete box with gates at either end. As we approach, the gates at the Pacific end are opened for us and we are towed into the lock by electric locomotives running on tracks at the top of the lock walls. The gates are shut behind us, and water is admitted from the higher level through the sides and bottom of the lock. The vessel rises with the water until it is on a level with the surface of the Canal beyond. Then the gates in front are opened, and we

419

sail out of the lock only to enter another one and be lifted to the level of Miraflores Lake ahead of us. What a wonderful invention it is by means of which vessels are able to travel uphill.

Leaving Miraflores Lake we are lifted by another lock to the level of the Gaillard Cut. This is the channel which was cut through the highest hills on the route. To dig away earth and rock for more than three hundred feet in depth and make a channel nine miles long and wide enough and deep enough for the largest ocean vessels to sail through was a stupendous task. The dirt which was removed would have filled a train of cars long enough to stretch four times around the earth at the equator. The task was made much more difficult because the hills on either side insisted on sliding down into the Canal, bringing tons of dirt to be dredged out

Figure 180—Digging Gaillard Cut

Figure 181—A Slide in the Cut and Dredges at Work

and carried away. As we steam slowly through the water-filled Cut we cannot appreciate the amount of work that has been done. To do that we should have visited the Canal while the labor was going on. Explosions of dynamite sounded like peals of thunder, and with each blast tons of rock and soil were lifted into the air. Thousands of tons of dynamite were used every year. Without this powerful servant the difficulties would have been greatly increased.

All through the Cut engines tooted, bells clanged, trains rumbled back and forth, and great steam shovels puffed and rattled with each mouthful of dirt which they removed from the gorge. To one standing on the top of the cliff and looking down into the cutting, the

421

men appeared like dwarfs and the big engines like toys. Dozens of huge steam shovels, looking like children's playthings, were at work in the Cut. Each one of them did more work in a day than several hundred men could do. There were thousands of visitors to the Canal when it was building, and one and all liked to watch the steam shovels. With a clatter and a bang the great shovel was lowered and pressed into the dirt. With short, angry puffs it rose, swung around over the waiting cars, and dumped its load into one of them. In a few minutes the long train was filled and pulled slowly away, while another was backed in to take its place. The amount of work which could be done in a day depended on the speed with which switches could be changed and trains shifted.

As we steam slowly through the winding channel it seems impossible to believe that the great gorge was eaten out by the huge mouthfuls of the steam shovels. The steep sides are now covered with a thick growth of tropical green, and the Canal seems like a winding river flowing between its high banks.

What to do with the Chagres River was for some time a puzzle to the engineers who planned the Canal. In the dry season it was a harmless little stream which flowed through its valley by Gatun into the Caribbean Sea. In the rainy season it was a torrent sweeping all before it. The tropical downpours which are common in Panama we should call cloud-bursts. It rains so that you cannot see through it. Dry brook beds become swollen rivers, and little streams mighty torrents. In one of these heavy rains the Chagres River rises more than a foot an hour. Now the great Gatun Dam cuts across its course and holds back its waters, making a huge reservoir of its valley. Gatun Lake covers the place that only a few years ago was green with the tropical jungle and dotted with little villages and scattered huts.

The building of the Gatun Dam was, so far as its size was concerned, as great a piece of work as the Gaillard Cut. The figures which describe it are so large that even when you hear them you cannot imagine how big the Dam really is. It is built across the valley between the hills on either side for a distance of a mile and a half. In the middle of the valley stood a rocky hill higher than the Dam would need to be. This made a good place for a spillway, through which the water in the lake can escape if the flooding of the Chagres River causes it to rise too high.

The Dam itself is more like a hill than a wall, for through the widest part of its base it is more than a third of a mile thick. It is a hundred feet across the top. Measure the width of some street near your schoolhouse and compare it with the width of the top of Gatun Dam. The sides of the Dam are now as green as the hills near by, and it is so flat, so broad, so solid, and so apparently a natural part of the region that it seems hard to believe that it was not made, like the land around, by the hand of nature rather than by the hand of man. Through many months the great valley behind the Dam slowly filled with water, and now vessels steam at full speed through the wide, deep lake and thus save much time in their passage through the Canal.

*Figure 182—The gates are the most
wonderful parts of the lock.*

As we near the northern end of Gatun Lake our steamer slows down, for we must now go downstairs through the Gatun Locks to the level of the Caribbean Sea. The gates swing open before us and the electric engines on the walls tow us slowly into the great concrete box. The locks in the Panama Canal are the largest in the world. Each one is more than a thousand feet long. The gates at either end are the most wonderful part of the locks. Each gate weighs several hundred tons and is composed of leaves of steel seven feet thick. They are really more like steel boxes than gates, for between these steel leaves there are air-tight compartments, so that when the gates are opened they float on the water and thus help to support their own great weight.

On the walls we can see the little engines, known as electric mules, which are towing us through the lock. There are two (one on each wall) to pull us ahead, and two (one on each wall) to keep the ship in the center of the lock and to stop it when required. Before entering the lock we must pass a heavy chain which is stretched from wall to wall. If everything is all right the chain is dropped to the bottom of the lock, but if it happened that the electric mules should lose control of a ship, this chain would be held by machinery directly across its passage and would be strong enough to stop the largest vessel before it reached the end of the lock.

Figure 183—On the walls one can see the electric engines which are towing the steamer through the lock.

While we are going through the three locks between Gatun Lake and the Caribbean Sea, other vessels southward bound are being raised into the lake. All the locks in the Canal are arranged in pairs, so that there may be as little delay as possible.

We steam slowly out through the great gates of the lock and through seven miles of canal to the city of Colon. This was once a dirty, unhealthy place, where malaria and yellow fever were common diseases, but it is now, like the other towns which we have passed, supplied with pure water, sewers that dispose of filth, paved streets, and copper-screened houses to protect the inhabitants from the mosquitoes.

As we leave Colon we meet ships coming into the harbor laden with foodstuffs for the people who live in the Canal Zone. Few supplies except fruits and vegetables can be obtained near at hand; nearly all the food for forty thousand people has to be brought hundreds of miles from different parts of the United States. The town of Cristobal near Colon is the kitchen and pantry of the Zone. Here there is a great cold-storage plant, where meat and eggs can be kept fresh in this hot country. Near by is an ice-making establishment, a huge bakery, and a laundry. Early every morning a train loaded with supplies for the towns along the route leaves Cristobal. On the long train are several refrigerator cars filled with ice, meat, eggs, and other perishable goods. All these and other supplies are sold to the people at cost, for the government does not wish to make money out of its employees. The people in the zone live well and have plenty of healthy, nourishing food, even if most of it comes from long distances and has been kept in cold storage for some time.

As we sail out into the Caribbean Sea we feel that at last we are really homeward bound. Nothing lies between us and the land of the Stars and Stripes except the blue ocean. Our trip has been interesting; we understand better the wealth and resources of the countries to the south of us and the part which the United States may have if she will in their development. We feel better acquainted with our neighbors on this side of the world; we appreciate more fully the beauty of the tropical lands of South America, the grandeur of its mountains, and the vast area and possibilities of its plains.

But the best part of any trip is the getting home. Our country never looked so lovely, our homes so pleasant, and our flag so beautiful as when returning from a journey to a foreign land. As we stand on the deck of the ship and catch our first glimpse of land—of the dear old United States—we realize the truth of the lines written by Henry van Dyke:

Oh, it's home again and home again, America for me,
My heart is turning home again to God's country,
To the land of youth and freedom behind the ocean bars
Where the air is full of sunshine and the flag is full of stars.

TOPICS FOR STUDY

I

1. Trade advantages of the Panama Canal.

2. The Pacific approach to the Canal.

3. The old city of Panama.

4. Work of Colonel Goethals and Colonel Gorgas in the Canal Zone.

5. Balboa, the home of government employees.

6. Old ideas concerning a canal across the Isthmus.

7. Ferdinand de Lesseps and the French Canal.

8. Advantages of a canal across Nicaragua.

9. The secession of Panama and the purchase of the Canal Zone.

10. A bird's-eye view of the Canal.

11. The locks in the Canal.

12. The Gaillard Cut.

13. Gatun Lake and Dam.

14. The cities of Colon and Panama.

II

1. Write as long a list as you can of the important canals of the world. Locate each one. Explain the advantages of each one.

2. For what other uses besides navigation do canals serve?

3. What countries have many canals? Of what use are they?

4. With the exception of the Panama Canal, what is the most important canal in America? Why was this canal built?

5. Where is the Suez Canal? What nation controls it?

6. Name the waters on the route from London to Bombay by way of the Suez Canal. Why is this a very important trade route?

7. If there were no Suez Canal, what would be the route for vessels from England to India?

8. Draw a diagram and explain the workings of a lock in a canal.

9. Make as long a list as you can of isthmuses; of straits. Locate each one and tell why it is important.

10. Is there any work that you can do in your home town or city to make it a more healthy place to live in?

11. Make a list of the places mentioned in Topic III which you think are so important that you should always remember them.

12. Describe the route from New York to Callao, Peru, by way of the Canal; by way of the Strait of Magellan. Compare the length of the two routes.

III

Be able to spell and pronounce the following names. Locate each place and tell what was said of it in this and in any previous chapter. Add other facts if possible.

Peru	Republic of Panama
Colombia	Caribbean Sea
Nicaragua	Chagres River
Central America	Miraflores Lake
Spain	Gatun Lake
France	Gaillard Cut
United States	Gatun Dam
Maine	Strait of Magellan
Pacific Ocean	San Francisco
Panama Canal	New York
Isthmus of Panama	Madrid
Canal Zone	Guayaquil
Suez Canal	Colon
Bay of Panama	Balboa
Pearl Islands	Cristobal
Taboga Island	Panama
Ancon Hill	

GENERAL REVIEW

1. Bound South America.

2. Name the countries of South America and their capitals.

3. What is the largest country? the smallest? the most northern? the most southern? the most eastern? the most western?

4. Name the two inland countries; the country which is not a republic; the country in which the most Portuguese live.

5. Name the countries in the torrid zone. What country lies wholly in the temperate zone?

6. Name the three largest rivers and the plains that they drain.

7. Name the three highlands; the highest mountain; two noted volcanoes; the highest lake.

8. Name the largest city; the largest seaport on the Pacific coast; the most southern city; two cities noted for rubber; the largest coffee port in the world; an important beef and wheat port.

9. Write a list of the important cities on the plains; of those on the highlands.

10. The three most progressive countries of South America are called the "A. B. C." countries. Give their names.

11. Tell why each of the following men is famous: Bolivar, Magellan, Cortes, Atahualpa, Pizarro, Colonel Gorgas, Colonel Goethals.

12. Use in sentences the following words: plaza, patio, selvas, pampas, llanos, gaucho, poncho, campo, frigorifico, quebracho, estancia, manto.

13. What country of South America do you think the most interesting? Give the reason for your opinion.

14. What country do you think the most important? Give the reason for your answer.

15. Give the reason for the heavy rainfall on the western slopes of the Andes in southern Chile and the lack of rainfall on the same slopes in northern Chile and Peru.

16. Write a list of some of the animals of South America.

17. Tell from what city or cities the following products might be shipped: wheat, rubber, gold, cattle, Panama hats, coffee, wool, copper, pearls, cocoa, silver, tagua nuts, emeralds, hides and skins, sugar, asphalt, borax, tapioca, quinine, quebracho extract, coca leaves, maté, iodine, dyes, Brazil nuts, nitrates, diamonds, tin.

18. Name the country or countries with which you associate the following: deserts, jungles, wheat fields, oranges, quinces, blowguns, sugar plantations, revolutions, floods, islands, sheep, guano, asphalt,

Gran Chaco, prison, condor, mountain sickness, railroads, grassy plains, high plateaus, blacks, Hindus, Italians, locusts, coal, alpaca, tapir, manioc.

19. On an outline map of South America show the countries, three highlands, ten rivers, fifteen cities, three islands, one lake, one canal, one strait, one cape, the equator, the tropic of Capricorn.

20. The following places have been mentioned in the text. Locate each place and tell some fact about it: New York, Omaha, San Francisco, Washington (D.C.), Grand Rapids, Plymouth, Los Angeles, Birmingham, Savannah, Philadelphia, Denver, Chicago, New Orleans, Boston, St. Louis, Atlanta, Portland (Oregon), Minneapolis, Baltimore, St. Augustine, London, Petrograd, Venice, Paris, Madrid, Cape Town, Cairo, Sitka, Alaska, Canada, Mexico, West Indies, East Indies, Java, Straits Settlements, India, Ceylon, Malay Peninsula, Central America, Hawaiian Islands, Philippine Islands, Suez Canal, Cape of Good Hope, Peninsula of California, Desert of Sahara, Burma, Banka, Tibet, Pikes Peak, Mount Washington, Nicaragua, Great Lakes, Lake Erie, Great Salt Lake, Rocky Mountains, Appalachian Mountains, Mississippi River, Ohio River, Hudson River, Columbia River, Rhine River, Rhone River, Niagara Falls, Trans-Siberian Railroad, Cape-to-Cairo Railroad.

21. Make a list of the products of South America which you think are so important that you should always remember them. Write beside each one the name of the country or countries from which the product comes. In a third column write the name of the chief city.

PRONUNCIATION GUIDE

KEY. āle, ăt, câre, ärm, finəl, All; ēve, ĕnd, hẽr, recənt; īce, ĭll, admîrəl; ōld, ŏn, fôr; ūse, ŭp, fûr; fōōd, fŏŏt; ch *as in* chop; g *as in* go; ng *as in* sing; N *as in* ink; th *as in* thin; *th as in* the; ñ *as* ny *in* canyon; oi *as in* oil; ow *as in* cow; ou *as in* noun; N (*the French nasal*), *nearly like* ng *in* sing.

Aconcagua (ä kŏn kä´ gwä)

Acre (ä´ krā)

Africa (ăf´ rĭ kə)

Agassiz (ăg´ ə sī)

Alameda de las Delicias (ä lä mä´ dä)

Alaska (ā lăs´ kə)

Alfalfa (ăl făl´ fə)

Alpaca (ăl păk´ ə)

Amazon (ăm´ ə zŏn)

Amazonas (ä´ mä zō´ näs)

Ancon (än kōn´)

Andes (ăn´ dēz)

Antartic (ăn tärk´ tĭk)

Antofagasta (än tō fä gäs´ tä)

Appalachian (ăp ə lā´ chĭ ən)

Araucanians (ăr ô kā´ nĭ ənz)

Arequipa (ä rä kē´ pä)

Argentina (är jĕn tē´ nə)

Arica (ä rē´ kä)

Asphalt (ăs´ fălt)

Asuncion (ä soon sē ōn´)

Atacama (ä tä kä´ mä)

Atahualpa (ä tä wäl´ pä)

Avenida Central (ä vē nē´ thə thĕn träl´)

Bahia (bä ē´ ä)

Bahia Blanca (blän´ kä)

Balboa (bäl bō´ ä)

Bangu (bän goo´)

Barranquilla (bär' rän kēl' yä)

Beira Mar (bā´ rä mär)

Biobio (bē ō bē´ ō)

Bogota (bō gō tä´)

Bolivar (bō lē´ vär)

Bolivia (bō lĭv´ ĭ ə)

Borax (bō´ răks)

Brazil (brə zĭl´)

Buenaventura (bwā´ nä vĕn too´ rä)

436

Buenos Aires (bwā´ nōs ī´ rĕs)

Cacao (kə kā´ ō)

Callao (käl yä´ ō)

Campo (kăm´ pō)

Canada (kăn´ ə də)

Caoutchouc (koo´ chook)

Caracas (kä rä´ käs)

Caracoles (kä´ rä kō´ läs)

Caribbean (kăr ĭ bē´ ən)

Cartagena (kär tə jē´ nə)

Cassava (kə sä´ və)

Cauca (kou´ kä)

Cayenne (kā yĕn´)

Cerro de Pasco (sĕr´ rō dā päs´ kō)

Chagres (chä´ grĕs)

Chile (chē´ lā)

Chimborazo (chĭm bō rä´ zō)

Chinchilla (chĭn chĭl´ ə)

Cholos (chō´ lōs)

Chuquicamata (choo kē kä mä´ tä)

Cinchona (sĭn kō´ nə)

Ciudad Bolívar (syoo thäth´ bō lē´ vär)

Coca (kō´ kə)

Cocaine (kō´ kə ĭn)

Colombia (kō lŏm´ bē ä

Colon (kō lōn´)

Concepcion (kōn sĕp syōn´)

Condor (kŏn´ dôr)

Corcovado (kôr´ kō vä´ thō)

Cortes (kôr´ tĕz)

Cotopaxi (kō tō păk´ sē)

Cousiño (kō sē´ nyō)

Cristobal (krĭs tō´ bäl)

Culebra (koo lä´ brä)

Cuzco (koos´ kō)

De Lesseps (dẽ lĕ sĕps´)

Demerara (dĕm ẽr ä´ rä)

Ecuador (ĕk wä dōr´)

Essequibo (ĕs sā kē´ bō)

Falkland (fäk´ lənd)

Flamingo (flə mĭng´ gō)

Fray Bentos (frī bĕn´ tōs)

Fuegian Archipelago (fū ē´ jĭ ən är kĭ pĕl´ ă gō)

Gaillard (gä yär´)

Gatun (gä toon´)

Gaucho (gou´ chō)

Goethals (gû´ tălz´)

Gorgas (gôr´ gəs)

Gran Chaco (grän chä´ kō)

Guano (gwä´ nō)

Guanaco (gwä nä´ kō)

Guayaquil (gwī ä kēl´)

Guayas (gwī´ äs) River

Guiana (gē ä´ nä)

Huanchaca (wän chä´ kä)

Illimani (ēl yē mä´ nē)

Incas (ĭng´ kəz)

India (ĭn´ dĭ ə)

Iodine (ī´ ō dīn)

Iquique (ē kē´ kä)

Italians (ĭ tăl´yanz)

Java (jä´ və)

Juncal (hoon käl´)

La Guaira (lä gwī´ rä)

La Paz (lä päs´)

La Plata (lä plä´ tä)

Lima (lē´ mä)

Llama (lä´ mə)

Llanos (lä´ nōz)

Loa (lō´ ä)

Los Andes (lōs ăn´ dēz)

Lota (lō´ tä)

Madeira (ma dē´ rə)

Magdalena (mäg dä lä´ nä)

Magellan (ma jĕl´ ən)

Malay (mə lā´)

Manaos (mä nä´ ōs)

Manioc (măn´ ĭ ŏk)

Manto (măn´ tō)

Maracaibo (mä rä kī´ bō)

Marajo (mä rä zhō´)

Maté (mä´ tä)

Matto Grosso (mät´ oo grōs´ oo)

Mendoza (mĕn dō´ sä)

Minas Geraes (mē´ näsh zhā rīsh´)

Miraflores (mē rä flō´ räs)

Misti (mēs´ tē)

Mollendo (mō lyĕn´ dō)

Montevideo (mŏn tē vĭd´ ē ō)

New Granada (grä nä´ dä)

Omaha (ō´ mə hä)

Orchids (ôr´ kĭdz)

Orinoco (ō rĭ nō´ kō)

Oroya (ō rō´ yä)

Oruro (ō roo´ rō)

Pacific (pə sĭf´ ĭk)

Paita (pī´ tä)

Pampas (päm´ päs)

Panama (păn ə mä´)

Para (pä rä´)

Paraguay (pä rä gwī´)

Paramaribo (păr ə măr´ ĭ bō)

Parana (pä rä nä´)

Patagonia (păt ə gō´ nĭ ə)

Patio (pät´ yō)

Pernambuco (pĕr näm boo´ kō)

Peru (pə roo´)

Petropolis (pē trŏp´ ō lĭs)

Pizarro (pĭ zăr´ rō)

Plazas (plä´ zäz)

Potosi (pō tō´ sĭ)

Puerto Cabello (pwĕr´ tō kä bĕl´ yō)

Punta Arenas (poon´ tä ä rä´ näs)

Quebracho (kä brä´ chō)

Quinine (kwī´ nīn)

Quinoa (kē´ nō ä)

Quito (kē´ tō)

Recife (rā sē´ fā)

Rheas (rē´ əz)

Rimac (rē mäk´)

Rio de Janeiro (rēo dā jä nā´ rō)

Rio Mar (mär)

Rio Negro (nā´ grō)

Roosevelt (rō´ zē vĕlt)

Rosario (rō sä´ rē ō)

Russia (rŭsh´ ə)

Santa Lucia (sän´ tä loo sē´ ä)

Santiago (sän tē ä´ gō)

Santos (sän´ tōs)

Sao Paulo (soung pou´ loo)

Savanilla (sä vä nēl´ yä)

Selvas (sĕl´ vəs)

Siberia (sī bē´ rĭ ə)

Sorata (sō rä´ tä)

Sucre (soo´ krə)

Suez (soo ĕz´)

Taboga (tä bō´ gä)

Tagua (tä´ gwä)

Tapajos (tä pä zhōsh´)

Tierra del Fuego (tē ĕr´ rä dĕl fwä´ gō)

Titicaca (tĭt ē kä´ kä)

Trinidad (trĭn ĭ dăd´)

Uruguay (oo roo gwī´)

Uyuni (oo yoo´ nē)

Valdivia (väl dē vyä)

Valencia (və lĕn´ sĭ ə)

Valparaiso (väl pä rī´ sō)

Venezuela (vĕn ə zwē´ lə)

Viacha (vyä´ chä)

Victoria regis (rē´ jĭs)

Vicuña (vĭ koon´ yə)

Xingu (shēɴ goo´)

Yerba maté (yĕr´ bä mä´ tä)

CPSIA information can be obtained
at www.ICGtesting.com
Printed in the USA
BVHW080027110821
614096BV00007B/186